The Folly of Preaching

The Folly of Preaching

MODELS AND METHODS

Edited by

Michael P. Knowles

WILLIAM B. EERDMANS PUBLISHING COMPANY
GRAND RAPIDS, MICHIGAN / CAMBRIDGE, U.K.

Published 2007 by
Wm. B. Eerdmans Publishing Co.
2140 Oak Industrial Drive N.E., Grand Rapids, Michigan 49505 /
P.O. Box 163, Cambridge CB3 9PU U.K.

Printed in the United States of America

12 11 10 09 08 07   7 6 5 4 3 2 1

Library of Congress Cataloging-in-Publication Data

The folly of preaching: models and methods / edited by Michael P. Knowles.
       p.   cm.
ISBN 978-0-8028-2465-3 (pbk.: alk. paper)
1. Preaching.   I. Knowles, Michael (Michael P.)

BV4211.3.F65 2007
251 — dc22

2007010246

www.eerdmans.com

Contents

Contents

"Not with Plausible Words or Wisdom": Homiletic Method

"Grace Sufficient": The Theology of Preaching

"Grace Sufficient": Sermons

Contents

Contributors

The Rev. Dr. Elizabeth R. Achtemeier (1927-2002) was widely known throughout the United States and Canada as a scholar, preacher, lecturer, and writer. She received her theological education at Union Theological Seminary in New York and completed post-graduate studies at the Universities of Heidelberg, Germany, and Basel, Switzerland, before receiving the Doctor of Philosophy degree in Old Testament from Columbia University in 1959. Dr. Achtemeier taught Old Testament theology at Lancaster Theological Seminary (1959-1973) and from 1973 to 1996 was adjunct professor of Bible and homiletics at Union Theological Seminary in Richmond, Virginia. She was the author of twenty-four books, four of them co-authored; her autobiography, *Not Till I Have Done: A Personal Testimony,* was published in 1999 by Westminster/John Knox.

The Rev. Dr. Charles G. Adams is a graduate of the University of Michigan and Harvard Divinity School. He recently celebrated his thirty-fifth anniversary as pastor of Hartford Memorial Baptist Church in Detroit, and his fiftieth year in ministry. He is past president of the Progressive National Baptist Convention, and was named by *Ebony* magazine as one of America's fifteen greatest black preachers and one of the one hundred most influential African Americans. The recipient of twelve honorary doctorates, Dr. Adams has preached, lectured, and taught around the world, including addresses to the United Nations, the World Council of Churches, and the World Congress of the Baptist World Alliance.

The Rev. Donna Eleanor Allen is an Itinerant Elder in the Fifth Episcopal District of the African Methodist Episcopal Church and founding pastor of New Revelation Community Church in Oakland, California. She is currently completing her Ph.D. at Vanderbilt University, in the area of Homiletics and African American Religious History.

The Rev. John L. Bell is an ordained minister of the Church of Scotland and a member of the Iona Community, where he develops resources in the areas of music and worship with the Wild Goose Resource Group. He is a past convenor of the Church of Scotland's Panel on Worship and more recently convenor of the committee revising the Church Hymnary. John has produced many collections of original hymns and songs (some in collaboration with Graham Maule) and two collections of songs of the world church.

The Rev. Dr. David G. Buttrick is Drucilla Moore Buffington Professor of Homiletics and Liturgics, Emeritus, at Vanderbilt Divinity School in Nashville, Tennessee. Educated at Union Seminary, New York, the Garrett Institute, and Northwestern University, Dr. Buttrick previously taught at Pittsburgh Theological Seminary and St. Meinrad School of Theology. He has written or edited sixteen books (including his major 1987 work, *Homiletic: Moves and Structures*), and published more than 150 articles and reviews. Dr. Buttrick is an ordained minister in the Presbyterian Church.

The Rev. Dr. Anthony ("Tony") Campolo is Professor Emeritus of Sociology at Eastern University, St. Davids, Pennsylvania, having previously served on the faculty of the University of Pennsylvania. A graduate of Eastern College and of Eastern Baptist Theological Seminary, he earned a Ph.D. at Temple University. Dr. Campolo is a frequent media commentator, is President and Founder of the Evangelical Association for the Promotion of Education (EAPE), has authored thirty-two books, and is ordained in the American Baptist Church.

The Rev. Dr. Stephen C. Farris is Professor of Homiletics at the Vancouver School of Theology and Dean of St. Andrew's Hall. He holds a B.A. (Honors) from the University of Toronto, M.A. and D.Min. from Union Theological College, Virginia, and a Ph.D. from Cambridge University. From 1986 to 2003 Dr. Farris was Associate Professor, then Professor of Preaching and Worship, at Knox College in the Toronto School of Theology, University of Toronto. He is the author of three books, as well as numerous articles and encyclopedia entries, was President of the Academy of Homiletics for the year 2002, and is ordained in the Presbyterian Church of Canada.

The Rev. Dr. John N. Gladstone (1921-2005) served as pastor of Yorkminster Park Baptist Church, Toronto, from 1965 to 1991. A graduate of Manchester Baptist College in 1950, he was honored with a Doctor of Divinity degree from McMaster University in 1970. Dr. Gladstone published four volumes of sermons, in addition to numerous individual sermons in collections and anthologies.

The Rev. Dr. Edwina Hunter is Joe R. Engle Professor Emerita of Preaching at Union Theological Seminary, New York City. She received her B.A. from Louisiana College, Pineville, Louisiana, M.R.E. from Southwestern Baptist Theological Seminary, M.Div. from Pacific School of Religion in Berkeley, California, and an M.A and Ph.D. from Northwestern University in Evanston, Illinois. Ordained in the American Baptist Churches/USA, Dr. Hunter has served as President of the Academy of Homiletics (1991); her teaching interests include the development of preaching curricula for women, and for African American, Asian, and Hispanic perspectives, as well as the incorporation of the creative arts within preaching.

The Rev. Dr. Michael P. Knowles holds the George Franklin Hurlburt Chair of Preaching at McMaster Divinity College in Hamilton, Ontario. Following undergraduate studies in Victoria and Québec City, Dr. Knowles received the M.Div. and Th.D. degrees from Wycliffe College, University of Toronto, where he taught evangelism and New Testament studies. In addition to book reviews, sermons, and adult education resources, Dr. Knowles has published in the fields of biblical and intertestamental studies, evangelism, and pastoral theology.

The Rev. Dr. Cleophus J. LaRue is Francis Landey Patton Associate Professor of Homiletics at Princeton Theological Seminary, and specializes in the theory and method of African American preaching. An ordained minister in the National Baptist Convention of America, Dr. LaRue received his B.A. and M.A. degrees from Baylor University, the M.Div. and Ph.D. from Princeton. Dr. LaRue's recent publications include *The Heart of Black Preaching* (1999), *Power in the Pulpit: How America's Most Effective Black Preachers Prepare Their Sermons* (2002), and *This Is My Story: Testimonies and Sermons of Black Women in Ministry* (2005).

The Rev. Dr. Thomas G. Long is Bandy Professor of Preaching at Candler School of Theology, Emory University, in Atlanta, Georgia. Formerly Francis Landey Patton Professor of Preaching and Worship at Princeton Theological Seminary and Director of Geneva Press, Dr. Long received the M.Div. degree from Erskine Theological College, South Carolina (1971), and the Ph.D. from Princeton Theological Seminary (1980). In addition to many articles and book chapters, Dr. Long is author or editor of fourteen books on preaching (notably, *The Witness of Preaching*, 2nd ed. 2005), and is ordained in the Presbyterian Church (U.S.A.).

The Rev. Dr. Martin E. Marty is the Fairfax M. Cone Distinguished Service Professor Emeritus at the University of Chicago. His editorial activities include *The Christian Century* (since 1956), the weekly e-mail newsletter *Sightings,* and the fortnightly newsletter *Context.* He was co-director of the project "The Child in Religion, Law, and Society" at Emory University, 2001-2004. The author of over fifty books and more than 5,000 articles, he is a winner of the National Book Award (for *Righteous Empire: The Protestant Experience in America*) and holder of the National Humanities Medal. He is an ordained minister in the Evangelical Lutheran Church in America.

The Rev. Dr. Haddon W. Robinson is the Harold John Ockenga Distinguished Professor of Preaching at Gordon-Conwell Theological Seminary, and was named one of the twelve most effective preachers in the English-speaking world in a 1996 Baylor University poll. He completed graduate studies at Dallas Theological Seminary (Th.M., 1955), Southern Methodist University (M.A., 1960), and the University of Illinois (Ph.D., 1964). Dr. Robinson taught homiletics at Dallas Theological Seminary for nineteen years, was General Director of the Christian Medical and Dental Society from 1970 to 1979, and served as president of Denver Seminary between 1979 and 1991. He served as president (1983) and remains on the executive committee of the Evangelical Theological Society, is currently editor of PreachingToday.com, and has authored numerous popular articles and six books to date.

The Rev. Dr. John R. W. Stott is an internationally known evangelist, preacher, author, and scholar. Educated at Trinity College and Ridley Hall, Cambridge, he has been awarded numerous honorary doctorates. Ordained in 1945, he began pastoral ministry at All Souls Church, Langham Place, London, which he served for twenty-five years as Rector (1950-1975), and where he remains Rector Emeritus. In addition to a worldwide ministry of preaching and evangelism, Dr. Stott is the author of more than forty books and hundreds of articles. He is founder and president of Langham Partnership International, which provides scholarships and educational resources for pastors and teachers in the two-thirds world.

The Rev. Dr. Diane McLellan Walker is a graduate of McMaster University; Emmanuel College, University of Toronto; and McMaster Divinity College. Having served pastorates in Quebec and Ontario, she is currently at Pelham Community Church in Niagara Presbytery and is Senior Editor of Fellowship Publications (representing a coalition of renewal groups within the United Church of Canada).

Introduction

The "folly of preaching" (1 Cor. 1:21) is a phrase taken from the Bible of English Reformer John Wycliffe (*ca.* 1330-1384), the earliest complete translation of the Scriptures into English. To speak of preaching as "folly" neatly captures the human difficulty of the task, the unexpected content of the gospel message, and the low esteem in which both preaching and preachers are often held by society at large. It also sums up a key theme of many of the lectures and sermons in this collection, all addresses presented by leading homileticians of our day to the Gladstone Festival of Preaching at McMaster Divinity College in Hamilton, Ontario. Selecting a quotation from First Corinthians seems all the more appropriate in that many of the presentations in this collection derive their inspiration from Paul's letters to the church at Corinth, in which the apostle vigorously defends both the message of the gospel and his own manner of proclaiming it.

It should not surprise us that, without exception, the speakers represented here argue for the centrality of preaching within the life and mission of the church. Although, as might be expected, there is often considerable overlap of themes, the material has been divided into three sections, which address in turn the social context, homiletic method, and theological content of Christian preaching. In the first section, "'New Creation': The Social Dimensions of Preaching," David Buttrick responds to the widespread loss of public confidence in Christian preaching by calling for a renewed appreciation of God's present self-revelation in the form of preaching itself. As distinct from the therapeutic emphasis of Harry Emerson Fosdick, on the one hand, and the biblicism of Karl Barth on the other, Buttrick argues that "preaching itself forms symbolic reality in the consciousness of Christian communities" as it articulates the concrete social implications of God's "new creation." Charles Adams writes eloquently of how African American spirituality, born of suffering and rejection, challenges the wider church to embrace a more holistic, socially conscious vision of the Christian life, and to discover the transforming power of Jesus' weakness. In a similar vein, Tony Campolo urges us to preach in such a way that our hearers will commit themselves to God's vision of the future, and become agents of transformation in the revolutionary new society that God creates by means of the church. "All of the world groans and is in travail," says Campolo, "waiting for us to move forward and to participate with God to deliver it from its sinful state." Finally, Tom Long situates preaching in relation to the need for North American congregations to regain a comprehensive theological self-understanding and a working theological vocabulary to describe their new identity as the people of God.

The title of the second section, concerning methodology, cites 1 Corinthians 2:1: "'Not with Plausible Words or Wisdom': Homiletic Method." Picking up on his previous discussion, David Buttrick draws out the methodological implications of the formation of meaning in human consciousness. Specifically, he proposes that the structure and movement of the scriptural narrative should determine the form of the sermon, which then becomes "a journey of ideas, moving from beginning to end." Also focusing on the preacher's engagement with the biblical text, a second address from Tom Long demonstrates the importance of historical, theological, and especially literary-critical considerations to a responsible reading of Scripture. Likewise concerned with the relation between Scripture and proclamation, Edwina Hunter reminds us that preaching is often akin to poetry, emerging out of a spirituality that finds inspiration by submitting creatively and imaginatively to the biblical text. Her first and foundational assumption, she says, "is that preaching is at its most communicative, its most incarnational, an artistic medium." By contrast, and in conversation with Aristotle, Paul Ricoeur, and Paul's argument about the offense and nonsense of the gospel in 1 Corinthians 1:18-31, Martin Marty explores the contribution of classical rhetoric to contemporary proclamation. Yet Paul, he ultimately concludes, is "against Aristotle's way of persuasion in order to make room for the persuasion of God in the pattern of the cross."

In 2 Corinthians 12:9, Paul reports the response of the risen Christ to his prayer for healing as, "'My grace is sufficient for you, for my power is made perfect in weakness.'" In the third section of this collection, "'Grace Sufficient': The Theology of Preaching," lectures and sermons alike revolve around the theme of abundant grace in the midst of profound human weakness, even failure. Thus, in two lectures from 1996, John Stott calls preachers to be faithful to the inspired text of Scripture and sensitive to our contemporary social context yet — appealing to Paul's argument in 1 Corinthians 1:17–2:5 — with a profound sense of reliance on God's power that manifests itself amidst weakness. By this he means "the weakness of the cross which is the power of God," the human weakness of "the converts who accept and embrace the gospel," and the exemplary weakness of those who preach the gospel, including Paul himself. Six years later, in the 2002 Gladstone lectures, Stephen Farris returns to First Corinthians to explore Paul's response to debilitating conflict in that congregation by reasserting the theological character of Christian identity (1 Cor. 1:1-17). Reflecting the same theme in a sermon reproduced in the final section of the anthology, Farris reminds us that we are "called saints" despite our own and the church's many shortcomings. Continuing with an exposition of 1 Corinthians 1:18-31, Farris then explores the apparent foolishness and futility of preaching in light of the wisdom and folly of the cross. In both instances, he admits, "It's foolishness, but it's *God's* foolishness."

Twelve sermons round out this collection, many of them continuing to reflect on the key theme of grace amidst weakness and need, and six in particular expounding passages from Paul's Corinthian correspondence. From 1993, David Buttrick offers a classic (Pauline!) appeal, based on 2 Corinthians 5:20–6:2, for us to be reconciled with God in Christ. In the same year John Gladstone, also citing 2 Corinthians 6:2, explores the past, present, and future dimensions of Paul's declaration, "Now is the acceptable time . . . now is the day of salvation." From 1994, Charles Adams takes Paul's assurance in 1 Corinthians 3:21, "All things are yours," as the basis for declaring the universal power of God to emancipate the poor, the powerless, and the oppressed. In his 1996 sermon, "Glorying in the Cross Alone," John Stott explains the centrality of the cross as the antithesis of human glory, and as the sole basis "for our acceptance before God, for our daily discipleship, and for our message [to] a needy, alienated, and lost world." My own sermon, offered two years later, sets out the challenge of preaching as that of declaring the "name" and reality of God, not on the basis of our own ability, but because — as Paul tells the Corinthians — Christ enables the foolish and weak to do so. Unfortunately it has been possible to include only one of Elizabeth Achtemeier's two sermons from 1999: in "What Are We About?" she compares Zechariah's vision of the new Jerusalem with Paul's assurance that, whatever difficulties the church may face, Christ remains its sole foundation (1 Cor. 3:11). From 2000, Donna Allen envisages God's call to Moses from the burning bush as the beginning of "a divine-human dance," an invitation to a liberating partnership with God in the work of ministry. Cleophus LaRue's 2000 sermon, "Why Bother?" reflects on the many difficulties Paul experienced in Athens. Noting that as preachers we sometimes "do our best work under life's most austere and trying circumstances," LaRue challenges us to rely amidst adversity on God's power to accomplish the salvation we proclaim. Then Stephen Farris, as we noted above, rounds out his 2002 lectures with a sermon entitled "And He Has . . ." based on 1 Corinthians 1:1-17. From the same year is a sermon by John Bell, "Not Peace but a Sword," which introduces Christ as one who confronts us with the challenge of God's love, and corrects us with his vision of God's purpose for humanity. Diane Walker's "The Power to Submit" (2003) also wrestles with the challenge of Christ's sacrificial love, particularly as reflected in the injunction of Ephesians 5:21, "Submit to one another out of reverence for Christ." Finally, as a fitting conclusion to this section and the volume as a whole, Haddon Robinson preaches on the parable of the Pharisee and the Tax Collector (Luke 18:9-14), citing the example of Paul and insisting,

> You never outgrow your need of grace or forgiveness. . . . The more you know of God's light, the more you see your own shadow. And the more you become aware of your need of God's grace, . . . the more you realize how much God gives you.

The annual Gladstone Festival of Preaching was established in 1992 in honor of the Rev. Dr. John N. Gladstone (1921-2005). For twenty-nine years pastor of Yorkminster Park Baptist Church in Toronto, Dr. Gladstone was an alumnus of McMaster University, a prominent figure in the Baptist Convention of Ontario and Québec, and — in the words of one contemporary — "a pulpit virtuoso." The purpose of the John N. Gladstone Festival of Preaching has been to encourage the ministry of Christian proclamation by inviting noted preachers and scholars to engage students and practitioners alike in reflection on the biblical, theological, pastoral, and practical dimensions of preaching.

Undoubtedly the most difficult feature of preparing the Gladstone addresses for publication has been selecting a representative sample of material. Of course, transcription of the original audio recordings has itself been a long and arduous task. For much of this work I owe a considerable debt of thanks to my student assistants over several years: Michael Ford, Luz Iglesias, and Matt Lowe each brought to their task cheerful willingness, patient good humor, and careful attention to detail. I am particularly grateful for the many hours they spent tracking down elusive references and preparing several of the transcribed texts for final editing. Alas, not all of their work has ultimately appeared in print. For although the Gladstone addresses have been both rich and varied, much that is excellent has had to be omitted because of space limitations. Even prior to the selection process, some original material was no longer available, while in other instances the speakers in question had already published the substance of their addresses in another form and preferred to avoid overlap. Nonetheless, the lectures and sermons presented here manage to convey the breadth of interest, as well as the depth of scholarship and spirituality, that the Gladstone Festival of Preaching has sought to foster. The printed versions also seek to retain something of the vibrancy of their original live delivery.

Tracking down references and compiling accurate footnotes to secondary sources has presented a significant challenge. While this has usually proven workable in the case of the lectures, it will be immediately evident that source citations for sermon illustrations are very incomplete. It is in the nature of their craft that preachers amass anecdotes and quotations for future use, but short of gaining access to a particular speaker's personal files, tracing the origin of such illustrations — and verifying their accuracy! — proves difficult. Since oral delivery does not require footnoting, the printed equivalent must in many instances yield to a similar limitation.

The following is a complete list of Gladstone Festival presentations from the years 1992 through 2004 (although, because they appear here in edited form, some of the addresses in this volume have been given a title that differs from the original).

1992   ***Preaching and Evangelism in Today's World***

William H. Willimon, Dean of Chapel and Professor of Christian Ministry, Duke University, Durham, North Carolina

a. "The Gospel: Call to Conversion"
b. "Evangelism: Linguistic Assault"
c. "Evangelism: Call to Counterculture"

With sermons by Kerr Spiers, John McLaverty, Wendy Roy, and William Willimon

1993   ***Preaching Toward God's Future***

David G. Buttrick, Professor of Homiletics and Liturgics, Vanderbilt University, Nashville, Tennessee

a. *Sermon:* "The Time Is Now" (Dr. John N. Gladstone)
b. "Preaching Today: The Loss of a Public Voice" (Dr. David Buttrick)
c. "Preaching Tomorrow: The Shape of the Gospel" (Dr. David Buttrick)
d. *Sermon:* "What Is God Like?" (Dr. John N. Gladstone)
e. *Sermon:* "The Model Legacy" (Dr. John N. Gladstone)
f. "Homiletic Method: Meaning and Consciousness" (Dr. David Buttrick)
g. *Sermon: "Quid Pro Quo:* Our Sins for Christ's Righteousness" (Dr. David Buttrick)

1994   ***Proclamation, Music, and Culture in the Christian Worship Experience***

Charles G. Adams, Senior Pastor, Hartford Memorial Baptist Church, Detroit, Michigan

Frederick Swann, Director of Music and Organist, the Crystal Cathedral, Garden Grove, California

c. "What the Bible Really Says About Women" (The Rev. Kate Penfield)

d. "Taking the Listeners Seriously in Sermon Design" (Dr. Tom Long)

e. "Taking the Listeners Seriously as the People of God" (Dr. Tom Long)

f. *Sermon:* "God Listens" (The Rev. William Turner)

1998 *The Word Made Flesh: Preaching in Christ's Body*

Edwina Hunter, Union Theological Seminary, New York, New York

R. Maurice Boyd, the City Church, New York, New York

a. *Sermon:* "On Not Being Taken In" (Dr. Maurice Boyd)

b. "Imagination, Creativity, and Preaching" (Dr. Edwina Hunter)

c. "The Many Voices of Preaching" (Dr. Edwina Hunter)

d. *Sermon:* "I Will Proclaim the Name" (Dr. Michael Knowles)

e. "Poetry and the Preacher" (Dr. Edwina Hunter)

f. *Sermon:* "How Shall We Go Out?" (Dr. Edwina Hunter)

1999 *Practical Lessons for Passionate Preaching*

Dr. Elizabeth Achtemeier, Union Theological Seminary, Richmond, Virginia

Paul Scott Wilson, Emmanuel College, Toronto School of Theology, Toronto, Ontario

a. *Sermon:* "What Are We About?" (Dr. Elizabeth Achtemeier)

b. "God the Literalist" (Dr. Paul Scott Wilson)

c. "God the Poet" (Dr. Paul Scott Wilson)

d. "God the Allegorist" (Dr. Paul Scott Wilson)

e. *Sermon:* "The Shape of Glory" (Dr. Elizabeth Achtemeier)

2000 *A New Homiletic for a New Millennium*

Eugene Lowry, Saint Paul School of Theology, Kansas City, Missouri

Donna Allen, St. Paul School of Theology, Kansas City, Missouri

a. *Sermon:* "A Divine-Human Dance" (Rev. Donna Allen)
b. "The New Homiletic" (Dr. Eugene Lowry)
c. "Options for the New Millennium" (Dr. Eugene Lowry)
d. "Strategies . . ." (Dr. Eugene Lowry)[1]

2001 *Preaching in Three Modes: Historical and Contemporary Addresses*

Martin E. Marty, University of Chicago Divinity School, Chicago, Illinois

Cleophus J. LaRue, Princeton Theological Seminary, Princeton, New Jersey

a. *Sermon:* "Why Bother?" (Dr. Cleo LaRue)
b. "Preaching Rhetorically: Thanks, Aristotle and Apostles" (Dr. Martin Marty)
c. "Preaching Ironically: Thanks, Reinhold Niebuhr and the Prophets" (Dr. Martin Marty)
d. "Preaching Post-Postmodernly: Thanks, Luke-Acts and Artists" (Dr. Martin Marty)
e. *Sermon:* "What Are You Afraid Of?" (Dr. Cleo LaRue)

2002 *Preaching for a Church in Conflict*

Stephen C. Farris, Knox College, University of Toronto, Toronto, Ontario

John L. Bell, Iona Community, Iona, Scotland

a. *Sermon:* "Blessed Be Jael Among Women" (The Rev. John Bell)
b. "The Identity Critis of a Troubled Church" (Dr. Stephen Farris)
c. "From Cross to Cruciform" (Dr. Stephen Farris)
d. "Idol Fancies, Solid Preaching" (Dr. Stephen Farris)
e. *Sermon:* "Not Peace, but a Sword" (The Rev. John Bell)

---

1. Dr. Lowry's lectures are listed as originally planned, although their presentation was significantly revised due to inclement weather and the resulting temporary closure of McMaster University.

"New Creation":
The Social Dimensions of Preaching

Preaching Today:
The Loss of a Public Voice

DAVID G. BUTTRICK

1993

Down in Indiana there was an old church, built when Abraham Lincoln was a boy. The church contained a few pews — enough to seat about seventy-five people — a potbelly stove, and an enormous pulpit. The pulpit was massive: wide as a truck, it towered over pews so that preachers in the old days could stand nearly a full storey above the people, tossing down the Word of God like tablets from Mt. Sinai. A few years ago, the congregation voted to tear the pulpit down. "Times have changed," they said. "These days preaching is less important." Well, probably they were being honest. Most of us would agree that preaching is no longer as important as once it was. What has happened to preaching?

I

By all objective standards, *the pulpit has lost public influence.* Certainly, preaching is no longer as socially significant as once it was. In the first

---

An earlier version of this lecture appeared in *The Spire*, a journal of the Vanderbilt University Divinity School and Oberlin Graduate School of Theology, vol. 13, no. 1 (Summer/Fall 1988).

years of the twentieth century, *The New York Times* reported sermons from city pulpits every Monday morning. For, seventy years ago, the pulpit spoke not merely to particular congregations but to entire cities. Sermons were heard, discussed, argued over; they had impact. Editorials were written in response to sermons. Votes were determined by sermons. In rural North America, surely the impact was greater. Usually the preacher was one of the few truly educated people in a village, so that when the preacher spoke, people listened. If we step further back through history, few historians would doubt the impact of preaching in the shaping of Puritan culture in New England, on the abolitionist movement leading to the Civil War, or on revivalism in the mid-South of the United States.[1] In Canada, Henry Alline's preaching stirred Nova Scotia.[2] And surely the sermons of James Robertson shaped faith in Canada's western provinces.[3] Most of us have heard the names of famous preachers — John Cotton, Jonathan Edwards, Charles Finney, William Ellery Channing, Henry Ward Beecher, Phillips Brooks, Dwight Moody, Walter Rauschenbusch, all the way to Martin Luther King Jr. These were learned people whose preaching did turn the course of our history. Once upon a time, preaching mattered.

Rather obviously, times have changed, and the pulpit is now scaled down in its public influence. People do not hang on every preached word as if their lives depended on sermons. The question is, Why? Shall we blame the arrival of new forms of public entertainment — movies, arena games, rock concerts, and the ever-flickering "boob tube"? Probably not. Or shall we point a bony finger at competitive denominationalism? If you are competing for pious consumers in a religious "marketplace," obviously you want your product to be palatable and you appeal to chronic self-interest. After all, young moderns these days do not seem to be naturally religious people. What about the Bible? Shall we argue that a more biblical pulpit might restore authority to the word preached? No, with the revival of lectionary use there is probably more "biblical" preaching nowadays then ever before, yet the pulpit may still be irrelevant. How can we account for the collapse of the pulpit? There

1. For examples, see Dewitte Holland, ed., *Sermons in American History: Selected Issues in the American Pulpit 1630-1967* (Nashville: Abingdon, 1971).

2. Robert T. Handy, *A History of the Churches in the United States and Canada* (New York: Oxford University, 1977), pp. 127-29.

3. Handy, *A History of the Churches in the United States and Canada,* pp. 347-48.

are at least a hundred and fifty thousand sermons preached each week in North America, but to what avail? How can we account for the loss of pulpit impact? What's the problem?

II

Let's step back in time. Let's go back earlier in our century to 1928. As the winemakers say, 1928 was "a very good year," for in 1928 two people published on the subject of preaching; the one, an American, was Harry Emerson Fosdick, and the other, a Swiss, was Karl Barth. These two men put their stamp on Protestant preaching for more than fifty years.

In 1928, Harry Emerson Fosdick wrote a short essay for *Harper's Magazine* entitled, "What Is the Matter with Preaching?"[4] He criticized the usual expository preaching which, he claimed, spent much time on historical study of a scriptural verse, "ending with some appended practical application."[5] His accusation: Such preaching was intrinsically irrelevant. "Only the preacher," he wrote, "proceeds still upon the idea that folk come to church desperately anxious to discover what happened to the Jebusites."[6] But Fosdick was equally dismayed by what he labeled "topical preaching," namely, discourse on public issues "such as divorce, Bolshevism, America's foreign policy, the new aviation, or the latest book."[7] Such preaching, he hinted, could erode a minister's sense of calling. Instead, Fosdick urged what he labeled "The Project Method." Preachers should begin with people, with the personal problems of actual persons, the immediate concerns of individuals. The test of a good sermon, according to Fosdick, was "how many individuals wish to see the preacher alone" for personal counseling.[8] "A sermon is meant to meet . . . needs," wrote Fosdick, "the sins and shames, the doubts and anxieties that fill the pews." Even when a

4. Harry Emerson Fosdick, "What Is the Matter with Preaching?" *Harper's Magazine* CLVII (July 1928); also in Lionel Crocker, ed., *Harry Emerson Fosdick's Art of Preaching: An Anthology* (Springfield: Charles C. Thomas, 1971), chapter 2.

5. Crocker, *Fosdick's Art of Preaching*, p. 29.

6. Crocker, *Fosdick's Art of Preaching*, pp. 30, 54.

7. Crocker, *Fosdick's Art of Preaching*, p. 31.

8. Crocker, *Fosdick's Art of Preaching*, p. 40.

preacher speaks to thousands, according to Fosdick, the preacher "speaks to them as individuals and is still a personal counselor."[9]

Let us make no mistake here. We are not suggesting that preaching should not relate to human beings, to their immediate problems, their struggles, agonies, or large-looming anxieties. We are not saying that preaching should not care and, indeed, care deeply for individuals; Fosdick's own preaching was undeniably helpful. Nevertheless, you can trace a direct line from Fosdick's "Project Method" to a "positive-thinking" pulpit on the East Coast, a "possibility-thinking" pulpit in a West Coast "Glass Cathedral," and "the triumph of the therapeutic" from many if not most North American mainline Protestant pulpits in between. Now, preaching to personal, psychological problems isn't necessarily bad — most of us need all the help we can get — but it can be dangerous. Question: Is God, the holy God of Israel, nothing more than a free therapist for individual problems? Question: Is Jesus Christ only a nice one-to-one carer, handing out "God Loves You" buttons on Sunday mornings? The problem with therapeutic preaching is not that it's bad — no, it is often tender and helpful, but (1) it may limit theological meaning and (2) it can excuse our silence about public affairs, which is exactly what's been happening in most "mainline" pulpits — a huge silence about public affairs. Most North American pulpits, following Fosdick and fanned by the existentialist Fifties, have tumbled into a narrow personalism. As a result, the God the pulpit announces is a God no larger than the reflection of a particular range of psychological needs, a God who has no concern for social justice. To put it bluntly, psychological adjustment is okay, as long as you don't mind living with Pharaohs!

Karl Barth was a different matter.[10] In Germany he had witnessed

---

9. Harry Emerson Fosdick, "Personal Counselling and Preaching," *Pastoral Psychology* 3, no. 22 (March 1952); reprinted in Crocker, *Fosdick's Art of Preaching*, p. 55.

10. Karl Barth's *The Word of God and the Word of Man,* trans. Douglas Horton (New York: Harper, 1957), was published in German in 1925. The first American edition appeared in 1928. Barth also discussed preaching at length in his *Church Dogmatics,* particularly Vol. I, Part 1, *The Doctrine of the Word of God* (Edinburgh: T. & T. Clark, 1936). Barth's work on homiletics, *The Preaching of the Gospel,* trans. B. E. Hooke (Philadelphia: Westminster, 1963), includes the following paragraph (pp. 42-43):

> The purpose of preaching is to explain the Scriptures. What ought to be set forth in this human discourse? Since the only reason for preaching is to show

the catastrophe of World War I. In 1914, ninety-three intellectuals signed a manifesto supporting the war policies of Kaiser William II. Among the signers were nearly all of Barth's theological teachers. Barth was appalled.[11] How could Christians be kept from selling out to every social or political movement that came along? That was Barth's question.[12] For Barth the only answer was the Bible. Barth believed that God was not revealed in nature — nature may be lovely but it can also be lethal. And God is not reflected in the mirror of religious feeling — we may have all sorts of religious feelings that have nothing whatsoever to do with God. To Barth, God was revealed in history, and history was written down in the Bible. Therefore the Bible, by God's own design, is the objective witness to revelation, Jesus Christ, and God's Word for us to preach.[13] Of course, for Barth, the biblical word was always a dialectical word, a word that counters every worldly wisdom, every political power, every cultural moment. So, above all, Karl Barth was committed to biblical preaching. He was convinced that the Bible alone could keep the church faithful in the midst of a world tossed by changing tides of thought. Preachers, Barth wrote, "must accept the necessity of expounding the Book and nothing else."[14] No

---

God's work of justification, the preacher is not required to develop a system of his own, to enlarge on what he thinks about his own life and that of his neighbor, his reflections on society or the world. If he lives by justification, he cannot take account of human ideologies. Men do not live by the intrinsic values of things. If we ask what we are justified by, we are always recalled to the four keynotes of Holy Scriptures, which bear witness to Revelation, establish the Church, hand on the mission (the power to bear witness), and create vocations. There is, therefore, nothing to be said which is not already found in the Scriptures. No doubt the preacher will be conscious of the weight of his own ideas which he drags after him; but ultimately he must decide whether he will allow himself to compromise or whether, in spite of all the notions in the back of his mind, he will accept the necessity of expounding the Book and nothing else.

11. "Disillusioned by their conduct, I perceived that I should not be able any longer to accept their ethics and dogmatics, that at least for me the theology of the nineteenth century had no future"; quoted by Herbert Hartwell, *The Theology of Karl Barth* (Philadelphia: Westminster, 1964), p. 7.

12. See T. H. L. Parker, *Karl Barth* (Grand Rapids: Eerdmans, 1970), chapter 1.

13. See Karl Barth, *Evangelical Theology: An Introduction* (New York: Holt, Rinehart, and Winston, 1963), pp. 15-59.

14. Karl Barth, *The Preaching of the Gospel,* p. 43.

wonder that, reading Barth, many of us were led to the protest marches of the 1960s; we heard a word of God that spoke against the way of the world!

Nowadays as we reread the early Karl Barth, we may be shocked by his extreme commitment to Scripture. Barth likened preaching to the lip movements of someone reading Scripture with care; preaching was recital, the recital without addition or interpretation of the biblical message alone. He did not trust "application." Barth gives an example: "If a fire broke out in the community last week, and church members are still suffering under its awful impact, we should be on guard against even hinting this theme in the sermon. It belongs to everyday life, but now it is Sunday...."[15] As a result, Barth, who preached in a local German parish when World War I was on everyone's mind, confesses that he is sorry he ever mentioned the war in his preaching.[16] "Pastors," he says, "must aim their guns beyond the hills of relevance."[17] Will you notice that by Barth's logic, Bishop Tutu in South Africa should never refer to racial segregation from the pulpit? Yes, Barth seems extreme and is extreme, but his influence on preaching during the mid-twentieth century has been equally extreme.

So even the best guides can mislead us. Barth helped us to turn back to the Bible from a thinned-out early twentieth-century theological liberalism — good enough! But what happens to Karl Barth in a reactionary North America, a North America that can use the Holy Bible to support resurgent racism, to endorse the domination of women, or to prop up a demonic defense budget? The tragic fact is that Karl Barth has been co-opted by a reactionary, frightened people. The result is that the pulpit has tumbled headlong into a Barthian biblicism that is big on history but small on prophecy. A pulpit that does nothing more than to recite a past-tense Bible to pious present-tense people with no thought of the wider human world is a mighty small pulpit — about the size of a stained-glass phone booth! Barth was a good guide for churches trying to stand apart from the world, to disengage from a cultural "mind," but he is not

---

15. Karl Barth, *Homiletics,* trans. G. W. Bromiley and D. E. Daniels; Foreword by David Buttrick (Louisville: Westminster/John Knox, 1991), p. 118.

16. Barth, *Homiletics,* pp. 118-19.

17. Barth, *Homiletics,* p. 119.

much help when it comes to evangelism, and even less help when it comes to social protest against those who may have Bibles tucked under their arms but are still oppressors!

What has been the result of a Barthian definition of preaching? Well, Barth's biblicism — "the Book and nothing else" — bumped into a tradition of lectionary preaching revived by the liturgical renewal of the Sixties and Seventies; now mainline preachers preach from pericopes, units of the biblical text. Insofar as such preaching builds some grasp of the story of God-with-us, it may well contribute to the church's own sense of identity in the world. But, ultimately, the Barthian appeal to the authority of Scripture has all but destroyed lively preaching — prophetic, apologetic, edgy, future-oriented preaching. So the irony is that Barth, who wrote more on the subject of preaching than any other modern theologian, has contributed much to the demise of preaching and, at the same time, to the rise of a peculiar crypto-fundamentalism in the land. Under the aegis of Barth, the church has withdrawn from public discourse. Nowadays we bus people into church buildings where the Bibles are, and where the Bible can speak to baptized faith. If you compare published sermons in the 1930s and 1940s with published sermons in the 1980s, the most obvious change is a rise in biblical background and a sharp drop in what might be termed "cultural engagement." A pulpit plastered over with "Back to the Bible" bumper stickers without any regard for social correlation will be an arrogant, often irrelevant pulpit. We no longer have much sense of the moving purposes of God in public affairs.

So 1928 was a big year for the American pulpit. In 1928, patterns of preaching in mainline white pulpits were set: therapeutic personalism on the one hand and a biblical positivism on the other. What is not on hand is any sense of the awesome presence of God brooding over our broken world, or any prophetic vision of God's future coming toward us, or any real apologetic grappling with the mind of our age. No wonder the pulpit has become strangely irrelevant — insights from *Psychology Today* and little Bible lessons are poor substitutes for a contemporary word of God.

III

Now, let's turn around and ask what can be done to renew the usefulness of preaching. Is there any way that the pulpit may once again speak some clear "word of God" to the present age? The problem is, ultimately, theological. That is to say, a shift in homiletic procedures will scarcely suffice. Yes, preachers may read Fred Craddock or Clyde Fant, Canada's Paul Wilson, or David Buttrick and, I hope, improve rhetorical technique — at least sermons may be less tedious — but rhetorical technique is not a sufficient answer. If frightened white Protestant North American churches are playing trivia games, then well-formed, more amusing sermons may not solve anything: well-formed trivia is still trivia! Yes, we should attend to homiletic skills, particularly as the somewhat static homiletic of Bishop Whately will no longer serve our rather different human consciousness,[18] but if there is no depth to the word preached, then homiletic skills can be deceptive or even demonic. No, like it or not, we must move toward theology. In every age, the gospel once delivered must be turned so as to catch light in a different way. The speaking of the gospel to every new cultural moment is very much a theological task.

Let me venture some modest suggestions.

We must dare to reconsider our whole understanding of revelation. The notion that most of us inherited during our theological education, a "mighty acts of God" theology, may no longer be helpful.[19] In fact, the historical model of revelation may no longer serve at all. The problem can be stated simply: Where on earth is there any such thing as objective history? History is always history within some community's interpretative framework; it doesn't exist "out there" as some objective facticity. The children of Israel high-tailing it out of Egypt were dazzled by a remarkable Red Sea deliverance. "God," they announced, "God has acted." But was the Red Sea deliverance a self-evident act of God? Nowadays a naturalist could examine the facts and prattle wisely about radical drought conditions in the Sinai peninsula. Or an unreconstructed Marx-

18. Bishop Richard Whately (1787-1863) wrote his *Elements of Rhetoric* in 1828. He influenced North American preaching through a text by John A. Broadus, *A Treatise on the Preparation and Delivery of Sermons,* first published in 1870.

19. See the brilliant essay by James Barr, "Revelation through History in the Old Testament and Modern Thought," in Martin E. Marty and Dean G. Peerman, eds., *New Theology No. 1* (New York: Macmillan, 1964), pp. 60-74.

ist could read the same event as the rise of proletariat people against an Egyptian ruling class. But Israel read the event as an act of God. Why? Not because the event was somehow divinely self-evident; no, instead they attributed deliverance to God because such an understanding made sense within their religious symbolism. So, the question: Where is revelation? Is it in the historical event, or in the hermeneutic that grasps events? Is it not possible that God is revealed in the symbols that structure the minds of people in communities of faith? All we are saying is that perhaps it's time to reconsider revelation. Maybe God is not so much a God who acts — "the mighty acts of God" — as a God who gives us symbols and images through which we comprehend the world.[20]

There are some clear advantages to the model change. For one thing, the whole idea of a self-evident objective act of God in history is almost unintelligible. History itself is not an objective facticity, but rather is always history understood and interpreted by some kind of communal consciousness. When I was a second-year high school student in a rather small American History class, an innovative teacher handed out ten different American history books — one endorsed by the D.A.R.,[21] another purchased in the Communist Worker's Bookstore, still another written by a British author, and so forth. The readings of history were all different, though the seeming facts were often the same. Lesson: History is "soft"; it is always interpreted history and depends on the community that interprets — on its values, faith, and symbols. So does it not make much more sense to praise God as the fount of social images than to try to delineate a self-evident "act of God"?

Are there advantages to a change in the model of revelation? Yes, for then preaching itself can be a mode of God's self-revealing instead of the recitation of past-tense God-events drawn from the Bible. For preaching itself forms symbolic reality in the consciousness of Christian communities. Through preaching we receive the symbols and meanings of faith. In the Barthian model, preaching is a kind of recitation. Preaching studies the Bible, recovers events, and passes past-tense revelation to present-tense people of faith. Preaching is largely transmission from the Bible page and, because it's from the Bible, is only derivatively a "Word of God." But supposing that preaching itself forms

---

20. Avery Dulles, *Models of Revelation* (Garden City: Doubleday, 1983), chapter 7.
21. Daughters of the American Revolution. [*ed.*]

the faith-consciousness of the church; suppose it forms images and symbols by which we grasp and make sense of life, present-tense life. Then preaching itself may be God's right-now means of revelation. You participate in the revealing of God as you form symbols of Christ in contemporary consciousness — now. For as St. Paul proclaims, *"Now* is the day of salvation" (2 Cor. 6:2).

A second modest suggestion: *We must widen the focus of our preaching and address human beings as social beings.* Ever since the existential Fifties, we have lived in a "triumph of the therapeutic." We have preached to human beings as one-to-one people, one-to-one in their particular relationships and one-to-one in their inner conversations. The problem here is that we may be addressing an abstraction and not real people. Personalist preaching speaks to an unreality just as much as did turn-of-the-century "social gospelers." Personalism speaks to a self without a world, and the social gospel addressed a world without a self — both alike preached to unrealities. Young Richard R. Niebuhr argues that we are all "Radial People."[22] That is to say, we internalize symbols of a shared social world. For example, suppose you want to urge your congregation to live lives of simple poverty for the sake of the gospel (an amusing thought given the median income of Presbyterians!). Can your congregation even hear you? Their inner world is papered with pictures from *Better Homes and Gardens* — the firelit family room, the automatic kitchen, the gold-knobbed stereo — not to mention slogans: "High Standard of Living," "Free Enterprise," and the like. Somehow preaching must transform the social worlds we have internalized, the worlds in which we actually live! We cannot address problems in a world "out there" when the real problem is with our internalized world, the internalized world that attends church every Sunday. We cannot preach to a psychological self surrounded by feelings and psychic processes; that self is Narcissus. We must once more preach to a self who has a social world in consciousness.

If we widen the focus of our preaching, once more we will recover the gospel Jesus preached, namely, news of the kingdom of God! The gospel of the kingdom of God may not grip us; it may sound like a backward step toward theological liberalism — particularly to a Barthian reading of Christianity that seems devoted these days to

---

22. Richard R. Niebuhr, *Experiential Religion* (New York: Harper and Row, 1972), chapter 2.

churchly self-preservation. But news of the kingdom is not a liberal invention, for it happens to be the gospel Jesus preached, a glad gospel that shouts from every page in the New Testament. And in a time of terrifying social weariness, it is the gospel that the church is once more called to announce. Yes, our old order may well be tumbling down with a bang, a whimper, or the balance of trade payments, but ultimately God's new order shall be. The task of the pulpit at the tag end of the century may well be social vision; we must once more paint pictures of the new humanity to a hoped-out world.

Of course, there may be a reason for our silence. Put simply, we may not want to speak of God's new order, at least not in North America. So Canadian theologian Douglas Hall would argue.[23] News of a new order is good news if you live scratching dust for sustenance in Somalia, and it is certainly good news if you sleep in doorways, huddled homeless against the chill winds of economic chance, and it is a glad hope if you live under an old-order Apartheid. For the dispossessed of the earth, the gospel of the kingdom is always good news indeed. But what can news of a new social order mean to a North American continent bent on preserving its position, its "free enterprise," its political power and its cash? To a reactionary land, news of a coming new order is positively scary, if not downright un-American. Most of our "mainline" middle-class church members have built their lives into a hope of the *status quo;* they have secured themselves in the so-called "American dream." Have they not invested their future in property or, if not in property, then in what the bankers call an "Individual Retirement Account"? And have they not adapted themselves psychologically to get along in an all-American ethos? Thus, news of a new order sweeping out of God's future toward us will be threatening indeed. Ministers who dare to preach such a gospel are bound to be in jeopardy. Though our world seems to have banished crosses, it still has unemployment lines. Did you see that wonderful cartoon in the *New Yorker* magazine? It showed two clergy gazing sadly into an all-but-empty collection plate — a penny, two buttons, and a "Win with Willkie" pin. One of the ministers is saying to the other, "Well, so much for prophecy!" Preach the coming of God's new order in North American establishment churches and you can expect to encounter bristling resistance.

23. Douglas John Hall, *Confessing the Faith: Christian Theology in a North American Context* (Minneapolis: Fortress, 1996), pp. 462-69.

But, turn to the Christian Scriptures, and on every page there's good news. The news is not personal salvation. No, Christ is risen, Christ is regnant, and God's new order has begun. Doesn't the apocalyptic apostle Paul propose that a new humanity has begun in Christ, the second Adam? He seems to be shouting the joyful news: With Christ the whole wide world is beginning again. Evangelism in our age may propose a "personal relationship to Jesus," whatever that may mean, but in the first century the big news was social: it was news of a new creation. Oh, yes, by the time of Constantine, the apocalyptic dream had ebbed. To be honest, we modern-day Christians no longer cherish such a vision. We've pushed any hope of the kingdom of God into our small-scale hearts or into the hereafter — "Oh, that will be glory for me," with the word "me" underlined. But unless we want to picture Jesus as an excitable first-century nut, pleasant but deluded, we cannot let go of the kingdom of God. Now, between the ages, it may return once more to fill our preaching with the promises of God.

The wonderful British author, Joyce Cary, has a great scene in which an irascible artist named Gulley Jimson, half drunk on a high swinging scaffold, tries to paint a mural on the wall of a condemned building.[24] The image may sum up the world of the ministry at the end of an age. Yes, Western culture seems to be tumbling down, but our hope is not in Western society. No, Jesus came announcing a new creation. In a weary age, we are called to speak the vision of the kingdom of God. The promises of God are sure.

*   *   *

Remember the church that scaled down its pulpit? What has happened to preaching? Can the influence of the pulpit be renewed? Maybe and maybe not. North America may simply not want to hear from God these days. But we must seek to be faithful. In scaled-down pulpits, once more we can preach to full human beings in a full human world a lively, present-tense Word of God. Then maybe we can stand back and see what happens next!

24. See the final chapter of Joyce Cary's *The Horse's Mouth* (New York: Harper, 1950 [1944]).

The Burden of the Black Church

Charles G. Adams

1994

In Matthew, the twenty-seventh chapter and the thirty-second verse, we have the words, "And as they came out, they found a man of Cyrene, Simon by name. Him they compelled to bear his cross." We will not get into an argument as to Simon's alleged blackness or Africanity. Whether or not Simon was physically black like me is a question that we must leave open to further critical, historical, and exegetical investigation. But suffice it to say that for all practical purposes, Simon represented black humanity. Simon was identified with a disadvantaged segment of the human race. He was isolated, he was given no freedom of choice whether or not to bear the cross, his personhood was not honored, his manhood was not respected. His freedom to decide was not conceded, for they compelled him to bear his cross.

In his first book of twenty-five years ago, entitled *Black Theology and Black Power*,[1] Professor James H. Cone had this to say: "God's word of reconciliation means that we can only be justified by becoming black. Reconciliation makes us all black. Through this radical change we become identified with the suffering of the black masses." Then he goes on to clarify this for white people: "It is to be expected that many white people will ask, 'How can I, a white man, become black? My skin

1. James H. Cone, *Black Theology and Black Power* (New York: Seabury, 1969).

15

is white and there is nothing I can do to change it.'" But according to Cone's ontological definition of blackness, being black is not exclusively a matter of skin color. Cone says, "To be black means that your heart, your soul, your mind, and your body are where the dispossessed are." Simon was compelled to be where Jesus was because Jesus had decided to be where Simon was. Jesus had already decided to identify himself and his kingdom with Simon. Jesus had already counted himself among the despised, rejected, hated, exploited, excluded brothers and sisters. He sat where they sat. His heart was with Simon, because as the great physician, he knew that if he could heal the extreme case, all other cases would derive radical hope from that deep therapy. The privileged classes are included in any benefits that fall to the dispossessed, but the dispossessed are not included in the power prerogatives of their oppressors. There are no restrictions against lying down in a manger. There is no lock on the stable door. There is no lock on the door of dispossession. But there are numerous locks, and bars, and barriers, and policies, and customs, and covenants of restriction to keep the poor from moving among the rich. Simon was black due to his identity. Jesus was black due to his decision to be one in heart with the person farthest down on the social ladder. The black church is Simon. Not Simon Peter, but Simon of Cyrene. It was compelled into existence. It is a voluntary institution produced under the conditions of involuntary servitude.

The black church was compelled to be when, in 1727, the bishop of London declared that one's conversion and baptism were entirely inner experiences and individual matters that had no effect at all upon one's external status or condition. When he took from black slave Christians even the right to hope for freedom based upon their membership in Christ, he was promulgating the primary heresy of Western Christianity and compelling the black church into existence to confront or to challenge that heresy.

Even before 1727, the legislature of the colony of Virginia declared in 1667 that baptism did not alter the condition of the person as to his bondage or freedom. This started a process of enactments or rulings that essentially removed the Christian religion as a legal barrier to slavery in the colonies. In 1729, the Crown Attorney and Solicitor General ruled that baptism in no way changed a slave's legal status. Two years previously the bishop of London had declared,

> Christianity does not make the least alteration in civil property. The freedom . . . which Christianity gives is the freedom from the bondage of sin and Satan, and from the dominion of their lusts and passions and inordinate desires. But as to their outward condition they remain as before, even after baptism.

The black church was forced to be in order to repudiate that ruling, that assumption, that one's relationship to Christ does not alter one's relationship to others, especially those who are of the household of faith.

Black Christians contended that Christian conversion is a radical change that affects a person's total life. Things can never be the same as before. "If any person be in Christ, that person is a new creation: old things are passed away; behold, all things are new" (2 Cor. 5:17). And this radical change of relationships, this trans-valuation of values, begins in the church where the change was generated in the first place. Paul said to the churches of Galatia, "Let us do good to all persons, but especially unto them who are of the household of faith" (Gal. 6:10). If I am in Christ, a child of God, I cannot own a slave. If I am in Christ, a child of God, I cannot be a slave. If I am in Christ, a child of God, I cannot look down on any human being, deeming him inferior. If I am in Christ, a child of God, I cannot look up to any earthly master. I cannot use a fellow human being and I cannot demean myself to the status of being used by another human being. Paul said,

> As many of you as were baptized into Christ have clothed yourselves with Christ. There is no longer slave or free, there is no longer male or female. For all of you are one in Christ Jesus. And if you belong to Christ, you are Abraham's offspring, heirs according to promise. (Gal. 3:27-29)

The black church is predicated on the union that exists between the spiritual and the physical, the body and the soul, the individual and the communal. To be in Christ is to be free in a free church, attached to Christ who sponsors and empowers and enlists human freedom. As Martin Luther King Jr. said, "The freedom of God is God's image in us, and to deny or reduce that freedom is to sin against God." Simon was compelled into existence and Simon's burden first of all is to serve oppressed people everywhere. Because apart from Simon, oppressed people may have a hard time finding any hope in being generally accepted, liberated, and celebrated. Not only are Simon's people excluded from the mainline church, or given only token participation and power in the mainline church, but the same thing is true of all of our Western secular institutions. Although in the United States we boast of a number of black mayors of cities, a few black congresspersons, one black U.S. Senator, one anomalous black Supreme Court Justice, and one recent but still former black governor, the truth is, we still represent less than 2 percent of all elected officials in that country, and we are still isolated from the top reaches of political aspiration. Where does a black mayor go when he or she can no longer be mayor? Where does a black governor go when he can no longer be governor? Can they ascend to higher office, or do their political aspirations shrivel and shrink under a glass ceiling?

Simon must serve all people, who without him may become discouraged, depressed, and devaluated by inexorable social, economic, and political barriers. The black church, therefore, was compelled into existence. Black people, after an unsuccessful attempt toward Christian amalgamation, came to realize that either they would have their own religion, or no religion and nothing else. Either they would be accepted by Christ or they would be accepted by no one. Either they would be free, and loved, and wanted, and honored, and unshackled from the church, or nowhere. So, the black community formed a church in the eighteenth century and said to it in the words of the Psalmist, "Whom have I in heaven but thee? And there is none upon earth that I desire besides thee [Ps. 73:25]. There is none upon earth who will accept me as I am but my Christ, my church, my cross." This is what the slaves meant when they sang that spiritual, "Give me Jesus, you can have all this world, but give me Jesus." They were not giving up on the world, but they were saying, "Either I will have Jesus or I will have nothing but futility and frustration. Either I will find life and hope in the church, or I will find it nowhere."

Before we were allowed to identify with our families, we found refuge and healing with our churches. The foundation of our social solidarity is not our family, but the church. Our families were destroyed, our kinsmen were torn from us, our mothers and fathers and sisters and brothers were sold, from plantation to plantation, driven from one master to another, forcibly bred like cattle. Our families were torn asunder, our schools disallowed, our businesses crushed. Only the church endured. The church too was persecuted, but it endured because of its nature. It is the nature of the church to endure under persecution, to stand firm under fire, to walk through furnaces of trial, and come forth like gold. It flourishes under strife, it is strengthened through suffering, it is quickened under the heavy hand of oppression, it is more powerful in its hiddenness than in its openness. E. Franklin Frazier called the black church during slavery the "invisible institution," and yet the finest hour in the history of the black church is the hour of its invisible, underground manifestation. For it gave a despised people meaning and value, faith to persevere, courage to persist, and love to lift its sons and daughters from bondage to liberty.

This is still the burden of the black church: to make everybody somebody in Christ and in the church. Everybody is loved in the free black church, the low and the high, the young and the old, the rich and the poor, the blacks and the whites, those who think they are sophisticated and those who know they are not. The church loves them all, accepts them all. And that is why there is this phenomenon in the black church called "whooping" and "shouting." There is a point in the proclamation of the gospel when the sweetness of God's word transforms speech into music, and the minister continues to preach, but clearly his sermon has become a song, and the whoop becomes the highest note in the song which when reached is sustained in a beautiful way until people are caught up in ecstatic wonder and worship and praise. Now they call me the Harvard whooper because they say that I have done the impossible. I have taken a Harvard theological education and put a whoop to it. I clearly do not think that I deserve their accolades, but I have fun when people give me that name. In our tradition we call it "getting happy," expressing joy, openly, publicly, in a way that is not programmed, in a way that is not predicted, in a way that cannot be controlled, and yet it is not a negative disruption of the service but a positive incursion of something wonderful and lovely. Getting happy, shouting, not just speaking voluminously, but speaking ecstatically. Perhaps at no other time in the church are people more aware of being truly loved, completely accepted, and totally free.

Now, I have heard this kind of emotional expression explained by scholars and sophisticates in other terms. Terms that do not take into account that enthusiasm from the compound *"en theo,"* meaning "participation in God," for how can one participate in God and not blow all of one's circuits? For participation in God is by definition ecstatic, standing beyond the self, beyond the order of the day, beyond one's own racial or historical identity. To participate in God means to break out of the steel case of the imperious ego. But most scholars do not appreciate that explanation, and they explain these emotional outbursts in different terms, whether they are black scholars or white. They have a tendency to refer to this kind of thing as a negative manifestation of ignorance and frustration, which will disappear as blacks become more educated and assimilated into the mainstream. One black lady who was totally educated and totally assimilated came to our service, and when she saw some of these goings on she wrote me a letter in which she called them "the anguished outpourings of troubled spirits." Persons who think like her say that shouting or emotionalism is compensatory because through it impoverished blacks enjoy a certain satisfaction that is denied them in their physical and social circumstances. They say that shouting is anticipatory in that it savors in advance, via the imagination, the glory and joy of a delayed heaven. They say that it is a relief valve through which blacks can let off the built-up steam of their accumulated miseries, misfortunes, and frustrations. They say it is an escape system, an exhaust pipe, a temporary relief from earthly misery. They say that it is a reaction formation, an expression of misplaced aggression, and suppressed anger. Instead of cursing the white man, shout at the Lord. Instead of kicking Whitey, knock over the bench.

That is what they say, but they who explain it like that have never done it. How can one explain a feeling that one has never felt? Or analyze an overwhelming, inscrutable experience that one has never experienced? I think it might be better to let someone who knows something about it tell us what it is. And if you really want to know what it is, what all the fuss is about, you might begin by asking me, for I have been known to be in this state from time to time, though not as often as I would like. It is ecstasy, it is positive, it is reassuring, it is self-transcendence, it is race-transcendence, it is a rendezvous with absolute love which is absolute reality and absolute power, the Holy Spirit, God, giving God's self to us in freedom, power, and love. It is affirmation, it is joy, it is a high and holy gladness, it is perfect peace, abounding confidence, incomparable hope, unquenchable fire, internal, eternal, ecstasy. It is insuppressible enthusiasm, surging gratitude, blessed assurance, ceaseless praise, hallelujah love, unyielding faith. It is a powerful love that will not let us go and will not let us hate. It is a deep, unsearchable, inestimable, and abiding joy that the world cannot give and the world cannot take away. Storms cannot sweep it, trouble cannot overwhelm it, problems cannot prevent it, burdens cannot crush it, sickness cannot defeat it, death cannot destroy it, the grave cannot hold it, for something happens over which we have no control whatever. Somebody passes by, the unseen is felt, it is unpredictably gratuitous, God comes in, the Holy Ghost takes over, barriers disappear, shame vanishes, walls tumble down, love takes over, the Holy Ghost falls on every head and burns in every heart and stirs in every soul with cloven tongues of hallowed fire. And in this presence, in this incursion, there is reconciliation and an empowerment that sweeps through the church and people find themselves able to love without fear, and to rejoice without shame.

So the first burden of the black church pertains to the acceptance and healing of those persons whose rejection by the majority of society willed and compelled the black church into existence. When I was a child I met an old, shriveled-up, ninety-five-year-old man, W. H. Jernigan, who at that time was pastor of Mount Carmel Baptist Church in Washington, D.C. Dr. Jernigan boasted of having been born during slavery and having remembered certain things that occurred during slavery. He said that during the worship services the black slaves were compelled to sit in the gallery while the others sat on the main floor. The preacher would look up to those who were in the gallery after having preached to those who were on the main floor, and he would tell them, "You are sitting exactly where God had intended for you to sit." He said, "Just as you occupy the gallery on earth, you will sit in the gallery in heaven. You will not be permitted to sit on the main floor, you must sit in the gallery. On earth and in heaven." But as the black worshipers were tumbling from the gallery and leaving the church, an old white-headed black preacher stood at the door and told them as they passed out one by one, "I want all of you, my brothers and sisters, to meet me down at the brush arbor after dinner. I've got a very important announcement to make, and I want all of you to hear it. Meet me at the brush arbor after dinner." And when they had gathered there he said this: "We heard this morning that when we get to heaven we will not be permitted to sit on the main floor, but I'll tell you what I want you to do. When you go to heaven, don't be late. I want you to get there early and take your seat on the main floor, and if anybody comes in who doesn't want to sit with you, well then they will simply have to go to the sub-basement."

The first burden of the black church is not to be silent in the face of suffering and injustice. The black church attempts to equip people with truth and tongues to speak, and to work for the alleviation of pain and sorrow, unemployment and poverty, homelessness and unequal education. The black church sits in the midst of a troubled and tortured community in the middle of the dark ghetto. Everybody in the community does not belong to the black church, but the black church belongs to everybody in the community. It is the fulcrum of human hope, the nucleus of human life, the preserver of culture, the producer of genius, the power base for advocacy politics. It is the parent of black music and art, the incubator in the production of new leaders, the storehouse for the disinherited, the powerhouse for the disenfranchised, the headquarters for the advancement of poor people, the launching pad for social action, the hospital for wounded souls, the love tabernacle for the hated, the open door to the least, the last, the lost, the little, the unlucky and the left out, the biggest enemy to the status quo, the central agency in anti-segregation, anti-discrimination, and anti-defamation. It is a rock in a land of oppression. It is a shelter from a stormy blast of indifference. It is a house of prayer for all nations. It faces a frowning world and sings and shouts "Black and white together we shall overcome!" So the first burden of the church is to spiritualize, organize, and galvanize a new people of hope.

The second burden of the church has to do with Christ. Simon of Cyrene was compelled to bear the cross in order to reveal the real Jesus. And since the black church is Simon, it is the burden of black religion to reveal Jesus, that man among men in whom dwelt the fullness of God bodily. Who is Jesus? Is he the caretaker of the prevailing political order? Is he the sponsor of smug middle-class culture? Is he the blond, blue-eyed, effeminate, northern European seen in nineteenth- and twentieth-century portraits? Is he the guardian of private property values? Is he the night watchman for our vaunted way of life? Is he the ward of Western paternalism? Is he the king of the culture of contentment? Is he the tribal deity of the status quo? Or is he God's great "I am"? Is he God's Word, saying to us, "I am who I am"?

Who is Jesus? Could it be that the black church may be permitted to reveal his nothingness in terms of worldly values? Could it be that the black church in its weakness can leap to identify with a Christ who said, "Foxes have holes and the birds of the air have nests, but the Son of Man has nowhere to lay his head" (Matt. 8:20; Luke 9:58)? He owned everything; he possessed nothing. He was a king with no visible kingdom, a captain with no discernable troops, a pilot without a ship, a general with no army, rich without wealth, a doctor with no medical degree from McMaster; a surgeon with no surgical instruments, a preacher with no theological training, a lawyer who did not pass the bar. In terms of the way the world measures success, he was a complete failure. A political zero, a perennial flop, a nagging disappointment, a social misfit, a cultural dropout, a tragic victim of mistaken identity. He was what we would call definitely deprived socially, and culturally deficient, born in a stable, wrapped in undifferentiated rags, laid in a manger, baptized by a rustic named John in the muddy waters of the Jordan, arrested by Roman soldiers, beaten by an angry mob, condemned by Pilate, mocked by the crowd, crucified on Calvary. Wounded in his side, he died in agony, buried in a borrowed tomb, sealed in his grave. Yet he lives, because God raised him up, gave him a name above every name that at the name of Jesus every knee should bow and every tongue confess that Jesus Christ is Lord to the glory of God. He identified with the lowest, and God raised him to the highest.

Simon and Simon's church can really reveal the depths that Jesus embraced, and perhaps Simon, proleptically celebrating his eschatological hope, may reveal the powerful heights in which Jesus is and shall be glorified. Two of the most precious hours of a sabbatical Merrill Fellowship that I had at Harvard Divinity School were spent in the company of my old and now very feeble, retired professor in Christian Social Ethics, James Luther Adams, no relation to me, who wrote the book on being human religiously.[2] I asked him, "Dr. Adams, will you please tell me what in your opinion is the hope of the world today?" And that sagacious, white-skinned, white-haired octogenarian looked

---

2. James Luther Adams, *On Being Human Religiously: Selected Essays in Religion and Society*, ed. Max L. Stackhouse (Boston: Beacon, 1976).

me straight in the eye and said, "The hope of the world today is the African American preacher." Now, I want to change that to the "African American *church*," because I think that is really what he was meaning to say. But can you imagine that a white Harvard scholar who has spent all his life, more than ninety years, in celebrated white institutions, in a white academic world of power and privilege, a man who has never wanted for any honor or distinction, saying to me that the hope of the world is not white wealth, not white culture, not white America, not white academic institutions, not the white Republican Party, not white corporate America, not General Motors, not IBM, not Harvard University with its 5-billion-dollar endowment and 2.5-billion-dollar general campaign? None of these things that we respect and adore. But he said, "The hope of the world today is the black church." It was a shocking statement, both because of its source and its substance.

As to its source, I would not have been surprised at all if these words had come from a black demagogue, charlatan, or perennial presidential candidate. Wouldn't you expect people like me to make such a cavalier and off-handed assertion? Black preachers like me are often given to hyperbole, overkill, and media hype. All demagogues, politicians, and propagandists will claim that they and their ethnic group are the hope of the world, the source of a new world order. But this man is not a demagogue: he is too feeble. He is a seasoned, sober, reasoned, Harvard scholar. And he said with no uncertain sound and with no unexamined sense that the American African church is the hope of the church today. Now, I know that means all colors because the color black includes all colors and excludes none. But it's still a startling statement. It's like a Jew looking to a Gentile for salvation, or like the West turning to the East to find faith.

Secondly, I am startled by the substance of the statement. How can we who have received the least be expected, even required, to give the most? Are we who are crucified by the world now to become its saviors? Are we who have been left out of the structures and privilege now to be the key that unlocks the door to freedom and power and liberty and justice for all? It seems absurd, doesn't it? Yet perhaps the victims of society's injustice and indifference are the inevitable redeemers of the society that has rejected them. For when God was ready to build a new people to be the instruments of divine salvation, God chose not a yuppie or a buppie, but God chose those who were underprivileged. A one-hundred-year-old Abraham, and a ninety-year-old, shriveled-up Sarah. God made *them* the mother and father of a holy nation. Then when God was ready to draw Israel out of bondage in Egypt, God chose an eighty-year-old, tongue-tied fugitive from justice named Moses, and made him the first international leader and liberator in human history. As Gardner Taylor says, "Moses left Egypt as a fugitive from justice, and Moses returned to Egypt as the prosecuting attorney." When God was ready to break the back of the British Empire, God chose not the armies and generals of Europe, but a thin, gaunt, brown, praying man of peace named Mahatma Gandhi, who crushed the largest, most far-flung, most impressive empire in the world not by military might, but by prayer and fasting.

When God was ready to desegregate America, God chose as the leader not a privileged, preferred, pampered, honored person, but a hated, rejected, despised, exploited, excluded, segregated, dishonored man named Martin Luther King Jr., and made him the greatest moral and spiritual leader of the twentieth century. Does it take an exiled Moses to humanize and save a whole society? Does it take a blind Milton to see an invisible Paradise? Does it take a deafened Beethoven to hear a humanly inaudible symphony of brotherhood and peace and write it down on paper? Does it take a once-excluded Maynard Jackson and Andrew Young to recreate the urban vitality of Atlanta? Does it take a once-rejected Coleman Young to raise Detroit from pronounced social and economic death? Does it take an excoriated and vilified Harold Washington to transform Chicago politics? Does it take a crucified savior, a wounded healer, to redeem the world? And will it take ebony and ivory people of intelligence and spirituality and integrity to lift all of humanity to the light and life and love that are available in Jesus Christ? God has given us what we have, God has made us who we are, and even those who occupy the bottom of the social, political, and economic pyramid, the underclass of the world, even the nobodies of the earth have been called to be the somebodies of God and the instruments of life and hope.

Where is the one who is wise, where is the scribe, where is the debater of this age? Has God not made foolish the wisdom of the world? For since in the wisdom of God the world did not know God, through wisdom God decided, through the foolishness of our proclamation, to save those who believe (1 Cor. 1:20-21).

So the third and final, ultimate burden of the black church is to embrace the whole church and to challenge any residuum of the heresy of dichotomy, the heresy that says Christians can worship God with their tears and prayer and songs and sermons in the beauty of their buildings and paintings in the gilded sanctuary, and yet fail to serve God in their day-to-day relations with their brothers and sisters. The black church, at its best, will confront this heresy both in its own ranks and in the ranks of others: the heresy that theology has nothing to do with ethics, that the gospel is estranged from freedom, that the church must stay out of political engagement, that the soul has no communication with the body, that the spiritual has nothing to do with the physical, that the saved individual can continue to be insensitive to an unsaved economy and society, that religion is a personal matter only, that Jesus is a personal savior only, and has nothing to do with systems and governments, with structuralized evil and systematized injustice.

We must prove our authenticity, not by what we do for ourselves, but by what we do for others. Jesus lived and died for others, and we are not in Christ unless we have identified with others, with the empirical *other*. It is the nature of the church to give its life to those who need it. It does not take in wealth to keep it but to *give* it. Its life is preserved through giving, just as the survival of the amoeba is guaranteed as it divides itself and shares the substance of its protoplasm on behalf of others. And just as the life of the seed is ensured as it breaks itself and sacrifices its life for the sake of new life, so the life of the church is guaranteed as it empties itself in the world and pours itself out where it is needed. The church must pour out its strength among the weak, its wealth among the poor, its gospel among the estranged, its joy among the sad. We must pour it all out, every bit of it. If we are an authentic church, and I hope we are, we will not keep our religion to ourselves. We will not be esoteric, we will not become a closed community, we will never take on the form of country-club elitism or exclusivism, but we will take on the form and power of a servant and pour out the love and power of God all around us. To keep it is to lose it, to share it is to renew it. It is Simon's burden to save himself and others with him. Simon's religion sustained him through slavery and it will sustain anyone in the midst of the deadening cacophonies and tragedies of a civilization hung up on futility.

Jesus had to carry the cross on his naked back through the streets of

Jerusalem, from the judgment hall of Pilate to the hill outside Jerusalem where he was nailed to the cross and bled until he died. While on his way to Calvary, Jesus weakened under the weight of the cross. He had been up all night; he had stood more than one rigorous trial; he had taken more than one nasty beating. They had beaten his back until the blood spurted out and had begun to coagulate on the soft surface of his broken skin. And when he got to the gate of the city going out, he slumped under the load of the cross. He could not carry it by himself. The Roman soldiers began to search through the crowd, trying to find somebody to help Jesus bear the cross. The Jews wouldn't touch it because they were too religious. The Romans wouldn't touch it because they were too proud. Soldiers wouldn't touch it because they had too much power. The Greeks wouldn't touch it because they were too intellectual. The Asians wouldn't touch it because they were too conscious of status. The in-crowd wouldn't touch it because they were arrogant. His friends wouldn't touch it because they were scared. His enemies wouldn't touch it because they were indifferent. So the Roman soldiers kept scanning the scene and combing the crowd and searching the multitude to find somebody to help Jesus bear the cross.

Finally, they spotted the sun-crowned face of a slave from Africa. They found a man whose muscles had been strengthened by years of forced labor. They found Simon of Cyrene, a hewer of wood and a drawer of water. They compelled him to bear the cross. At first he resented it, did not want to do it. But he looked in the face of his strange partner, and saw cosmic victory written in his bleeding brow; he saw perfect love, power, pity and mercy, mingled together in the face of Christ. Instantly, he accepted the cross and he did not ask, "What will happen to me if I *do* bear this cross?" but, "What will happen to the world if I *don't* bear it?" He felt the surge of ultimate significance, and he said to himself, "Here I am at the focal point of history, at the center of the cosmos, at the fulcrum of the future. If I don't bear it the earth will be destroyed and the planet will be dissolved and all people will perish. If I don't bear it, the coupling pin will drop out of creation, the ozone layer will be eaten away, and the world will go back to chaos. If I don't bear it the land will be swallowed by the raging sea, hell will break the flood banks of containment and sweep the earth to ruin. If I don't bear it, right will lose and wrong will win, the mission of hope will be lost, the cause of life will fail, sinners will never be saved, the gospel will never be preached, people will never be reconciled to people, nations will never be reconciled to nations, races will never be reconciled to races. If I *don't* bear it, faith will go out of existence, love will turn to pretense and deception, hope unborn will die stillborn, darkness will rule over light, evil will reign over justice, hate will prevail over love, the devil will win over God. If I don't bear it, law and order will prevail over liberty and life, property values will predominate over human values, forgiveness will be lost in vengeance, violence will cover the earth with blood, the wicked will never cease from troubling, the weary will never be at rest, Handel will never write the "Messiah," Beethoven will never write the Ninth Symphony, Martin will never march on Washington, the oppressed will never be free, the globe will never be redeemed, sickness will never be healed, the hopeless will never find hope and the dead will never be raised."

"So," said Simon of Cyrene, "I'll cherish the old rugged cross until my trophies at last I lay down. I will cling to the old rugged cross, and exchange it someday for a crown."[3]

---

3. "The Old Rugged Cross," words and music (1913) by George Bennard (1873-1958).

Preaching to the Culture of Narcissism

TONY CAMPOLO

1995

The book of Hebrews tells us categorically that "faith is the substance of things hoped for, the evidence of things not seen" (Heb. 11:1). American and Canadian youth cultures have been highly affected by trends that are at work in society. For instance, the human potential movement has had a tremendous impact on determining how young people view themselves. Over and over again they have allowed themselves to be caught up in the value system that the human potential movement has communicated. I find them constantly unsure where they are going because they are too focused on becoming "complete" people. They are too focused on self-actualization. They are too focused on becoming rather than on doing. I ask them when they come out of high school, "You're graduating, so what are you going to do, what are you going to be?" You get one standard answer: "I don't know." So if a kid has no direction, no purpose, no goals, what do you do with him? You send him to university. Four years later you ask the question again, "You're graduating from university, so what are you going to do, what are you going to be?" You get the same standard answer.

They are all trying to find themselves. It comes out of a philosophical tradition that goes all the way back to the Greeks. The Greeks assumed that there was a self waiting to be found. The Greeks assumed that before we were ever born in time and space we lived in another world of pure archetypes, and that, at birth, something terrible happened; that the pure, essential self left the transcendental and entered into history and became incarnated in human flesh. Thus it becomes the problem from the time of the Greek philosophers to the present for us to look within ourselves to find out who we really are, because our identities and our essences are buried within. So the Oracle of Delphi says to Socrates, "Know thyself," implying that there is a self waiting to be known. The human potential movement has picked this up. We have to find out who we really are; we have to go through this process of self-discovery. It all suggests that there is a self waiting to be discovered through introspection.

Even Christian education becomes an attempt to nurture a psychological journey into the inner self to discover who the individual really is. Over and over I have youth ministers telling me that they are trying to help people find themselves. But a biblical perspective assumes that, rather than the self waiting to be found, the self is waiting to be created. And that the real task of Christian education is to facilitate in the lives of young people a process by which they create their identities rather than discover them. That is our great task: to facilitate the process of creating the self. My argument is that there is only one way to create a self; there is only one way to create an identity; there is only one way to create an essence to your humanity. And that is through commitment. In the end we become that to which we choose to commit ourselves, and our identities lie in our commitments. It is the uncommitted who have no identity. As T. S. Eliot says, we are like "hollow men," heads filled with straw, our dry voiced whispering meaninglessly like "wind in dry grass."[1] We have no essence. Ours is a generation of people who are uncommitted. When they asked John the Baptist what he was all about, he said, "I am the voice crying in the wilderness, prepare ye the way of the Lord — That is what I am, my mission is my identity." The very name of Jesus is "Deliverer." He was named in terms of what he was called to do — "For this purpose I came into the world" (John 18:37). His identity was wrapped up in his life commitment. There is no identity without commitments, and the task of those of us who are working with young people is to nurture commitment.

1. "The Hollow Men," lines 1-8 (1925), by Thomas Stearns Eliot (1888-1965).

A second problem with the human potential movement is that it has not only led us to believe there is an inner essence waiting to be discovered if we will just search and find it, but also that it encourages us to understand ourselves in terms of our past experiences. Whether one comes at it from a neo-Freudian position or a behaviorist position, the idea is the same: that who you are is determined by what you've already been. Or as the poet William Wordsworth says, "the Child is Father of the man,"[2] that in the end our past experiences mold us into who we are. In this struggle for identity, we look for the secrets of who we are; in our self-seeking we look to our pasts and try to find there the hints and suggestions that will tell us who we really are. We go through endless processes of unpackaging the past.

But what does it mean to be converted? It doesn't mean that your past is no more — it means that you give to the events of the past a whole new set of meanings. The events in the past are still there, with all their ugliness and tragedy, but one assigns them new meanings, and the new meanings that you assign to the events have the ability to impact you and mold you in a whole new way. This is our great deliverance from behaviorist psychology. Behaviorism says, "the events of the past — what happened yesterday — impacts you and determines what you are." If that's true, then there is no hope, and we are all victims of our yesterdays. But if the past can be redefined, if the events of the past are events to which we can give new meaning, then what the past is and how it affects us is always up for transformation.

That is the source of human freedom, to which my colleagues in sociology will ask the next question: On what basis will you alter the events of the past? What criteria will enable you to make the judgment as to what meanings you will give to the events of yesterday? Even granted that the events of yesterday do not determine who you are, what *meanings* do you give to those events that would lead you to define your future? The answer to those of us who ask such questions is this: we redefine the past in terms of what we hope for in the future. I redefine the events of my yesterdays, giving them new meaning, in terms of what I choose to become.

I find this orientation to the future throughout the entire New Tes-

---

2. "My Heart Leaps Up When I Behold," line 7 (1802), by William Wordsworth (1770-1850).

tament. "Forgetting those things that are behind," says the Apostle Paul, "I press toward the mark of the high calling of God in Christ Jesus our Lord" (Phil. 3:13). And that is the point with which I began, quoting Hebrews 11:1. Faith, when you really get down to the essence of it — faith which saves us by grace — "faith is the substance of things hoped for, the evidence of things unseen." Thus, in trying to escape from the narcissism of self-centeredness, our task as Christian leaders is not so much to help people understand how the events of the past have impacted them, but to define for them a new future that will enable them to go back and reconstruct the past so that the events of the past mold them into a person who is oriented to the future they have chosen.

The task, therefore, of someone in youth ministry, is to help young people define the future. And there is our problem, because for us the future tends to be defined in very individualistic terms. We constantly say to young people, "What do you want to be or become? How can we help you to realize your potential?" There is value in this, but again I come back to the Bible and would argue that the Bible asks us to define ourselves within a larger scheme of things. The Bible is about the unfolding of the kingdom of God — not an individualistic thing, but a social reality. God is at work in the world creating his kingdom. Thus, for me, becoming Christian is not getting saved so as to be ready to die. To understand ourselves as participants with God in the transformation of the world into his kingdom takes us out of that self-centered religiosity in which we see ourselves merely as people who need to get ready for heaven, to get our act together and become perfected in our own right. I would argue that the great emphasis of evangelical Christianity has become self-centeredness. Go to the Christian bookstores and see how many of the books are concentrated on how you can become more Christian, more spiritual, more holy, more sanctified, more joyful, and so on. It is totally self-centered, and the fact that you put Jesus into it doesn't change a thing. In the end, Jesus is only a means for you to become "all that you can be." But Jesus wants to save you and transform you so that through you he can be at work, transforming this world into the world that he wishes it to become.

All of his parables are about the kingdom, are they not? When he teaches us to pray he asks us to say, "Our Father who art in heaven, hallowed be thy name, *thy kingdom come,* thy will be done on earth as it is in heaven." The first words out of his mouth when he initiates his ministry in the Synoptic Gospels are, "Repent, for *the kingdom of God* is at hand" (Mark 1:15). It's the first thing he talks about and it's the last thing he talks about. In the book of Acts the last thing he does before ascending into heaven is this: "he taught his disciples the things concerning *the kingdom of God*" (Acts 1:3). His whole ministry was about a kingdom. We often mistake what he was all about, because what we like to say is, "Jesus came into the world and people misunderstood him. They thought he came into the world to create an earthly kingdom, a kingdom in this world. But he didn't, and that's why they crucified him. They thought that both in social and in political terms, Jesus wanted to transform society. But his kingdom wasn't really about this world, it was about another world, and people didn't understand him."

I think that those who crucified Jesus understood him perfectly. When he said, "I have come into this world to declare the kingdom of God, which is already among you," I think they read him right. I think that when those people put Jesus on the cross they did it for good reason. You may say that Jesus went to the cross in spite of the fact that he didn't commit a crime, but from a sociological point of view he committed a very serious crime. He didn't break the law of God; he just broke the law of society which says, "Don't mess with the system." It was said of him, "This is the man who stirs up the people" (Luke 23:5). And he did: he held before the people an alternative vision of the future, an alternative vision of tomorrow, and he asked people to come and join him, to participate with him in creating a new world, a new society, a new era in human history.

When I call young people to become Christians, I do not call upon them to get spiritual so they can go to heaven when they die. Rather, I call them to become participants in a revolution, in a movement that is designed to transform this world into the world it ought to be. In this process, I want them to separate themselves from a generation of people who are continually saying, "I am trying to find myself." Jesus says, "Whoever tries to find themselves will lose themselves" (Matt. 10:39). Where we are self-nurturing and self-seeking, Jesus says, "The more you try to find yourself, you're going to lose yourself. But those who are willing to lose themselves for my sake and for the sake of the kingdom will find themselves." The only real actualization of our humanity comes not through introspective self-discovery but by the losing of the self into the design of God for history, by becoming a participant in history for the transformation of the earth.

I believe that God's purpose will be realized in history. I believe that God is already at work in his people. When I remember Martin Luther King Jr. standing on the steps of the Lincoln Memorial and saying, "I have a dream," I know it is not a futile dream. To say, "I have a dream of a world in which there is no more racism, no more sexism, no more homophobia, no more militarism," is a statement of hope. I read in the sixty-fifth chapter of Isaiah, with its vision of the kingdom of God that is to come, that children do not die in infancy, that people live into old age, becoming everything that is joyful and good, that men and women work and enjoy the fruits of their own labors, and all have decent housing. So when I ask young people to escape from the culture of narcissism, I do it by saying, "Come, let us change the world." Let's build housing for poor people; let's deliver the street people from the obscenity of their lives; and let's get global. Let's look at the people in Rwanda, let's look at the people in Haiti, let's look at the people in Bolivia, and let us become agents of God who, transformed by his Spirit, are ready to move into this glorious life of commitment to the kingdom.

I said that we are not defined by the events of our past but by the meanings that we give to those events, and that the meanings we give to those events are totally determined by the commitments that we make to the future. The future is the kingdom of God. Contrary to what T. S. Eliot thought, the world will not end with a bang, nor will it end with a whimper. This is how the world will end: the kingdoms of this world will become the kingdom of our God (Rev. 11:15); and he shall reign forever and ever. In the end, he shall bring all principalities and all powers into submission to his will. All things will be brought under his control: all principalities, all powers, all dominions, all corporations, all publishing companies, all television networks.

When Hendrikus Berkhof wrote his essay, *Christ and the Powers,* he said something that we need to learn.[3] When I read in Ephesians 6:12 that we wrestle not only against flesh and blood but against "principalities and powers," I think this makes it clear that there are demonic

---

3. Hendrikus Berkhof, *Christ and the Powers,* trans. John Howard Yoder (Scottdale, Pa.: Herald, 1977 [1953]).

forces in history and in the world that have seized control of the principalities and powers. The demonic has seized control of the media, has it not? In the United States, more than in Canada, it has gained control of the educational process. In Camden, New Jersey, and in Philadelphia, Pennsylvania, where we work in the inner city, only half of the children who enter high school will ever graduate. And, of the half who graduate, two thirds will graduate as functional illiterates. Hundreds of thousands of kids who are graduating are incapable of functioning in this high-tech society. Is there any wonder that they resort to drugs and crime? The principalities and powers have gained control of this system.

Berkhof says that any supra-human entity (be it the media, corporations, ideas, magazines) and all of the cultural factors of society must be looked at as principalities and powers. Satan has gained control of them. The principalities and powers, governments and corporations, newspapers and media, all were created by God to serve us in his name and to serve his kingdom. What was created by God for good has been taken over by the demonic, and is now being used to destroy people. Your task, should you choose to accept it — and this is *not* a mission impossible! — is to become the people of God who move forward and take over the principalities and powers in a loving way, so that they are transformed into agencies that foster the good in people. So when you are working with young people, you must get them to define themselves not in terms of actualizing their own potential, but in terms of asking, "How do I contribute to the creation of the kingdom of God?"

If I understand that this is my task, I must see my vocational choices in terms of which of the principalities and powers I can enter into as leaven, as transforming salt, as a presence that works to make the world more like what God wants it to be. So, for example, if one becomes a steel worker and joins the labor union, one must ask, "How do I, along with others who believe with me, transform this labor union into the kind of labor union that Jesus wants it to be? How do I speak, how do I say 'Thus sayeth the Lord' at the next union meeting?" Perhaps within that union I have to find other people who have the same commitment to Jesus Christ that I do and with them form a little caucus, a support group that studies Scripture and tries to understand what the Bible has to say about the issues with which our union is dealing. Then we can address these issues and become agents of transformation, for God's will is not to *destroy* the union but to *transform* the union into the kind of union that God wants it to be. God's will is not to destroy General Motors, for to destroy is not God's motive. Jesus did not come to condemn and destroy; he came to redeem, to save, to transform.

When we are working with young people we need to get them to define themselves in terms of the future, in terms of the kingdom of God and the role they can play in transforming the society that is into the kind of society that ought to be. In short, the most important thing that you have to do as a youth leader is not to get people to believe certain propositional statements. The truth is, in almost every instance, those young people already believe that God is God and that Jesus is God. Your job is to help them decide on their vocational commitments, to help them ask, "What am I going to become, and how does that fit into the kingdom of God? How do I choose a vocation that enables me to participate with God in the transformation of this society?"

That means, of course, that we have failed miserably in youth work in the following way. We constantly concentrate on trying to discern what kinds of people God wants us to be as individuals. We have tremendous discussions on personal ethics and on personal sanctification. Nothing wrong with that. But when was the last time you sat down with your young people (as I have with my students in sociology) and asked, "What kind of world is Jesus trying to create?" My sociology students want to study how society changes, and I say that the first thing they have to do is answer the question, "If you want to change the world, what do you want to change it into?" Please give me a definition of God's kingdom. If God could transform the educational system of Canada, what would it be like? How would it be different than it is today? If God could change the labor movement, how would it be different than it is today? There have to be clear definitions of the future because if you don't know what you are trying to achieve, it is very hard to become committed to it.

That is what great biblical scholarship is about. The Bible should not only help us understand the past; it should also help us understand the future. That is why I get very upset about prophecy conferences, because all they ever do is look for evidence of when it is all going to end. They are all trying to figure out the date. But I don't want to know the date, I want to envisage the image of the kingdom that is to come. Jesus began to give us hints in his parables when he tried to tell us that the kingdom is likened unto this, and unto that, and unto the other thing. What is the kingdom of God like? That is a theological problem, and we have only to look at the past to understand where we are going. The Bible ultimately points to the future. The book of Romans says that we are not simply saved by faith, but we are saved by hope (Rom. 8:24). Just as when you talk about faith and you ask what faith is, the book of Hebrews says that faith is the substance of things hoped for, the essence of things unseen.

In what ways have we helped young people define the future, the kind of world that ought to be? Why is it that I have to go to secular musicals to get my inspiration? "Les Misérables" did for me what I ought to get in church — when those revolutionaries dream of a world without hate, a world without oppression, a world where people are not in need; when they are willing to die in that cause, then come back from the dead in that last scene on stage and the chorus sings:

> They will live again in freedom
> In the garden of the Lord.
> They will walk behind the plough-share
> They will put away the sword.
> The chain will be broken
> And all men will have their reward.
>
> Will you join in our crusade?
> Who will be strong and stand with me?
> Somewhere beyond the barricade
> Is there a world you long to see?
> Do you hear the people sing?
> Say, do you hear the distant drums?
> It is the future that they bring
> When tomorrow comes. . . .[4]

4. Act 2, "Finale," lines 9-22, from Alain Boublil and Claude-Michel Schönberg, *Les Misérables;* lyrics by Alain Boublil, Herbert Kretzmer, and Jean-Marc Natel (© Alain Boublil Music, 1985 ASCAP).

If you go to see the musical, the only thing that will disappoint you is that when they hit that crescendo at the end, the revolutionaries do not sing, "Amen." It would seem the most natural thing in the world for them to do that.

I go to see "Man of La Mancha," and the woman next to me starts yelling at her husband, "Stop it, you're exposing yourself!" So I lean forward and there's this guy crying his eyes out in his three-piece suit, shaking uncontrollably, and I know why he is crying:

> To dream the impossible dream,
> To fight the unbeatable foe . . .
> To run where the brave dare not go . . .
> This is my quest, to follow that star,
> No matter how hopeless, no matter how far,
> To fight for the right, without question or pause,
> To be willing to march into Hell, for a Heavenly cause . . .[5]

I know why he was crying, because he too once had dreams, he once had visions, and he sold them out for a Porsche and a Jacuzzi. He sold out to the system, he lost his dreams, he lost his visions. The Bible says that when people no longer have dreams, and when they no longer have visions, there is a deadness about them. I want to tell you what delivers people from deadness: what delivers them are dreams and visions.

All the great prophets of God wept, not only over what was going on in the world, not just over sin, but because there were no dreams about the future. The great prophets not only condemn the sins of the past but hold before the people a vision of the world that ought to be. When you read Isaiah, you will get that vision. Not only does Isaiah write about the sins of history, but he holds before the people of Israel the future that could be. When the prophet Jeremiah gets carried off into slavery, the last thing he does is to buy a piece of land, a symbol of the kingdom which is yet to come. God is angry, but it's not over till it's over. God is at work in the world through his people, and that is where we can get kids turned on. When we say to them, "Come join the movement, participate with us, and together we can change the world; we

---

5. "The Impossible Dream (The Quest)," lines 1-4, 9-12, lyrics by Joe Darion, music by Mitch Leigh (used by permission © 1965).

can deliver the world from the effects of the demonic. God is with us and he will deliver us into victory." We need to make young people into dreamers and visionaries about the future. Do we define the future? Do we make them believe that Jesus who is at work in them can achieve through them incredible things in history? The great news of the gospel is not just that you are loved, that your sins have been forgiven, and that Christ is at work in you to sanctify you. When God called Abraham in Genesis 12, God didn't just say, "I'm going to be a real blessing *for you*. I have something wonderful in store *for you*. Something really good is going to happen *to you*." No, God said, "through you all the nations in the world are going to be blessed" (Gen. 12:3).

The great problem with Jonah was not just that he disobeyed God, but that he did not want to carry out God's mission to bring good news to the Ninevites. Whenever someone says that he or she is "chosen," I always ask the question: "Chosen for what?" For you were not saved for your own sake. You were saved to carry out a mission. That is the escape from narcissism. We have made salvation into an instrument of self-actualization and personal fulfillment, when in fact Jesus saves us, sanctifies us, and fills us with his Spirit so that through us he might be at work in the world, transforming the world into the kind of world it ought to be. We've got to create visionaries, dreamers.

Let me tell you what I think is wrong with the church: our best young people are not interested in religious vocations. They think that religion is about getting people saved so that they go to heaven when they die; they think that religion is about becoming spiritual and sanctified. But the brightest and the best want to go into the world, to do something significant in the world, and they do not understand that the Christian calling is exactly that. The Christian calling is to do something significant in the world, to be agents of transformation. Down through the years I have been accused of being a social activist. My answer is, "Can you be anything else?" If there is a movement to eliminate racism, I ask a very simple question: "Does God want to eliminate racism?" Does God want to eliminate war? Does God want to redeem and reconstruct his environment? Does God want to elevate the state of women? Does God want people who are oppressed, as are homosexuals, to discover that they are loved and affirmed? Yes to all of the above. So, to me, the Christian vocation is to participate with God in all of these activities for the transformation of society. I am not saved to go to Heaven. I am saved, filled with the Spirit, so that God may have instruments through whom he can effect things in history. The escape from the narcissism of our culture is not a Christianity that offers personal fulfillment and personal happiness, but rather a Christianity that calls us to sacrifice all and if need be to suffer for the sake of creating the kingdom of God. It is a societal reality that Christ came into the world to initiate, which he is working through us to complete, and which will be completed on the day of his coming.

In every war, says Oscar Cullmann, writing in the context of World War Two, there is a decisive battle, and after that battle the inevitable works itself out.[6] In the American Civil War it was the battle of Gettysburg, because when the battle of Gettysburg was over, the South knew that they could no longer win. In World War Two, it was D-Day. It was an incredible day. I am old enough to remember sitting by the radio in school: we stopped classes and listened to the reports coming to us from Normandy, because everybody knew that all the chips were down. Both sides had bet everything on that struggle, on that one day. And when the dust had settled that day, the one they called the longest day, the beachhead had been established. D-Day had been a success. But let me point out something interesting. More people died after D-Day than before D-Day. There was a greater loss of life and greater destruction between D-Day and V-Day than there was before D-Day. But here's the important point that Cullmann makes: the outcome was never in doubt. Once the decisive battle had been fought and won, the outcome was never in doubt. There was suffering, there was pain, there was destruction, there was horror, but the outcome was never in doubt. Once there was a D-Day we knew there would be a V-Day, when the victory would become complete.

Cullmann gives this illustration for a very obvious reason. The Bible also describes a D-Day and a V-Day. The cross and the resurrection is God's great D-Day. The eagle has landed, the battle is fought, Satan and all his legions have come face to face with our Savior on a hill outside a little city. When the dust has settled it looks as though the evil one has won, that Satan is victorious. It looks like he has a throne, but three days later Jesus stages a coup, and up from the grave he arises. He

---

6. See Oscar Cullmann, *Christ and Time: The Primitive Christian Conception of Time and History,* trans. Floyd V. Filson (Philadelphia: Westminster, 1964), p. 84.

comes forth, and now we know that what looked like a defeat was actually the greatest victory in human history. So now, say the Scriptures, as we fight against the principalities and the powers, as we struggle against the demonic, we do not struggle as those without hope, because D-Day is a done deal. We know how it will end, so that even when we are knocked down we are not cast out because we know who will win. Even if we die, we die in a cause that ultimately wins, which is better than winning in a cause that ultimately loses. We know that ultimately we will win.

The good news is that the day of victory is coming. If you had talked to people in the French Underground, and asked them a very simple question, "Do you really think you can beat the Nazis with their power, their organization, their structures?" — they would have said, "I know we look like a rag-tag force that has no effectiveness whatsoever, but what you don't know is that across the English Channel, even as we talk, a huge invasion force is being assembled. We don't know when it is going to happen, because nobody has told us the day, but a signal will be given, and on that day that huge invasion force will come across the Channel and join up with our feeble efforts and carry us to victory."

We are God's underground. People laugh at us when we try to move into society and change the world without using power. When we try to change the world through sacrificial love, through giving, through ministry, they say, "You can't win, because evil is too strong, Satan is in control; darkness rules." But we say in reply, "I know it looks bad, but what you don't understand is that there is a huge invasion force being assembled. I do not know when the signal will be given, but one of these days a trumpet is going to sound, and Jesus is going to come back. He is going to lead us, so you'd better join us now because we're going to run over you on that great day. Nothing can stop us when that day comes."

To help young people assume their identity as participants in the transformation of the world, rather than through self-actualization and self-definition, we must define ourselves in terms of that to which we are committed and that which we are committed to change. Who we are is to a large degree influenced by the events of yesterday, but we can give new meaning to those events so that they affect us differently. And the meaning we give to the events of the past that mold us into who we are is determined by what we imagine by the grace of God, and believe

God is calling us to in the future. For me, conversion is the reconstruction of the past, giving to the yesterdays of our lives new meaning so that we begin to see those things in the past that were so destructive as part of a process whereby God is using us to do his good in the world. All of the world groans and is in travail, waiting for us to move forward and to participate with God to deliver it from its sinful state. Like that one line of the sermon in the story I always tell: "It's Friday, but Sunday's coming."

Taking the Listeners Seriously
as the People of God

THOMAS G. LONG

1997

In my doctoral program at Princeton Seminary, I had a teacher named Seward Hiltner. He was in the field of pastoral care, and he used to talk about a concept known as "dated emotion." A "dated emotion" was when somebody went though a crisis and psychologically formed a reaction to it, but then the psychological reaction persisted after the crisis had passed. The illustration he used was that of a man standing in a field when a flash flood comes through. In order to save his life, he climbs up on a rock and clings there for dear life as the waters rush by. But then the waters subside, the sun comes out, and the land becomes dry, parched, and baked. But the man won't let go of the rock. He stays there perched on top as if the crisis still persisted.

I would like to suggest that homiletics and the practice of preaching have been experiencing a "dated emotion." In order to demonstrate this, I want to take a very brief journey all the way back to the very beginning of the homiletical tradition. The oldest homiletical text that we know anything about is Book Four of Augustine's *On Christian Doctrine*. At one point in this book he asks, "What is the sermon for?" The purpose of a sermon, says Augustine, is "to teach, to delight, and to persuade."[1] Now,

---

1. Saint Augustine [354-430 CE], *On Christian Doctrine,* trans. D. W. Robertson (Indianapolis: Bobbs-Merrill, 1958), XVII.34 [p. 142].

he stole that from Cicero, but by the time he put it into his context he had redefined the words. If the purpose of the sermon is to teach, to delight, and to persuade, what he meant by that was that the first responsibility we have as preachers is to teach: to give people the content, the vocabulary, the narratives of the Christian faith. We teach the inner-doctrinal connections of the fabric of the faith. But we don't teach in some dry, didactic fashion. We teach in a way that inflames the heart and the imagination. We teach delightfully, and if we teach delightfully, then our teaching is persuasive. By "persuasive," Augustine did not mean what Billy Graham means by persuasion. What he meant was ethics. If I learn the Christian faith in a way that lights up my imagination, it opens up opportunities for ethical obedience. We can see this in Jesus' own teaching and preaching. Remember when Jesus was trying to explain the reign of God in the Sermon on the Mount?

> "Look at the birds of the air; they neither sow nor reap nor gather into barns, and yet your heavenly Father feeds them. . . . Consider the lilies of the field, how they grow; they neither toil nor spin, yet I tell you, even Solomon in all his glory was not clothed like one of these." (Matt. 6:26, 28-29)

I never liked that text because it always dies the death of a thousand qualifications. I understand that the birds of the air and the lilies of the field neither work nor spin. But they also don't have college tuitions and mortgages. Robert Tannehill says that Jesus does not simply teach, he teaches delightfully, because the verbs here are strong: not just "consider" but "look carefully." Really *look,* he says, at the birds of the air.[2]

One night in Atlanta I went to see "The Cotton Patch Gospel," the play that sets the Gospel of Matthew in the rural south of America.[3] Tom Key was playing the part of Jesus; it was the last night of the run and the actors were a little frisky. They got to that point in the Gospel

---

2. Robert C. Tannehill, *The Sword of His Mouth* (Philadelphia: Fortress; Missoula: Scholars, 1975), pp. 62-63.

3. See Clarence Jordan, *The Cotton Patch Version of Matthew and John; Including the Gospel of Matthew (Except for the "Begat" Verses) and the First Eight Chapters of the Gospel of John* (New York: Association, 1970); stage adaptation by Harry Chapin, Tom Key, and Russell Treyz.

where Jesus was doing the Sermon on the Mount. Tom Key walked to the edge of the stage, made a sweeping motion with his hand, and said "Look at the birds of the air." Then he stopped as if he couldn't remember the next line. He started over: "Look at the birds of the air." He stopped again. The other members of the cast were beginning to fidget and get a little nervous. He acted as if he couldn't remember. So he did it again: "Look at the birds of the air." Finally he stopped, turned around to the other cast members on stage, and said, "I can't get these people to look." The next time he spoke his line, we all looked at the birds of the air. Tannehill says that if you actually look at the birds of the air and the lilies of the field, suddenly you begin to wonder, "Which world is real? The world of mortgages, tuitions, anxieties, threats, and fears, or the world of carefree providence?" So look. Because when you look hard enough, what you see relativizes the world in which you live. You still have to live with mortgages and tuition fees, but maybe underneath there is providence. And that opens up possibilities for ethical obedience. Therefore the purpose of preaching is to teach, to delight, and to persuade.

Augustine thought that every sermon ought to do all three. I sometimes say that if Augustine preached in your church on Sunday morning, do you know what he would like to hear, standing at the door afterwards shaking hands? "Thank you preacher, I learned something this morning, I was moved by what you said and I intend to do something about it." But I also think that Augustine's categories are descriptive of moments in the history of preaching. There are times when the pulpit bursts forth with teaching, the Reformation being one of those moments. I grew up in the rural south of the Fifties and Sixties, when some preachers lost their pulpits because it was a time of ethical persuasion on the civil rights issue. It was a season when the pulpit moved into persuasion. But for the past thirty or forty years, we have been in the season of delight. In the Fifties, the pulpit in North America was very didactic: the Christian faith was complete, and all that remained was for it to be taught. Preachers were trained in a pedantic, content-oriented, propositionally based preaching style. The pews were full, but suddenly preachers began to sense that their congregations had stopped listening. They weren't tired of preaching in principle. No, they were tired of *our* preaching. So a 911 call went out to homiletics, and homiletics began to generate a new style.

One of the first signs of the new style was *Design for Preaching,* published in 1958 by a Lutheran homiletician named H. Grady Davis.[4] For fifteen years, it was the most popular homiletical textbook in North America. What Grady Davis said was, "Look, don't think of the central idea of the sermon as a thesis that is to be sub-divided into supporting points, because then you will inevitably produce a stale, static, dry sermon. Instead, think of the central idea of the sermon as an acorn, and of the sermon as the oak tree that grows from the acorn." He changed the primary metaphor of the sermon so that preachers began to think about sermons as living, breathing, moving, rolling organisms. The totality of the sermon was alive in a way that the old didactic, pedantic style did not allow. Squeeze *Design for Preaching* really hard, and you will not get a drop of Bible or theology out of it. It is not because Davis, a good Lutheran, was not concerned about Bible or theology; no, he could assume it. The teaching had been done, but the delight was missing.

The real blow, however, was achieved in 1971 when a then relatively unknown homiletician by the name of Fred B. Craddock published *As One Without Authority.*[5] In that book, Craddock wanted to know how it was that the sermons of creative, energetic, responsible ministers were often so dull. He was not interested why the sermons of irresponsible, uncreative ministers were dull: there was no mystery in that. But how come the good ones were boring their congregations? He decided that it was due to a difference in the logical style applied in the study and the logical style applied in the pulpit. In the study the minister has the Bible open, along with a few commentaries and a blank tablet. The minister does not know what the text will yield or what the sermon will be, so the minister engages in a process of discovery. The minister is a detective — sleuthing, following clues and leads, doing word studies and pursuing this idea or path until finally at the end of the process there is a moment of discovery: "Oh yes, that'll preach, that'll preach." It is an exciting process. But the minister takes that insight into the pulpit, says, "My thesis for this morning is . . ." and then unpacks it in the form of three deductive points. The process in the study is inductive; the process in the pulpit is deductive. Why not, said Craddock, bring the induction out of the study and into the pulpit, so that the

---

4. Henry Grady Davis, *Design for Preaching* (Philadelphia: Muhlenberg, 1958).
5. Fred B. Craddock, *As One Without Authority,* rev. ed. (St. Louis: Chalice, 2001).

preacher engages the congregation in a kind of replicated, open-ended process of discovery with the insight of the sermon coming near the end? You can imagine what that created in homiletics. It spun off all the Lowrys and the Buttricks, the Patricia Wilson-Kastners, all of the Chris Smiths and the Tom Longs. All of us got into the business of creating homiletical styles and preaching techniques that were designed to infuse the sanctuary with delight. We were like crazed electricians popping pennies into the fuse box: anything to keep the juice on in the sanctuary.

In 1978, Fred Craddock published *Overhearing the Gospel.*[6] It was based on a line from Kierkegaard, complaining about Christianized Denmark and, saying, essentially, "There is no lack of information in a Christian land. What is lacking is something else, and that something else cannot be communicated directly. It can only be communicated indirectly." There is no lack of information: we've done the teaching. What is lacking is something else: delight. And you can't communicate delight directly. You have to do it with poetry and imagination, narrative and image, indirectly.

But now there *is* a lack of information, and ours is not a Christian land. The crisis of the Fifties is not the crisis of the turn of the century. The crisis of the Fifties was boredom. I am not saying that we have overcome the boredom, but if we define our preaching over against a crisis of boredom we will miss the new and larger crisis that is looming before our very eyes. The crisis of the Nineties and the turn of the century is incompetence. I don't mean that in the pejorative sense, but in the technical sense. What I mean is that our congregations have lost the ability to be competent as Christians. When you stand in your pulpit, what do you see as you look out at your congregations? I think that you see a congregation, whether you know it or not, that is more tentative than they have been before. In *Why Preach? Why Listen?*[7] William Muehl says, in essence, "If you are standing in the pulpit of a North American church, be assured that you are looking out at a congregation of people, many of whom almost did not come this morning. And of those who did come, many secretly fear that everybody else in the sanctuary is more confidently Christian than they are." I don't think it

---

6. Fred B. Craddock, *Overhearing the Gospel,* rev. ed. (St. Louis: Chalice, 2002).
7. William Muehl, *Why Preach? Why Listen?* (Philadelphia: Fortress, 1986).

is nostalgia to say that seventy-five years ago the average Christian lay person had a working theological vocabulary. Christians could use words like "faith" and "hope" and "salvation," maybe even "justification" and "sanctification." Not only that, they needed such language to make sense of their lives. But now those images, that vocabulary, those metaphors have slipped away from us like the robes of kings and queens.

You may know the work of Don Luidens, Dean Hoge, and Benton Johnson on the state of the laity in typical Protestant churches in North America.[8] By tracking people who were confirmed in Protestant churches when they were middle or older teenagers and following them into their thirties and forties, they have discovered that fewer than half are involved in the church any longer. Those who are still involved have an unofficial creed that these researchers call "lay liberalism." As a kind of lay approach to religion, it is not "liberal" in the classic, nineteenth-century sense, but in the sense that people say, "Hey look, we are all autonomous people who are trying to work toward the best balance in life that we can, and I want my kids to be exposed to religion, but when they are old enough I really want them to make their own choice as to whether they want to be Christian or not." It is a sort of laissez-faire approach to the training of the faith.

Leander Keck, who teaches at Yale Divinity School, says that when the New Haven Educational Board gets together annually to set the calendar for the following academic year, the Muslims are absolutely shocked that the Christians and the Jews trade holidays ("Give us Christmas and we'll call it winter holidays and we'll give you . . ."). The Muslims are astounded at the ability of their Christian and Jewish counterparts to view religion as a negotiable quantity, as a set of opinions that you can swap back and forth, rather than as a comprehensive way of viewing self, other, world, God, and life. How did we lose that comprehensive ability? We have lost our theological vocabulary and competence in two kinds of ways, depending on whether we are liberals or conservatives. Those of us in the liberal tradition have lost our theological competence because we have stopped using our theological vocabulary. When I graduated from seminary in 1971, I had a kind of

---

8. Dean R. Hoge, Benton Johnson, Donald A. Luidens, *Vanishing Boundaries: The Religion of Mainline Protestant Baby Boomers* (Louisville: Westminster/John Knox, 1994).

modified Tillichian approach to preaching that went something like this: "My congregation cannot possibly understand crusty old theological words like 'grace' or 'faith,' so I am going to translate them into existential qualities they do understand." So in my preaching, "grace" became "acceptance," and "faith" became "trust." But as Peter Berger says, that's playing poker with the house. You end up squandering the one thing theological vocabulary does that existential vocabulary cannot, which is to point to the transcendent.

When I was in seminary, I spent a summer as an apprentice minister in a little town in North Carolina, where I was given pastoral care responsibilities over half a dozen families or so. One of these families had several children, the youngest of whom was a victim of cerebral palsy. Visiting this family was a strange experience. It was almost as if everyone in the family was in a circle of light except this youngest kid, John. He stood literally and figuratively outside the circle, watching the rest of the family. One afternoon I went to visit the family, and only John's mother was at home. I sat down in the living room and we had a conversation in which she told me about a religious experience she had had only a couple of days before. She had been in the same room reading, or knitting. It was late in the afternoon, the light was dim, and John was down at the end of the hallway watching her from the shadows. She said she felt a shift in the room. She looked up, and, she said, "I saw Jesus with his arm around John. I looked away, I looked back, and there was only John. But for the first time since he'd been born, I began to understand that John was already healed in the power of God."

I don't know what exactly went on there, but I do know what she and I each did with that experience. She turned it into ethics. If you were to visit that town today, you would find programs in place for kids with disabilities, programs she started because of that visionary experience. I had just had a course in clinical pastoral education, and what I did was to say (fortunately, to myself), "My God, this woman is feeling so guilty about this kid's relationship to the family that she is taking the vocabulary and symbols of the Christian faith and projecting her guilt on the screen of . . ." In other words, I took an experience that she needed theological vocabulary to describe, and I reduced it to psychological categories so that I could manipulate it on the chessboard of manageability. Now, if her minister does that, think what her culture does, constantly eroding confidence in religious experience. According to Peter Berger, either people do not have experiences of God as much as they used to, or they have them as much as they ever had, but they doubt them, even to themselves, and deny them, because the culture puts cognitive pressure on all of those experiences. Allan Gurganus, the novelist, once wrote in *The New York Times* that we used to name our daughters Faith and Hope, but now we name them Tiffany, and we don't know why. We have lost our theological vocabulary.

If we are in the conservative tradition, however, we lose our theological vocabulary and competence not because we stop using the words, but because we make the words too small. The great words of the faith, such as "the Lordship of Jesus Christ," describe large, public categories. But we reduce them to interior states of piety:

> He lives, He lives, Christ Jesus lives today!
> He walks with me and talks with me
> Along life's narrow way.
> He lives, He lives, salvation to impart!
> You ask me how I know He lives:
> He lives within my heart![9]

True, but too small. An American televangelist who specializes in reducing the Christian faith to the American dream was being introduced on the BBC. The interviewer was sharp: she said, "You preach a gospel of success, don't you?" "Yes I do," he replied,

> "I think Jesus helps you sail, not tail or fail."
> "Well, didn't your own Lord die a shameful death on a cross? How do you fit that into a gospel of success?"
> "Oh, like all successful men, Jesus had his setbacks, but on Easter he put that all behind him."

Too small. Some of us lose our theological competence through negligence and others through reductionism.

If our congregations don't have theological competence, what do they lose? The first thing they lose is that the Christian faith collapses

9. "He Lives!" (1932), by Alfred Henry Ackley (1887-1960).

in on a narcissistic self. Looking out on our congregations, we see people who, because they have lost their theological competence, can only describe the Christian faith in highly individualistic terms. I have spent the last year researching funerals. An amazing shift has taken place. Instead of the gospel story, we now tell the biography of the deceased, so that funeral services have become monogrammed experiences. I once heard about a funeral at which they sang the two favorite hymns of the deceased: "Amazing Grace" and "I Did It My Way." What that turns our preaching into, of course (and this is where Buttrick is absolutely right), is exclusively autobiographical, experiential self-revelation. I was talking to a friend who saw a faculty colleague next to him in the pew one Sunday after the service, so they struck up a conversation. The congregation began to drift out and finally the sanctuary was mostly empty except for these two people and a couple of kids running around. One of them, a little boy, climbed up into the pulpit. The little boy saw his mother in the back of the church and shouted out, "Mommy, Mommy, look at me, look at me." To which the colleague responded, "I think I've heard that sermon before."

Not only is there a curving-in on the self, there is a loss of the capacity for a religious and theological interpretation of life. After I had preached one Sunday on the Harvard campus, Peter Gomes and I were walking to lunch. While admiring the architecture at Harvard I saw a building that didn't fit in, a modern glass and concrete structure several stories high. "What in the world is that?" I asked. As Peter explained, it used to be that the sociology department, the anthropology department, the psychology department, and the other human sciences were all lodged in separate little buildings. Talcott Parsons, head of sociology, had a great idea: "What if we built a building for all of the human sciences, but without segregating them into separate departments? We could build a building with wide corridors and open spaces to encourage interdisciplinary interaction. We could build a dining room so that we would eat together, so that the greatest scientists in the world would be in conversation every day. And the result of that would be a new and better society." So they built it. It wasn't long before they began to squabble over secretaries, typewriters, and space. The sociologists and anthropologists and psychologists and others divided at lunchtime into separate little groups, and finally they had to build partitions to Balkanize the thing and keep the various academic disciplines apart from one another. Another member of the Harvard faculty observed that what Talcott Parsons lacked was a doctrine of sin. When you lose your theological vocabulary, you can no longer make meaning out of the depth of human experience.

You also have a loss of mission. I serve on the Princeton University Chapel Advisory Council. Once a year, the University chaplains report on their work to us, and we can ask them any questions we want. One year after we had heard the reports from the chaplains, a member of the council, an old tiger who is a Wall Street lawyer, said, "I have a question. What are university students like these days?" The chaplains looked at each other as if to say, "Who wants to answer that one?" Finally the Methodist chaplain said, "Well, I think you'd be pleased. They are very career-oriented and ambitious, but that's not all. They work in soup-kitchens; they tutor after school; last week they protested apartheid . . ." As she began to go down the list, Eddie Feld, the Jewish chaplain, began to grin. The longer she went down the list, the wider he grinned. Finally she said, "Eddie, am I saying something funny?" He replied, "I'm sorry. I was just thinking that what you are saying is that the university students are good people. You're right. And they do good things: you're right about that too. I was just thinking, though, that the one thing they lack is a vision of salvation." We all looked at the Jewish university chaplain. "It's true," he said. "If you do not have some understanding of what God is doing to repair the creation, you can't get up every day and go to a soup kitchen because the world finally beats you down."

Now, if there is any truth at all in what I have been saying, what that means is that if you look out on the horizon of preaching, the word "teaching" is coming over the edge. I am fully committed to inductive preaching, to imagination, to story, to image, but I now want to harness those images toward re-equipping the communion of the saints and the competent community of the church. Imagine that you stand in the pulpit on Sunday morning and there is a target superimposed on your congregation. In the bull's-eye are the saints, those who know the vocabulary, who know the story, who carry on the mission of the church. The next ring represents the seekers, those who are, as it were, "in and out." The third ring represents the people who are there because their kid sings in the junior choir: they are largely marginal to the purposes of the church. To whom do you preach? Some say that you preach to the outer ring in order to bring them in. You dumb down the vocabulary of the faith in order to attract people who do not care about the vocabulary of the faith. I would like to say, to the contrary, "Preach to the bull's-eye." But preach to the bull's-eye in such a way that those in the other rings can overhear and also acquire the vocabulary of the faith.

Think of it this way. If a family adopts a teenage boy who does not know the family jokes, who doesn't know about the family vacations to Nova Scotia, who doesn't know about Aunt Myrtle, do you stop telling the family jokes, stop going to Nova Scotia, and forget about Aunt Myrtle? No, you keep telling the family jokes, but in such a way that brings him into the family conversation. You keep going to Nova Scotia, and you tell him about Aunt Myrtle. We make the vocabulary of the faith *porous* for those who need to acquire it. Take the issue of inclusive language. Why should I be bothered with inclusive language in worship? Some people say that you should use inclusive language because otherwise, feelings will get hurt. That is true but not very persuasive. Others say that you must use inclusive language because kids in school are using it and they might as well learn to do so in church. But that's just following the drumbeat of secular culture. Still others say you must use inclusive language because it is an issue of justice and ethics, and you are a bad person if you don't. I don't want to be a bad person, but I get grumpy if that is my only motivation. I want to use inclusive language because a day is coming when people will come from East and West and North and South, and sit down together in the kingdom of God — men, women, children, young, old, red, yellow, black, and white. The conversation at that great banquet is going to be inclusive, and the church is the language school of the reign of God. I want to learn to talk today the way we are going to talk then. I want to equip a community with the vocabulary of the future, because the vocabulary of the present is obsolete. And I am stammering at it, I really am stammering at it, but every vocabulary word that I acquire liberates me and deepens my participation in the messianic feast.

We also need to give them back their Bibles, and there are several concrete ways we can do that. First of all, whenever we read Scripture, let's acknowledge that the reading of Scripture is one of the low moments in worship. People listen episodically, and have no idea what they are hearing. So before we read, we need to set the context. Give them some hooks on which to hang what they are about to listen to, so that gradually they will begin to understand the continuity of the biblical story. Likewise, even though we use historical-critical, theological-critical, redactional, and literary-critical tools to get at the text, we hide all those things when we get to the pulpit because we worry that the congregation couldn't handle it, or because they might think we doubt the inspiration of Scripture. No. As Judge Oliver Wendell Holmes once commented, "Even a dog knows the difference between being tripped over and being kicked." It is vital for the preacher who shares critical information with the congregation to give them their Bibles back. Whether we know it or not, there are people who are clinging onto their faith in the Bible by their fingernails, and we need to help them know that you can love God with mind as well as with heart. Give them the critical information that helps us to see the Word of God.

We also need to exegete the practices of the church. The church is a living theological community, and underneath the practices of the church is a biblical, theological, exegetical foundation. In one of his books, Stanley Hauerwas tells of a Mennonite farmer who makes cheese. He takes the cheese to a convenience store on the main highway in Lancaster County, Pennsylvania, where a lot of tourists come through to see the Amish and the Mennonites, and the convenience store operator sells the cheese on consignment. When the farmer goes to collect his money at the end of the year, the convenience store operator says "I've sold a lot of your cheese, and I owe you six thousand dollars, but I don't have it, and I don't think I'm ever going to have it. I've had a bad year in the rest of the store." End of story. Hauerwas says that whenever he tells that story, people say, "The farmer ought to sue the convenience store operator." Someone told that to the farmer, who answered, "Mennonites don't sue." That's all the farmer knows, that Mennonites live in a community where the practice is, "We don't sue." What isn't obvious is that underneath that practice is an exegesis of 1 Corinthians 6:1-8. His preacher needs to bring into visibility the exegetical, biblical, and theological foundations that underlie the practices of the community. You may not serve a community that doesn't sue, but you do serve a community with distinctive practices of its own, and underneath those practices are theological foundations. Bring them into visibility to create theological competence in the church.

Finally, consider your congregation to be saints in the making. It is not just Martin Luther King Jr. and Mother Teresa who put the faith in action, it's the Millers and the Joneses. Therefore, when we give them

54

the intrinsic illustrations of which I spoke in my previous lecture, what we are doing is dress-rehearsing a faith in action that they will put into practice during the week. In *A Whole New Life,* Reynolds Price writes about his struggle with spinal cancer:

> My presiding oncologist saw me as seldom as he could manage. He plainly turned aside when I attempted conversation in the halls; and he seemed to know literally no word or look of mild encouragement or comradeship in the face of what, as I later learned, he thought was a hurried death. . . . It's often said by way of excuse that doctors are insufficiently trained for humane relations. Well, for complex long-range interaction with damaged creatures, they may well need a kind of training they never receive; but what I wanted and needed badly, from that man then, was the frank exchange of decent concern. When did such a basic transaction between two mammals require post-graduate instruction beyond our mother's breast milk?[10]

The nurses, on the other hand, were as full of grace as the oncologist was of disinterest. They were able, "by something more than accidental grace . . . to blend their profession with the oldest natural code of all — mere human connection, the simple looks and words that award a suffering creature his or her dignity." Price goes on to say, "Many times since, I've thought that if I were ever to donate a work of art to Duke, I'd commission a realistic statue of a black woman in a nurse's uniform and ask that it stand by the hospital door."[11] Make no mistake, it would be a statue of a saint. Think of our congregations as saints in the making.

Taking our listeners seriously as the people of God means reminding them of which world is real. Reaching all the way back to Augustine, this will require us to recover the element of teaching in our proclamation, and that in turn will help our congregations begin to recover their theological vocabulary, their theological perspective on life, their understanding of Scripture, their sense of mission, and their appreciation of the unique character of the Christian community. Preaching takes listeners seriously because they *are* the people of God.

10. Reynolds Price, *A Whole New Life* (New York: Atheneum, 1994), p. 56.
11. Price, *A Whole New Life,* pp. 132-33.

"Not with Plausible Words or Wisdom": Homiletic Method

Homiletic Method:
Meaning and Consciousness

—————

DAVID G. BUTTRICK

1993

Some years ago, there was a satiric review called "Beyond the Fringe."[1] A smash hit in London, the show was sent to the States. In the review, there was a spoof of a typical Anglican sermon. The text was a single verse from Genesis: "Behold, Esau my brother is an hairy man, and I am a smooth man" (Gen. 27:11). The homily began with the text, moved along by whim and association through one pulpit cliché after another and finally, concluded minutes later with a ringing repetition of the text, every word weighted with significance, "Behold, Esau my brother is an hairy man." A British bishop visiting the States was asked for his reaction: "I laughed," he said, "but not loudly." "The satire," he added, "was too close to the mark." Of course, the bishop may have indicted not merely the Anglican pulpit, but Protestant preaching in general. Is

---

1. Alan Bennett, Peter Cook, Jonathan Miller, and Dudley Moore, *Beyond the Fringe* (New York: Random House, 1963). The skit was entitled, "Take a Pew."

This lecture was prepared for two engagements a few weeks apart, for the Gladstone Lectures at McMaster Divinity College and for the "College of Preachers" Festival Lectures at the University of York in England. Subsequently, the lecture, edited and much amplified, appeared as chapter 4, "Preaching and Method," in *A Captive Voice: The Liberation of Preaching* (Louisville: Westminster/John Knox, 1994).

there any way, any new way to preach that will speak God's good news to our word-weary age? Today, we shall talk of method.

I

Anyone who preaches regularly wants a method. We need method simply to survive. The average preacher produces the equivalent of a book a year in sermons; a daunting task, week after week, month after month, year after year. Therefore, however freewheeling ministers may be, they soon become methodical if only in self-defense. There has got to be a way of preaching that gets the job done faithfully, without hair-tugging, endless rewriting, and sweaty last-minute desperations. Of course we know that method can stifle. Method can turn into an every-week, repetitive formula that congregations soon pick up, if only subliminally. Like Erle Stanley Gardner detective stories — if you've heard one sermon, you've heard them all. No, we need a method that marshals our energies, but sets us free from enacting ourselves psychologically on a weekly basis.[2] After all, our lives are already crowded with parish busyness and the tears of the broken-hearted. There are never enough hours in a day for the work of the Lord! So preachers need a method, some sure way of doing sermons.

But push the matter deeper. Yes, all of us would like a quick and easy way of preparing sermons. But crowd us into a corner, and maybe we'll admit the truth: we'd like to be able to prepare not just quick sermons but good sermons, sermons that can reach deep into the lives of our people and be useful. We know that in preaching, we ought to love our neighbors — specifically our neighbors in pews. Moreover, we know we ought to love God. What makes slap-dash, hasty sermons intolerable is that they are a sure sign of unbelief. Let me repeat: careless preaching is a testimony to unbelief. For if we truly believe that we preach in the presence of God, how can we ever let ourselves be careless? Surely one of the purposes of preaching is *invocation*. Our sermons

---

2. Could sermon design be a form of psychological enactment? The literature is sparse, but see Leslie J. Tizard, *Preaching: The Art of Communication* (New York: Oxford University, 1958) and, more recently, Hans van der Geest, *Presence in the Pulpit*, trans. D. W. Stott (Atlanta: John Knox, 1981).

should be fit offerings to God in whose awesome presence we dare stand to speak. So, yes, we'd like a quick and easy way of preaching but, more deeply, we want our sermons to be worthy of God and useful to our neighbors. So please, in our harried parishes, how do we prepare ourselves to preach and preach well? Give us a responsible method!

II

These days the problem of method is more complex than we know. Human consciousness is historical. Consciousness is not fixed forever; it changes from age to age.[3] Rather clearly we are speaking to a different human consciousness than did preachers a century or so ago. Look at paintings painted in the "Age of Reason," which all display the same perspective. They are painted as if by a third-person, objective viewer; in a way, they are a testimony to the style of the age, which is Rationalism. The world is there, ordered by a detached, objective reason. But wander any Toronto art gallery these days and the canvases are quite different. In a single painting there may be several different perspectives, angles of vision, imposed one upon another. Artists now are opening up a world beyond the objective, a world that includes memories and fantasies, swirls of feeling and strange, compelling myths.[4] The same sort of change has occurred in fiction, hasn't it? Thackeray could describe the world of Becky Sharpe in *Vanity Fair* by telling a third-person chronological story from start to finish, "Dear reader."[5] But nowadays, authors imitate consciousness. Memories merge and fantasies occur — day dreams, feelings, urges, and all — even as we meet and speak with others in a present-tense world.[6] We live at a time when definitions of reality

3. For discussion, see Emil L. Fackenheim, *Metaphysics and History* (Milwaukee: Marquette University, 1961).

4. Compare the painting of an ordered Dutch kitchen by Jan Vermeer (1632-1675) with Marc Chagall's astonishing *I and the Village* (Museum of Modern Art, New York: Mrs. Simon Guggenheim Fund).

5. William Makepeace Thackeray, *Vanity Fair: A Novel Without a Hero* (London: Bradbury & Evans, 1848).

6. For example, see Edoardo Sanguinetti, "Capriccio Italiano," trans. Raymond Rosenthal, *The Award Avant-Garde Reader,* ed. Gil Orlovitz (New York: Universal Publishing Award Books, 1965), pp. 210-38.

are wider and more complex than in earlier eras. The scientific world-view is fading fast; we realize now as not before that reality is beyond both objective and subjective. Reality is defined by consciousness.[7]

Now, when a world's understanding of reality changes, so does language. Every major language family in the world has been changing radically since the beginning of the twentieth century. Dwight McDonald suggests that the English language was shrinking until the late 1950s, shrinking and becoming more abstracted. If there were 450,000 words in the big *Webster's Dictionary* in 1934, McDonald suspects that more than 175,000 words simply dropped from common vocabulary in the first half of the century. But then, with the Sixties, though another fifty thousand words may have slipped away, language began to enlarge again.[8] New words invaded common English as sub-cultural speech was heard and copied: words from Hispanic culture, from black communities, not to mention third-world countries. The language began to enlarge again and to become more metaphorically alive. Some lexicographers suppose that more than half of the standard vocabulary will be altered in less than a single century. Well, ever since Wilhelm von Humboldt we have known that worldviews are embodied in language. So what's going on in the world today? Why, a whole wide world is changing its mind! We live in the midst of an epochal event similar in scope to the collapse of the Greco-Roman world and the fragmentation of the Medieval synthesis. No wonder we reissue dictionaries and rewrite liturgies. To repeat: we must find a way to preach in a world that is changing its mind.

Please note, I said "changing," not "changed": a *changing* consciousness. Rather obviously, to borrow Barth's phrase, we live "between the times," in the midst of tumbling paradigms. Normally preaching finds method as well as rhetorical convention in the high periods of cultural synthesis, not usually in the moments of change. As we noted earlier, in the early 1800s Bishop Whately framed a way of preaching that has lasted, and is still very much with us. Yet Augustine wrote in a time of radical change and set patterns for the Medieval church. Likewise the Reformers, Luther and Calvin, preached in a turbulent era and, again,

7. See Aron Gurwitsch, *The Field of Consciousness* (Pittsburgh: Duquesne University, 1964).

8. Dwight McDonald, "The String Untuned," *The New Yorker* (March 10, 1962).

set precedents for years of Protestant preaching. The task of our age is not only to speak the gospel but to find and form new ways of preaching for an emerging new human consciousness. Biblical study is now working beyond the supposed objectivity of the historical-critical method in various new literary-critical ways, not to mention procedures that work from sociologies of knowledge.[9] Likewise, many theologians have moved quite beyond the neo-orthodoxy of the past fifty years. At minimum, they are "revisionist," if not deliberately post-Protestant. So homiletic method is much more than a "how-to" program for desperate preachers; it is strategy for the presentation of the gospel in a strange, turbulent new age. So questions of method are not merely practical matters; we are asking how to present the gospel message to an emerging new human consciousness.

III

Turn back for a moment to review the past. Many of us who preach were trained to speak from one-verse texts. Though liturgical tradition provided lections during the Thirties, Forties, and Fifties, single-verse texts were common: "Esau . . . was an hairy man." But if we did not preach from snippets of Scripture, we operated by what might be described as a "method of distillation": we distilled *topics* from biblical passages. We looked at a biblical passage objectively, and then took out something on which to preach. Methods of distilling topics from passages developed in the eighteenth century with the rise of Rationalism.[10] For example, if you dared to preach on the stilling of the storm, some surly rationalist would protest the miracle; but if you distilled a topic from the story — "Our Fears and Jesus" — you could sidestep the embarrassments of the biblical narrative. What's more, you might even get a reputation for psychological acuity at the same time. Not only did the method of distillation avoid embarrassments in the biblical text, in

9. See Walter Wink's critique of historical-critical method in *The Bible in Human Transformation: Toward a New Paradigm for Biblical Study* (Philadelphia: Fortress, 1973). For a broad survey of various literary-critical approaches, see Edgar V. McNight, *The Bible and the Reader: An Introduction to Literary Criticism* (Philadelphia: Fortress, 1985).

10. See my article, "Preaching and Interpretation," *Interpretation* 35, no. 1 (January 1981): 46-58.

itself it parodied scientific method. After all, scientific method is based on isolation and observation. You isolate an object for study, for example, my watch. You venture a general hypothesis — "It is a timepiece" — and you follow with "points": "It is square, It has numbers, It is cheap!" The word "point" was a tip-off, wasn't it? We "pointed at." Sermons were exercises in rational observation. Most of us were trained in a method of distillation. If we didn't pick out a single-verse text, we distilled topics from lections.

What did we lose? In fact, we lost the "whole story." We discarded both narrative structure and rhetorical movement. Let me see if I can explain. Rational homiletics treated biblical passages as if they were still-life pictures. You could study them, comment on the details within the picture, and then take something out of the picture to talk about in a sermon. In our efforts we were supported by erudite historical-critical commentaries. They too isolated a passage and then, verse by verse, explained each detail philologically or historically; the commentaries often concluded with a sentence or two on the topic they found in the passage. Notice that both the "scientific" commentary and the rationalist preacher observed the passage as if it were a still-life picture full of things to isolate and talk about. But suppose that biblical passages are much more like motion-picture film clips; suppose they move like stories, or travel along like the give-and-take of lively conversation, moving from one idea to another. Suppose that what characterizes any language is not still-life meaning, but movement. Why, we might have to learn to explore Scripture in a new way and, yes, to preach quite differently. Meaning occurs in a movement of thought or event; it is never static truth. No, meaning is structural, and structure is shaped by movement.

So instead of "point-making" sermons, often categorical in design, we will be developing something like a journey of ideas, moving from beginning to end. An older homiletics would distill a topic from a text — let us say, "Love" — and then develop the subject matter categorically: let's love in the family, love in the church, love in the world, and sometimes throw in a poem by way of conclusion! What's wrong with categorical, point-making sermons? Well, at the outset, they are intrinsically tedious. They are static and didactic at the same time. Though a minister can jot down points with ease, people in the pews find categorical homilies almost impossible to hear. But probe further: ask yourself, do you speak of the deepest, dearest moments in your life by listing? No, you tell what happened like a story or you try to open up a meaning by a moving description. We human beings save categorical thinking for trivia, for grocery lists, or for sorting laundry — so many bras, so many shirts, so many socks. We are not speaking some sort of fixed word-of-God truth which, hung up before us like a poster, we can discuss by pointing. No, as preachers, we are journeying into the mysteries of God! And journeying requires a very different homiletic method indeed.

IV

There has been another change we need to notice. Let's call it the importance of form. Preachers must take form seriously in Scripture as well as in sermons. An older homiletics indulged in what might be termed a "shell game," in which meaning was viewed as a kernel within a shell-like form. God's truth could be wrapped up in all kinds of shells. The task of an interpreter was to crack the shell and thereby liberate truth. What were the shells? Why, they were the stories, the parables, the epigrams, the poetry that encased the pithy truth. Fortunately the kernel/shell model has disappeared. Long before Canadian Marshall McLuhan, scholars had begun to sense that form was not a disposable shell; no, form is part of meaning. For example, would you attempt to write a treatise on thermodynamics as if it were lyric love poetry? No, the results would be astonishing. Likewise would you try to preach a parable with categorical points? Scarcely, for parables have a narrative plot. So a newer homiletic will brood on matters of form. Not only will we study the forms of Scripture, we will begin to sense the forms we human beings use in the everyday living of our lives.

Actually, most biblical scholars suppose that form is a clue to intention. To say it simply, form is something we choose in order to *do*. Think of the many language forms you bump into every week: "Once upon a time there was a beautiful woman who sat on a bench that, in sunlight, seemed made of gold" — you are hearing a fairy tale. Or, "Mr. and Mrs. Smith request the pleasure of your company at . . ." — you are reading a formal invitation that requires an answer. "Hey did ya' hear the one about the bishop and the actress?" — you brace yourself for a raucous joke. Notice that the forms are not interchangeable. You can't tell a racy joke as if it were a formal invitation; it simply would not work. "Work" — did you pick up the word? The linguistic forms in any culture are designed to work; they accomplish things, they are *performative*. Perhaps all biblical language is performative; though written down, biblical language is made up of oral forms designed to *do*. So, can the intentionality of scriptural language be realized in the standard form of a Protestant sermon? If meaning is not a kernel that can be crammed into any shell, then perhaps as preachers we must find different forms for the biblical passages we preach. Think how bracing it might be for pew sitters if the sermons they heard had different forms — at times sounding like stories, at times moving along from one poetic image to another like verse or prophecy, or perhaps sounding sometimes like the exchanges in a sharp debate. A modern homiletic will have to attend to matters of appropriate form. Form and meaning are inseparable.[11]

Of course, there's one aspect to form we scarcely notice. We shall call it "point-of-view."[12] We have already mentioned that rationalism viewed reality objectively; that every painting in the "age of reason" was painted as if seen by a detached, third-person, objective observer. Oddly enough, sermons were written from the same position. Even today most sermons speak as if we were observing. So we talk of God as if God were an observable object. We even speak of our own religious experience by describing ourselves objectively. In our speech we are very much like the early days of motion pictures. Old films were made with a fixed-point camera in front of which actors moved and spoke their lines. We see such films on late-night television, and giggle; they seem quite artificial. Nowadays films are fashioned by a camera on a moving boom so that our angle of vision keeps changing; there may be a hundred such shifts in point-of-view within a single minute. The reason for the shifting camera angles is that human consciousness has changed; we view reality quite differently. The relativity of consciousness has al-

11. For a study of homiletic theory and biblical form, see Thomas G. Long, *Preaching the Literary Forms of the Bible* (Philadelphia: Fortress, 1989).

12. The term "point of view" is borrowed from literary criticism. The following studies will be helpful: Wayne C. Booth, *The Rhetoric of Fiction* (Chicago: University of Chicago, 1961); B. Uspensky, *A Poetics of Composition* (Berkeley: University of California, 1973); S. S. Lanser, *The Narrative Act* (Princeton: Princeton University, 1981).

ready shaped changes in the way we converse with one another. If you wore a tape recorder for a day, you would discover that your ordinary conversation displays all kinds of shifts in your angle of vision. So we are dealing with a major alteration in language — except in preaching! Preaching is still relentlessly a fixed-camera, third-person objective language. Perhaps in the future our sermons will move through a series of moves, each with a differently defined point of view.[13]

V

Now, before we venture a method, we must deal with a kind of shibboleth. Let us label it "the Myth of Biblical Preaching." The biblical theology movement has dominated our thinking for most of the midtwentieth century. As a result, a great many books have been written on "Biblical Preaching," specifically on how preachers can move step by step from the biblical passage to a sermon. Many of these works — from Reginald Fuller to Ernest Best — have been helpful. They have explained exegetical procedure in great detail: translating, word study, checking related biblical references, doing commentary research, and so forth. They have also described a set of homiletic procedures from an initial outlining down to a final speaking. But have you noticed that in all such books there's a gap? There's something left out. The crucial shift from exegesis to homiletic activity is not described. The shift itself — perhaps it occurs in a flash of imagination — is never discussed. So alert readers are left with the odd impression that we move from the Bible to a contemporary sermon by some inexplicable kind of magic!

Let's admit the truth: in one way, none of us preach from the Bible. Not really. Perhaps the whole notion of biblical preaching is a popular fallacy. Instead, here's what happens. As you translate, study, and consider a text, the structure of the biblical passage forms a contemporary structure of meaning in your mind. As a result, what you preach from is no longer the Bible, but the structure of contemporary meaning produced by your study. Suppose you were to preach on the stilling of the storm. To a first-century mind, storms were probably produced by demons. But you are scarcely going to preach about demons. The word

---

13. See my *Homiletic: Moves and Structures* (Philadelphia: Fortress, 1987), chapter 4.

"storm" will have a different set of meanings to you, perhaps informed by childhood fears of rumbling thunder or pictures of brave British Admirals defying the waves. Notice what occurs. As an interpreter, you automatically move the text into a contemporary range of understanding. You are "demythologizing" without even trying.[14] So what do you preach from? Not the Bible at all, but a structure of contemporary meaning produced by the study of a text, a contemporary structure of meaning that has already been demythologized. The fact is, true biblical preaching is impossible because something called "original meaning" can never be our meaning or the subject of our contemporary preaching.

VI

Now let's set down some rather concrete methodological procedures. Let's begin where most of you begin: with a blank sheet of paper and a biblical passage. In a few weeks, the Prayer Book lectionary will hand you a parable, the story of the Rich Man and Lazarus. How are you going to preach the parable? Yes, you could distill a topic: "Beggars at Our Gates — The Problem of Urban Homelessness." Or perhaps, "Rich and Poor: Our World Today." Or even, "Charity — Christ's Call to Compassion." Instead let's see what we can learn from the parable itself.

Structurally, the parable is quite simple. There are two men. One is rich: he dresses in purple and feeds on gourmet foods. The other man is poor. He is too weak to beg. So he lies at the gate to the rich man's house and feeds on scraps of garbage. Then, there is a sudden twist to the plot: both men die. The poor man ends up at table with Father Abraham while the rich man lands in hot Hades. So far, the parable's movement is a description first of one man, then of another, followed by a dramatic role reversal.[15]

---

14. On "demythologizing," the debates with Rudolf Bultmann are edifying: *Kerygma and Myth: A Theological Debate,* ed. Hans Werner Bartsch (New York: Harper, 1961) and *Kerygma and Myth: A Theological Debate,* vol. 2, trans. R. Fuller (London: SPCK, 1962).

15. The Jesus Seminar noted that the parable (vv. 19-26) is followed by an addendum, vv. 27-31. Members dismissed the addendum as a later addition to an original parable. Preachers may preach the parable with or without the addendum. The Seminar split on whether the parable was original Jesus material. Certainly it is tricky enough to be from

In Hades, the rich man begs Abraham to send Lazarus with a finger-dip of water to assuage his thirst. But Abraham announces that, No, the request is impossible because "a great chasm has been fixed" between the two men. There is then a somewhat ruthless extra scene added to the parable, but most scholars believe the original story ended with Abraham's flat statement. We will have to decide whether to include the postscript or not. But structural options are limited: we have two descriptions, a role reversal in the afterlife, and Father Abraham's blunt announcement of a "chasm fixed between." So either you will begin at the beginning and design your sermon to match the episodes in the parable itself, or perhaps you could begin in the afterlife and look back at the previous condition of the two characters, before beginning to understand Father Abraham's pronouncement. There do not seem to be many structural choices.

Exegetically there are nuances we can spot. Notice the rich man has no name! No, he is known only by his station — namely "richman" — maybe we should call him merely "Richman" in our sermon — "Richman" without an article. He dresses in purple and, therefore, is possibly a *nouveau riche* social climber who aspires to royalty or, more likely, a court official. By contrast, note that the poor man has a name, Lazarus, which ironically means "one whom God helps." Lazarus is a beggar and, at the time of Christ, beggars were regarded as sinners. Their poverty was divine punishment. [Wasn't it a wealthy American essayist who announced "The only sin is being poor!"?] Please notice Lazarus lies outside the rich man's gate and grovels for table scraps in the garbage. He is so weak that he is helpless when vicious wild street dogs lick his sores, waiting to gnaw his bones. The contrast between the rich man within and the poor man outside the gate is carefully drawn. But, watch out, keep your eye on the symbol of the gate!

In the afterlife Lazarus ends up in Abraham's bosom while the rich man is consigned to Hades. Notice that the rich man never deigns to speak directly to Lazarus. Instead he asks Abraham to send Lazarus over with water to cool his lips. What is the chasm fixed between Laza-

---

Jesus. For discussion, see Robert W. Funk, Bernard Brandon Scott, and James R. Butts, *The Parables of Jesus, Red Letter Edition: A Report of the Jesus Seminar* (Sonoma: Polebridge, 1988), p. 64. On the parable itself, consult B. B. Scott's brilliant *Hear Then the Parable* (Philadelphia: Fortress, 1988).

rus and the rich man? Why, it is the gate that in an earlier life was never opened to offer Lazarus charity. The gate of indifference has become eschatologically permanent!

So, how to design a sermon? The sermon will need an Introduction and a Conclusion and in between, a series of moves. Probably we will need an Introduction that will define the parable's genre. Perhaps something like the following:

> Have you ever heard a joke about the "pearly gates"? There used to be stories about the two Irishmen, Pat and Mike, meeting St. Peter at the gates of heaven. Well, guess what? There were stories about heaven's gate at the time of Christ. Perhaps Jesus borrowed one of them, for he told a story about a rich man and a beggar meeting Abraham in the afterlife. So now, listen again to the strange parable Jesus told.

Why would we want such an Introduction? Why, to get rid of any tendency to read references to a literal afterlife in the parable. Jesus is merely playing around with a folktale tradition.

Now, the first two paragraphs of your sermon will introduce the two characters in a kind of storytelling style. Of course you will be smart enough to begin and end each of these moves with mention of the gate — "Behind a high gate, a rich man lived . . ." "Outside the gate, down on the ground, a beggar lay . . ." "See the picture: a rich man, a poor man, and a gate, a big gate in between."

Your third move can be surprised by the reversal. Does God automatically reward the poor of the world? In capitalist countries, we tend to regard poverty as the ultimate sin. But Lazarus ends up feasting with Father Abraham as if he were a good and faithful Jew — which, by the way, the parable does not say. And the rich man, think of it, does he end up in hell simply because he's rich?

A fourth move will introduce the pleading by the rich man. Now he appears to be down, but looking up to Lazarus. Maybe we rich nations can never understand the agony of the poor until somehow we suffer hunger and thirst. Then, suddenly, we cry out for compassion.

Finally, we will face Abraham's terrible reply. We build fences to protect ourselves from hearing the cry of the hungry, from catching sight of the desperate Lazarus people of Somalia. But, tragically, fences can become eschatologically permanent. So what can we do? How would we rewrite the parable if we could? Why, we'd walk out of ourselves into a world where folk hunger and thirst, and claim them in love as our brothers and sisters in Christ.

Notice, first, a hermeneutic observation: you do not merely retell the parable in some modern way. You do not try to write an updated parable. No, you listen to the parable in a modern way. You preach as if you and your people were hearing the parable together and together re-acting. How else can you get at contemporary meaning?

Secondly, please note, there are no points, no moral lessons. Instead, you let the structural movement of the parable do its work. Oh yes, you help it along. For you define each episode sharply like separate scenes in a drama — never smooth transitions like a storyteller. Parables, as Bertolt Brecht surmised, are closer to drama than the flow of storytelling. And in your sermon, you will deliberately picture the rich man and Lazarus; they are defined by up and down and in and out. Of course, you will carefully design the gate symbol in your sermon, for it is central to the meaning. There is an old Romanesque stone carving of the scene.[16] In the upper right hand, there is Richman at table, hoisting a goblet. In the lower left, there is Lazarus curled in a fetal position with a dog crouching beside him. In between the artist has left a wide sweep of stone gate. A picture of the parable.

Above all, you won't look at the parable as an object of interest and then pedantically draw a moral conclusion — first the story and then, dear children, a moral lesson. No, your sermon will be plotted like the parable so that the plot of the parable can do its work. You, along with your congregation, will discover that the wall has grown large, terribly, tragically large. And, with your congregation, you will struggle to understand. What you are doing is letting the intention of the parable be fulfilled. You are letting the parable do what it wants to do.

Think of it: the gate of our everyday indifference, the gate to and from heaven!

So have fun with your sermon.

---

16. From the Abbey church of St. Pierre at Moissac in southern France (*ca.* 1125-30); see Brian Young, *The Villein's Bible: Stories in Romanesque Carving* (London: Barrie and Jenkins, 1990), p. 84.

*　　*　　*

So what have we argued? Oh, we've asked for structural movement —
no static, point-making sermons, please. And we've urged you to think
of preaching not only as instruction but as doing what the Scriptures
want done! A faithful preacher will try to let Scripture fulfill itself
through preaching. And you will choose vivid imagery because nowadays people think through imaging. Homiletic method has to change
because *we* have changed.

Taking the Listeners Seriously
in Biblical Interpretation

Thomas G. Long

1997

I was preaching about a year ago as a guest minister, and after the service I was standing at the door shaking hands with the congregation when I caught on my preacher's radar screen someone moving towards me with an air of mission and purpose. I looked over: there was a seventy- or seventy-five-year-old woman with a face like a hatchet dipped in vinegar, moving towards me with — obviously — something to say. When she got near, I finally looked up. She demanded, "You teach preaching at the seminary, don't you?" "Yes, I do," I said. "Well, I have something that I want you to tell your students. Tell them to take me seriously." And with that she walked out into the street.

What did she mean? Take me seriously as a woman? Maybe. Take me seriously as a senior citizen, as a person of age? Maybe. Probably both those things, but even more than these, it was clear that somehow she had not been taken seriously from the pulpit. She had not been taken seriously as a thinking, feeling, faithful human being by those of us who preach. I have been thinking about what she said and what it might mean if those of us who preach genuinely take seriously the peo-

---

An earlier version of this material appeared in C. J. A. Vos, *Proclaim the Gospel* (Pretoria: Etoile, 1994), pp. 101-9.

ple who sit in the pews. I want to think, first, about what it means to take the listener seriously when the listener is not literally present; when we are in our studies doing biblical interpretation in preparation for preaching. What does it mean to have them with us and to take them seriously?

I think the first thing it means is that we have to get over the notion as pastors that when we take time to do serious and prayerful interpretation and engagement with the biblical text, we are somehow stealing time from serious and real ministry. My wife is a pastor who has the kind of job description that those of you who are pastors have, and the effort to squeeze into her busy week time for brooding, thinking, praying, and studying the biblical text is a major achievement. But the bad news is that good preaching is exactly what it appears to be: hard work under pressure that takes time. There is no way to cut around it. We simply have to realize that when we are engaging the text, we are doing ministry. In his book, *The Purpose of the Church and Its Ministry*,[1] H. Richard Niebuhr wrote that if you really want to know what the church expects of its ministers, look at architecture. In the Medieval period we built cathedrals because we expected ministers to be pastoral rulers who sat on the *cathedra*. Then at the time of the Reformation we began to build sanctuaries like auditoriums because we expected ministers to be teachers and preachers of the Word. In the Fifties, we built sanctuaries connected to suites of offices with secretaries and telephones because we expected pastors to be "pastoral directors," the CEOs of small, struggling corporations. So you are under pressure to be administrative and programmatic, as if when you retreat to study and immerse yourself in the Word, you are stealing from the people. It is wrong. If we are going to take the listener seriously, one of the things we will have to do is to carve out time for brooding and thinking and studying.

It also means that we are going to have to do a different kind of Bible study than we have done in the past. When I was in seminary I was taught that the biblical text is a jar with a theological nugget inside. It is my job as preacher to put on a pair of sterile, surgical gloves, gingerly

---

1. H. Richard Niebuhr, *The Purpose of the Church and Its Ministry; Reflections on the Aims of Theological Education. In Collaboration with Daniel Day Williams and James M. Gustafson* (New York: Harper, 1956), esp. pp. 59-63, 80-83.

approach the vessel of the text, reach inside with word studies and critical examinations of the contours of the text, until I find the theological idea in the text, lift it out, compare it to other references in Kittel, then carry it intact to the congregation without damaging it. But I was lied to by my professors. First of all, those gloves are not sterile: they never were. Secondly, that text is not an inert container. It is something more like a dance partner: I want to lead, but it summons me from the congregation and engages me in a movement of interpretation and meaning that is different every time I go to it. When I come to the text, I bring with me the circumstances of my people in this time and this place. That is why I tell my students, before you look at Raymond Brown and C. H. Dodd and Rudolf Bultmann, look at the text. They can't tell you what you are to preach on Sunday. You are the only person who has the authority and the positioning to be able to know what this text wishes to say to these people whom you love in this time and this place. If you go to Bultmann first, you will be intimidated. Go to the text first: let it move you and speak to you. Then summon Bultmann and Brown as your consultants to clarify what you have heard there, but first go and be engaged by the text.

Walter Brueggemann wrote an interesting article in *Theology Today* in which he uses a concept from family therapy called "triangulation," when two people in a family system, perhaps a mother and a father, go up against a third member, a child.[2] Or a mother and a child go up against a father, two against one. Brueggemann says that we preachers sometimes triangulate the congregation. We go to the text, we get a theological idea, and then on Sunday morning we say, in effect, "The text and I have something to say to you." Brueggemann says that what we ought to do is to stand with the congregation and let the text speak to us both. We bring the congregation with us, engage the text, and then, in an imagistic way, sit back in the pew and listen to how the Word summons and speaks to all of us.

If we are going to take the listener seriously, we've also got to take seriously the fact that we and they as members of the church are heirs to three big revolutions in biblical interpretation, all three of which need to be employed in our engagement with the text. The first of

2. Walter Brueggemann, "The Preacher, the Text, and the People," *Theology Today* 47 (1990): 237-47.

these, the historical-critical revolution, occurred some three hundred years ago. It understands that biblical texts did not drop down from heaven, apart from human chance and circumstance, but that they sprang up in concrete historical episodes, and have the fingerprints of those episodes all over them. My dentist back in Princeton is an agnostic. He puts cotton wads and cubes in my mouth and then says something like, "Dr. Long, if there really is a God, how come there's tooth decay?" The last time I went to see him, my dentist told me with some excitement that he has become very interested in reading about historical Jesus research. He has gotten all intrigued about Funk and the Jesus Seminar. I happen to stand with Luke Timothy Johnson and Richard Hays and others who are sharply critical about the Jesus Seminar. Its methodology is flawed and its results are questionable, I think, but I was intrigued by the fact that my dentist is so excited about it. I think he is excited because he was raised in a Roman Catholic family, and the only Jesus he ever heard about was the Jesus who floated six feet above time and circumstance, and spoke in spooky, eternal verities. To find a body of scholarship that attempts, to his mind, to plant Jesus in historical circumstances apart from his Sunday School bodyguards is refreshing! I think that when we take listeners seriously, we recognize that they themselves are planted in historical circumstances and so is the text.

For example, we think that the Gospel of Mark comes from a lower socio-economic level, the Gospel of Matthew comes from an affluent socio-economic level, and the Gospel of Luke looks like it comes from a mixed socio-economic community. Jesus sends out the disciples two by two in all three of the synoptic Gospels, and when he does, he says to them, among other things, "Take no money." In Mark's Greek, he says, "Take no copper" (Mark 6:8). Luke 9:3 reads, "Take no silver." In Matthew, it is "Take no copper, silver, or gold" (Matt. 10:9). They are going out with Gold Visa cards from the church of Saint Matthew.

How does taking the historical circumstance seriously help us to interpret a text for preaching? In the Gospel of Mark, the disciples are debating among themselves who is the greatest, and when Jesus asks what they were talking about, embarrassed, they tell him. So he says, "If you want to be great, you must become as one who serves" (Mark 10:43). Note the language. "If you want to be great." What does that imply? That the people in Mark's community aren't great. What a surprising word: "If you want to become great — those of you who aren't — become lowly, become as slaves." The same conversation takes place in the Gospel of Luke, but in a different setting, at the table of the Last Supper. Again, the issue is which of them is the greatest. Jesus responds in the same way but with different language: "Those among you who are great must become as those who wait on tables" (Luke 22:26). There *are* some great ones in Luke's congregation. The image here is that up at the big house there are some who are waited upon and some who are waiters. But when you come to the Lord's table, you reverse the roles. Those who have sat at table in the big house are deacons, and those who have been deacons at the big house are waited upon in the kingdom of God, a reversal of economic issues.

The second revolution to which we are heirs came about some seventy-five years ago, and understands that the biblical writers were not just historically grounded, they were also theologians. Matthew is a different theologian than John, and Mark is a different theologian than Luke, and Paul is a different theologian than James. So in order to understand the biblical text, we need to understand that the biblical witness is a chorus of theological voices, all working on the same anthem, but not necessarily singing in the same voice. For example, Matthew, Mark, and Luke have one view of time, and John has a different view of time. To exaggerate slightly, if you ask Matthew, Mark, and Luke, "When is the kingdom of God?" they will say, "In the future." We don't live in the kingdom yet. To borrow the language of Paul, we see through a glass darkly, but *then* we shall see face to face. For the writer of the Gospel of John, however, it is almost as if he reaches out and takes that future kingdom and stretches it as a canopy over ordinary time. If you ask Matthew when and where the kingdom is, he says, "Ahead of us." But if you ask John, he says, "Above us." Like the needle of a sewing machine, it keeps striking down into ordinary time, so that we can see signs of the fullness of the kingdom itself. You can see this in the story of Lazarus. Because Jesus is in a holding pattern outside of Bethany, Martha finally comes out to him and says, "If you had been here on time our brother would not have died." To which Jesus responds, "Your brother will rise." Martha answers, "I know he will rise again at the last day" (John 11:21-24). And Jesus says "No, no, Martha, that's the Gospel of Matthew. We're in the Gospel of John. I am the resurrection and the life." The Gospel of John is for those moments and experiences in the Christian community when we catch a glimpse of the fullness of things. But if that were all, we would soon grow discouraged because the Christian community doesn't always live in the fullness of things. Matthew, Mark, and Luke are for those times when we have to put one foot in front of the other, trudging through the muck and the mire of human circumstance. Thank God for both of those theological angles of vision.

We are inheritors of a historical revolution. We are inheritors of a theological revolution, and in the last twenty-five years we have become the inheritors of another revolution in biblical understanding that in its own special and emphatic way helps us to take the listener seriously. I am speaking of the literary-critical understanding of Scripture, the understanding that biblical writers were poets and artists who chose language, images, metaphors, and syntax in order not simply to say something, but to generate an impact on those who read and listened to what they wrote. They were not simply trying to make statements, they were preachers, trying to generate faith and insight and understanding in their readers and listeners. They took their listeners seriously, and biblical interpretation that wants to take contemporary listeners seriously looks at the patterns they have woven into the text. For example, the writer of the Gospel of John has a literary pattern that I call "question, answer, dumb response." It occurs half a dozen times in the Gospel of John: somebody will ask a question of Jesus, a good question but at the ordinary, mundane, everyday level of life. Jesus will answer the question, but not at the same level. He answers it at the level of the Johannine *logos,* the Christological level, causing the answer to whistle right past the person who asked and evincing from them some banal, insipid response. For example, the woman at the well asks, "Hey, why is it that you, a Jew, ask me, a Samaritan woman, for a drink?" (John 4:9). Good question. Why would a Jewish male crack through all kinds of racial and gender barriers and speak a word to a Samaritan woman? Answer: "If you knew who was asking, you would have been free to have asked him, and he would have given you living water" (John 4:10). But then she responds, "Where are you going to get this water? You haven't even got a bucket" (John 4:11). This is a literary device, and in your laughter you discover the ironic theological point of the writer of John. You say, "He doesn't mean that kind of water, he means . . ." and when that happens, the miracle of the Gospel of John has begun to work in you.

Or take the description in the Gospel of Luke where the writer says that at the time of the crucifixion, "the women and the others who followed Jesus watched these things [the crucifixion] from afar" (Luke 23:49). The Greek word is *macrothen,* "from a distance." I wonder if he ever used a word like that again. "I will arise and go to my father. I will say to him, 'I am not worthy to be treated as a son; treat me as a slave.' But while he was still far off, *makran,* his father saw him and was filled with compassion" (Luke 15:18-20). "Two men went up to the temple to pray, one a Pharisee, one a Publican. The Pharisee stood and said, 'O God I thank thee that I am not like other men.' But the other one stood *macrothen*" (Luke 18:10-13). This vocabulary is not a tape measure, but a theological symbol for where you stand in relation to the grace of God. Luke also wrote the Book of Acts, so Peter's Pentecost sermon ends by saying, "This good news is for you and for your children, and for everyone who stands *macran,* far off" (Acts 2:39).

When I taught the baby preaching course at Columbia Seminary, we would say to them, "You may preach your sermon from any text in the Bible . . . as long as it comes from the first chapter of Mark." The interesting thing is that 70 percent of them preached from the very same text, starting at verse 35:

> In the morning, while it was still very dark, he got up and went out to a deserted place, and there he prayed. And Simon and his companions hunted for him. When they found him, they said to him, "Everyone is searching for you." He answered, "Let us go on to the neighboring towns, so that I may proclaim the message there also; for that is what I came out to do." And he went throughout Galilee, proclaiming the message in their synagogues and casting out demons. (Mark 1:35-39)

Why did 70 percent of my students pick that text? The reasons became obvious when you heard the sermons, which were as predictable as the choice of text. The sermons sounded like this:

> Jesus had had a busy day in Capernaum. He'd been working, teaching, preaching; he was tired and exhausted. Jesus was burnt out. So what did he do when he was burnt out? Early in the morning, he went to a lonely place and he prayed. He had a

Quiet Time with his Father. And you know friends, when we are burnt out we need to get up in the morning, open our Bibles, and spend some time . . .

Good sermon, but not on this text. The problem is that my students did not take seriously the way in which the biblical writer, as a poet, had planted here an explosive word. The English translators don't help, but in the Greek that explosive word is *erēmon,* "wilderness" or "desert place." What do you know from the Old Testament about the wilderness? It is the place of wandering and of sin, where the holy and the demonic vie for the vocation of God's people. The writer of Mark has already hit that word like a drumbeat several times before we encounter it in verse 35. Look at verse 3: "The voice of one crying out in the *erēmon,* 'Prepare the way of the Lord.'" John the Baptizer appeared where? "In the *erēmon*" (Mark 1:4). Verse 12: "The Spirit immediately drove Jesus — where? — into the *erēmon*." "He was in the *erēmon* forty days, tempted" (Mark 1:13). This is not an azalea garden: it is the wilderness, the desert. You expect Jesus to be tempted out there, and he was. So back to the passage that all the students preached on: was Jesus going to go back to Capernaum, or was he going to go on to the fifteenth chapter of Mark where they nail him to a tree? I know which way I'd go. But Jesus says, "Let us go on to the other towns, for that is why I came out." The Gospel is here because Jesus went forward, rather than back. Out in the wilderness. Now that is a sermon on this text.

In addition to the business of repeated language making a cumulative impact on the listener, occasionally a writer will insert a speed bump into the text. You're driving along the road and when the front end of your car hits the asphalt strip it says to you, "You're going too fast; slow down." Likewise writers insert literary speed bumps to make you slow down, as if to say, "Pay attention right here." There's a speed bump in the sixth chapter of Mark, verse 39: ". . . and they sat down on the green grass." Mark is not a Technicolor kind of writer. He does not say things like "Jesus was wearing a brown robe with matching tan sandals as he stood under the azure sky." That's not his style, so we've suddenly gone from black and white to green. If you are original readers or listeners to the Gospel of Mark, you are extremely competent in the Old Testament. So as a reader of the Old Testament, when the desert turns green on you, where does your mind go? It goes to Isaiah, where "the desert shall blossom" in the messianic age (Isa. 35:1-2). Not only that, but listen to this: "He ordered them to have all the people sit down in groups on the green grass." Oh yes, that's from a Psalm, isn't it? "He maketh them lie down . . ." How does that one start? "The Lord is my shepherd." So look at verse 34: "He had compassion for them because they were like sheep without a shepherd." With a single phrase, Mark has galvanized two significant Old Testament images around Jesus.

While we are in Mark, let's look at an example of foreshadowing. Foreshadowing is a literary technique whereby a writer involves a listener by planting in the text something that will blossom later on in the story. This example comes at the end of the little apocalypse in Mark 13:

> But about that day or hour no one knows, neither the angels in heaven, nor the Son, but only the Father. Beware, keep alert; for you do not know when the time will come. It is like a man going on a journey, when he leaves home and puts his slaves in charge, each with his work, and commands the doorkeeper to be on the watch. Therefore, keep awake — for you do not know when the master of the house will come, in the evening, or at midnight, or at cockcrow, or at dawn, or else he may find you asleep when he comes suddenly. And what I say to you I say to all: Keep awake. (Mark 13:32-37)

"I could come back in the evening," says the Master. In his next chapter, Mark writes, "When it was evening, he came with the Twelve, and . . . said, 'One of you will betray me'" (Mark 14:17-18). "Or I could come back at midnight." Later that night, "they went to a place called Gethsemane; and he said to his disciples, 'Sit here while I pray'" (Mark 14:32). But he comes back and finds them sleeping: "Couldn't you stay awake one hour?" (14:37). "I could come back at cockcrow." The serving girl asks, "Weren't you with him?" "No," says Peter, "I wasn't with him." "Then the cock crowed" (14:68). "I could come back in the morning": "And when it was morning they handed him over to be crucified" (15:1). Mark has used these temporal references to organize the Passion. The reader or listener discovers that if you want to look for the kingdom, you don't just get up on your tiptoes and look over the horizon: you look for the advent of God in every tick of the clock. Moments of loyalty and betrayal, denial and faith come with the passing of every hour.

Now in addition to foreshadowing and speed bumps and repeated symbols, there is the matter of words that create an emotive impact. Look at this famous passage from Philippians:

> If then there is any encouragement in Christ, any consolation from love, any sharing in the Spirit, any compassion and sympathy, make my joy complete; be of the same mind, having the same love, being in full accord and of one mind. Do nothing from selfish ambition or conceit, but in humility regard others as better than yourselves. Let each of you look not to your own interests but to the interests of others. Let the same mind be in you that was in Christ Jesus. . . . (Phil. 2:1-5)

At this point I have to start singing. Why? Because Paul is not composing here, he is quoting a fragment of an early Christian hymn to the Philippian congregation. Historical critics will tell you that, then promptly drop it and move on to more interesting questions such as whether this is a Persian, dying/rising god myth that has been taken over by the Christian community. But what I want to know about is the emotional impact created by a pastor who writes a letter to his congregation and quotes a hymn that they sing on Sunday morning.

Susan has been away at college for some months and now she is homesick. Every day she goes to the campus center and checks for mail. There never is any. One day, however, she sees through the little glass slot the diagonal outline of an envelope. With excitement she opens up the campus box and takes out a personal letter, written especially to her. She can tell that it is from her pastor back home:

> I know these are difficult days for you, but I just wanted you to know that you are in my thoughts and in my prayers. But more than that, you are in the care of God. "Grant us wisdom, grant us courage for the living of these days."
>
> Your pastor

Historical critics finding that letter would say, "We have here a fragment of a twentieth-century hymn by Harry Emerson Fosdick." But what is its impact on Susan? She is suddenly transported back to her home sanctuary, where she hears the congregation singing. It's all there, the entire ethos of worship. "Have this mind among you," Paul writes, then he takes them into the sanctuary for worship. It is not just a theological, cognitive point that Paul wants to make: he creates an affective experience of worship.

Sometimes writers will use repeated patterns. That is to say, they will tell you one thing and then — like a Budweiser commercial — they will tell it to you again and get you to sing the last part of the jingle: "This Bud's for you." One of these is in Luke 17:26-30:

> Just as it was in the days of Noah, so too it will be in the days of the Son of Man. They were eating and drinking and marrying and being given in marriage until the day that Noah entered the ark and the flood came and destroyed all of them. Likewise, just as it was in the days of Lot, they were eating and drinking and buying and selling and planting and building, but on the day that Lot left Sodom, it rained fire and sulfur from heaven and destroyed all of them. It is going to be like that on the day that the Son of Man is revealed.

Robert Tannehill tells us to listen to the poetry of the text.[3] The words in Greek — *ēsthion, epinon, egamoun* — are designed to create the rhythms of ordinary life: shopping, watching TV, eating, drinking, marrying. Then the crisis comes right in the middle of the ordinary. Second time around: "Just as it was in the days of Lot, eating and drinking, buying and selling, planting and building." We've heard this list before and we know what comes at the end of it. I know the crisis is coming, but I don't know when. Right in the middle of the ordinary rhythms of life, the repeated patterns of this text make me poised in anticipation of the advent: "It is going to be like that on the day that the Son of Man is revealed."

Finally, an interpreter who takes the listener seriously will take seriously the contours of the biblical text. Let's try a close reading of Deuteronomy 6:20-25:

---

3. See Robert C. Tannehill, *The Sword of His Mouth* (Philadelphia: Fortress; Missoula: Scholars, 1975), pp. 118-21.

When your children ask you in time to come, "What is the meaning of the decrees and the statutes and the ordinances that the LORD our God has commanded you?" then you shall say to your children, "We were Pharaoh's slaves in Egypt, but the LORD brought us out of Egypt with a mighty hand. The LORD displayed before our eyes great and awesome signs and wonders against Egypt, against Pharaoh and all his household. He brought us out from there in order to bring us in, to give us the land that he promised on oath to our ancestors. Then the LORD commanded us to observe all these statutes, to fear the LORD our God, for our lasting good, so as to keep us alive, as is now the case. If we diligently observe this entire commandment before the LORD our God, as he has commanded us, we will be in the right."

Now, a broad, non-close reading of the text says that what we have here is a script for a family liturgical event: the family is seated around the table and the oldest child takes his three-by-five card and says, "Papa, what is the meaning of the commandments, statutes, and ordinances that the Lord our God has commanded?" And the father takes his three-by-five card and says, "We were slaves in Egypt . . ." But Rabbi Michael Fishbane says that, on a close reading, what we have here is the split that happens between the younger generation and the older generation in the household of faith, and in order to hear it you have to read the question with a kind of adolescent slouch. Built into a close reading of this text, says Fishbane, is a command to the elders to tell the stories of the faith not only so our children hear them, but so they know they are a part of them, to retell the narratives in such a way that the "you" of whom the son speaks becomes the "we" and "us" of whom the father speaks.[4]

Once when I was working on that text with a group of ministers, one of them came up afterwards and said, "You know, every night my daughter and I read this passage to each other before she goes to bed. I don't know why we've done that; it's just been our ritual to read this as a bedtime devotion. One afternoon when I went to get my daughter for

4. Michael Fishbane, *Text and Texture: Close Readings of Selected Biblical Texts* (New York: Schocken, 1979), pp. 79-83.

supper, she was in the front yard playing with some of her friends. When I came to call her in, she didn't hear me coming, but I heard what she was telling her friends. She said to them, 'You know, I used to be a slave in Egypt, but the Lord took me out of it, but I don't really remember it because I was asleep and being carried in my father's arms.'" That's what it means to retell the narratives, to take them so seriously that you and your hearers become part of the contours of the text.

And that's our task: taking our listeners seriously in biblical interpretation will mean taking time to study the text, taking seriously its historical circumstances, its theological vision, and its literary artistry, and allowing all three to speak both to them and to us as we prepare to preach.

Imagination, Creativity, and Preaching

EDWINA HUNTER

1998

What is the role and purpose of preaching? You must have heard people say as often as I have, "I don't come to church on Sunday to be disturbed or upset. I get enough of that during the week. I come because I want to be made to feel good." Love for one's congregation, understanding of the pain of individual members, and identification with wanting to be made to feel good can lure us into preaching pastoral, compassionate, "feel-good" sermons every week to the detriment of everyone. I'm not saying there isn't a place for that kind of pastoral sermon, because I think there is. But I have been brought up short by some questions in a book by my friend, Charles Rice, from Drew University, who wrote,

> Might it be that many Christians do not come to the table because preaching does not create sufficient hunger and thirst, or satisfies superficially? Do we assume, to our loss, that preaching should meet our needs, answer our questions, come to satisfying conclusions, rather than sharpening our hunger, deepening our thirst? Is not the role of preaching to make us newly aware of our need for the saving presence of Christ, and of our own embodiment of that saving Word in the world?[1]

1. Charles L. Rice, *The Embodied Word: Preaching as Art and Liturgy* (Minneapolis: Fortress, 1991), pp. 137-38.

Rice quotes poet Anna Kirby:

> We are the Incarnation,
>   all living things,
>   word made flesh;
> transcendent thought of God.
> The Holy Spirit by inspiration
>   immanent,
>   revealed by grace,
> and flesh enfolds the living Deity,
>   translating Him and us,
>   a glorious Epiphany,
> a suffering, transfigured, human face.[2]

Can you see it in Jesus? Can you see it sometimes in the people you meet on the street? Or in a brother or sister sitting next to you? We are the incarnation. Are those words we really believe? Deep inside us, are those words that we believe and can say?

Word and Words of God

Lately I've been doing a great deal of thinking about preaching and the word of God, and about the preacher as God's messenger. In the first chapter of John, we're told that "the Word was made flesh, and dwelt among us" (John 1:14). The *Logos* — for some of us, believe it or not, that also means the *Sophia* — spoke the created universe *and us* into existence. That has led me to formulate a syllogism: since the *Logos*, the Word of God, is incarnational, relational, and dialogical, then when our preaching is incarnational, relational, and dialogical, preaching itself becomes the word of God. How long has it been since you claimed that *your* preaching is the word of God? I'm not sure I ever have. It feels like we're taking too vast a step; it's too awesome. The Bible is the Word of God, Jesus is the Word of God, but the preaching *I* do?

I know I get upset when only the Bible is spoken of as *the* Word of God, because for me, the Christ incarnate in Jesus of Nazareth is the

---

2. Anna Kirby, "Epiphany I," cited in Rice, *The Embodied Word*, p. 138.

living Word of God. Or as a friend of mine says, "Jesus is God's exegete." He is the Word made flesh. And who are we? Either we continue to be the Word made flesh, or we are not Christ's body in the world. Someone has said, "God made the Word flesh, and we have made it words, and words, and words, and words." As I say that, I realize that I am going to be using many words, but I hope that somewhere through it, together we may get in touch with a word of God.

What do we do as preachers? What do we do to embody the Word of God, to speak the Word of God, to call people to hunger and thirst for the Word of God, the very voice of God in their hearts and lives? In the *Cotton Patch Parables of Liberation,* Bill Lane Doulos says, "the biblical imagery of hungering and thirsting after justice conveys an intensity that we often lack. Hungering and thirsting call forth the necessity for daring action."[3] Have you ever been really, really thirsty? Really hungry? Did you take action? Did you try to do something about it? I want to propose that God's first action was the action of creation — a daring action. You and I are created in the image of God. Surely a main part of that image is creativity and imagination: the ability to imagine, to lead others to imagine; to call forth in people's minds pictures, smells, tastes, sounds, tactile impressions, and even muscle responses, such imaginings that cause our listeners to hunger and thirst for justice. They won't hunger or thirst unless they can see and hear and touch and feel, unless their response is a whole response to the sermon. I think that so often many of us are like talking heads, and what happens to the congregation? They become listening heads. I'm not talking about using a great many gestures or being flamboyant. I used to teach interpretation of literature on the college and university level. One of the questions we would talk about was, "How do you feel the poem from the tips of your toes to the top of your head?" Even if you stand still as you preach, let there be motivation in it, because if you feel your sermon, your whole body will be telling the same story your words are. But there can be double messages and great distraction when the message, the Word of God, does not come through us as an embodied word. Authenticity consists at least in part of feeling, experiencing what we are doing.

3. Clarence Jordan and William Lane Doulos, *Cotton Patch Parables of Liberation* (Scottdale, Pa.: Herald, 1976), p. 74.

Preaching as an Artistic Medium

Surely creativity itself is part of our being made in the image of God. If God's first act was that of creation, then surely we are most in the image of God, most like God, when our creative juices are flowing, when something creative is happening. It's a way of helping others embody God's image for themselves, a way for us to call for daring action, as well as to engage in it ourselves, and a way for us to preach incarnationally for transformation, relationship, and dialogue. In saying this, I make a number of assumptions. My first assumption is that, at its most communicative, its most incarnational, preaching is an artistic medium. So many of our revered, older books on preaching set things up very much in a kind of scientific order. But I am asking you to look at preaching — although the science, the order, and the intelligence will still be present — as an art form. In the 1970s, a number of people started writing about the role of religious imagination. One of the earliest was Robert D. Young. I had never seen anything like his *Religious Imagination;* I devoured it.[4] It was long and somewhat dense, and when I was finished, I thought, "He said some really good things: I wish he had *written* with religious imagination." But he was still, as most of us are, into a different kind of order, a different way of speaking and writing. Others, such as Charles Rice and Tom Troeger, came along with splendidly creative ways of saying what Robert D. Young had struggled to say and to inspire. Already in 1970, Charles had written:

> The saving grace of Christian communication today is imagination, that habit of mind which can move from one's own situation into a new frame of reference, enriching both "worlds" by the very movement.[5]

He made this claim for the imagination almost three decades ago. Since that time a number of others have hailed the imagination as a metaphorical weapon to be wielded in the battle against sermonic dull-

---

4. Robert Doran Young, *Religious Imagination: God's Gift to Prophets and Preachers* (Louisville: Westminster/John Knox, 1979).

5. Charles L. Rice, *Interpretation and Imagination: The Preacher and Contemporary Literature* (Philadelphia: Fortress, 1970), p. xi.

ness and aridity. If you've ever looked at the history of preaching, almost every time a revival of preaching broke out, it happened because the people in the pew got bored. They were tired of going to sleep, tired of feeling that they were not being addressed. Are we at a place again where lay people are going to have to say, "We're tired of this, enough! We want to hear the word of God!"?

Creativity and Spirituality in Parallel

Here's a second assumption: that creativity and spirituality derive from the same source or from a similar inner disposition. Karen Laub-Novak, writing in *Art, Creativity, and the Sacred*, says,

> The overarching metaphor for both the life of the spirit and the life of art is "the quest." We speak of the journey of the soul, the way, the pilgrimage. The power of this image is that it aptly describes the life of the spirit as a process, not static, but changing, developing. The spirit is energetic, not stagnant. It explores, questions, and moves, directly or indirectly, toward a goal.[6]

Let me see if I can demonstrate the parallels between the creative process and the spiritual quest, drawing on the work of Betty Edwards[7] and Karen Laub-Novak. Think about your sermon, and what the creative process is for you. Edwards lists the stages in the creative process as these. The first stage is what we call the "first insight," the solving of existing problems and the asking of new questions. The second stage is "saturation," prolonged study and research. The third is "incubation," and there is no way I can stress that enough: time to mull over and to gestate. The creative artist has to have time, often silent, sometimes listening to music, sometimes reading poetry. Was it Winnie the Pooh who said, "Sometimes I just sits and thinks, and sometimes I just sits"? I think that sometimes the creative artist has to do just that. The

6. Karen Laub-Novak, "The Art of Deception," in *Art, Creativity, and the Sacred: An Anthology in Religion and Art,* ed. Diane Apostolos-Cappadona (New York: Crossroad, 1984), p. 20.

7. Betty Edwards, *Drawing on the Artist Within: A Guide to Innovation, Invention, Imagination, and Creativity* (New York: Simon and Schuster, 1986).

fourth stage is "illumination," a sudden solution. What that means for me is a willingness to be awakened at three o'clock in the morning with a sermon direction after I've been blocked for days. Have you ever struggled so hard to wrest a sermon from a text and been blocked? You know the time is coming that you're going to have to preach. Have you ever prayed just before going to sleep and asked for something and been awakened at two or three o'clock in the morning? Ahh! There it is! But if we insist on staying asleep, if it wears us out too much to be awakened, then we may miss out on some wonderful dreams and some wonderful sermon ideas. The last stage, according to Edwards, is "verification," putting the solution into concrete form while checking it for error and usefulness. That sounds almost scientific, rather than artistic. But when Michelangelo referred to the sculpture as being already present within the stone, and having to be called out, somehow that was both very concrete and very artistic, amounting to a process of verification. Then Laub-Novak offers five matching stages in the spiritual quest: insight, preparation, discipline, dark night of the soul, and unity.[8]

Language and Structure as Artistic Tools

One of my favorite poets of all time is Gerard Manley Hopkins, and it's very clear from some of his dark poems that he went through dark nights of the soul. As preachers, we too go through dark nights of the soul. Yet sometimes it's out of those darkest nights that the greatest resurrection comes, the greatest renewal of life. The similarity between the artistic and the spiritual, and the contribution that each makes to the process of preparing to preach, leads to a third assumption: that the imaginatively and spiritually awakened preacher can learn to use language and structure to create an artistic sermon much as poets and novelists use language and structure, but also in ways similar to those of a painter or a sculptor, a composer or a potter. The reality is that the creative process — whether for poems, for sculpture, or for preaching — is very much the same. Let me give you an example from the works of Robert McAfee Brown, who is a good friend and was a teaching colleague for

---

8. Laub-Novak, "The Art of Deception," p. 12.

quite a while. This relates directly to the preacher's imagination concerning Scripture, and the way that the creative spiritual process worked for him. In *Unexpected News: Reading the Bible with Third World Eyes,* McAfee Brown retells the biblical narrative. So, for example, after prayerfully submitting himself to the story of Shadrach, Meshach, and Abednego during a time when McAfee Brown was working closely with Elie Wiesel, this is the story that emerged:

> Now in those days King Adolf made a graven image called a swastika. And he summoned all the members of his party, all the leaders of his government, all the officers and enlisted personnel of his military forces, all the teachers, all the businessmen, all the church members, and he said to them, "This image, and my person, represent a new era for our country. When you greet one another you shall say 'Heil Hitler!' And when you leave one another you shall say 'Heil Hitler!' In every home, in every church, in every place of business, in every classroom, you shall display the swastika and my picture, and for them you shall be prepared to make any sacrifice, even of life itself. And whoever does not do so shall be sent to a burning fiery furnace or a gas chamber."
>
> And the people did as he commanded them, and worshiped the images he had set up, and behold, the few who did not do so were sent to the burning fiery furnaces and the gas chambers.
>
> But it came to pass that informers came to him and said, "Heil Hitler! There are certain people, beloved leader, who do not worship as you command."
>
> And he said to them, "Who are they?" And they said, "The Jews, beloved leader. And what is more, they claim to worship a different God from yours."
>
> Then Hitler was in a furious rage and said, "We know already of these people, and how they contaminate life and debase the blood of our race. Since, therefore, they worship another God and will not bow down to our god, and since they have always been a pestilence on the earth, let us send them *all* to the fiery furnaces and the gas chambers and rid the earth of them forever." And he commanded new fiery furnaces and gas chambers to be built especially to destroy the Jews. "And then we will see,"

he shouted, "whether their God will save them from the burning fiery furnaces and the gas chambers."

And it was as he commanded, and the Jews were shoved into the fiery furnaces and the gas chambers, fifty at a time, then a thousand a day, then ten thousand a day, until a million Jews had been destroyed, and then two million, and finally six million.

And as the Jews went to the burning fiery furnaces and the gas chambers, some went in faith, and some went in disbelief to the very end that such things would happen, and many went with the *Shema Yisrael* — "Hear, O Israel: The Lord our God, the Lord is one" — their ancient affirmation of faith in the living God. It was their way of saying, "The Lord our God, *Adonai Elohenu,* can save us from the burning fiery furnaces and the gas chambers, but if not, be it known to you, O Hitler, that we will not serve your gods or worship the image which you have set up."

But this time no one was saved.
And six million times no one was saved.
And forty years later the *Shema Yisrael* is still on the lips of Jews . . .
It is a cause for wonder and tears and questions and yearning
　　　and angry hope.[9]

One of the greatest sermons I ever heard as a young person was from the great Scottish preacher, James Stewart. Its title was "But If Not . . ." I will never forget it, because as a Southern Baptist I had been taught over and over that when you pray, you receive. All the "victory stories" of the Bible had been told us in Sunday School. For the first time I was forced to think, "But what do we do if not?" And this is McAfee Brown's suggestion.

Imagination as Incarnational Hermeneutic

A fourth, and closely related assumption is that imagination is a vital component in what might be called an incarnationally artistic herme-

---

9. Robert McAfee Brown, *Unexpected News: Reading the Bible with Third World Eyes* (Philadelphia: Westminster, 1984), pp. 150-52.

neutic. Scripture interpretation that leads to holistic, embodied, artistic preaching demands that the preacher submit imaginatively and prayerfully to the scriptural text. To see how this is so, we may choose a familiar text such as the story of the paralytic lowered down through the roof by his four friends (Mark 2:1-12), and meditate imaginatively on it in order to get in touch with the temperature, the sights, the smells, the tactile experience of the people who inhabit the narrative. Just for a few moments, you go inside yourself, into your own imagination, so as to be there in that scene. You feel the pressure of the bodies, perhaps unwashed bodies, after they have traveled long, hot distances. Or you feel the tug on your arms as if you were carrying this man's pallet. You experience something of the consternation of the crowd, or the anger of the scribes. In other words, you taste it, smell it, touch it, see the scene and feel it in your deepest being. I dare you to try this some time in the middle of a sermon with your congregation, and to let them take the text with which you are working and tell it to each other.

I got the idea of using the story in this fashion from Walter Wink's little book, *The Bible in Human Transformation*[10] — although Wink does it more from a psychological point of view. I think it's a wonderful way for preachers, working with any biblical narrative, to begin to get into the narrative, taking the different parts. I try to get my students to carry the Scripture around with them for days and days before they ever go to a commentary, to begin to feel the story and to live with it until something in their own experience, their own story, surfaces in memory and connects them with the text. At that point you move into a sense of ownership with the text, whether you ever tell that story to your congregation or not. The fact that you have lived with the text until something in your own life and experience has come to memory means that when you preach from it, even if you never tell the story, someone will say to you, "You sounded like you knew what you were talking about." The Scripture has become your own.

10. Walter Wink, *The Bible in Human Transformation: Toward a New Paradigm for Biblical Study* (Philadelphia: Fortress, 1973).

Incarnation as Dialogue and Collaboration

At the same time — as a fifth assumption — it is important to foster a collaborative approach to preaching, rather than a competitive one. Over years of teaching preaching, I have allowed the students to divide into groups of three to five that meet together for two hours a week outside of class. They pray together; they work on sermons together; they practice; they brainstorm for sermon ideas. Together, they watch the videotape of each one's sermon, to help each one see why the instructor and why the other members of the class made the comments they did. In this way they begin to feel almost as if each person is preaching *our* sermon. Again, I challenge you to experience working with other people in that fashion, perhaps exegeting the text for the following Sunday, perhaps getting them to give you feedback afterwards. I met one man who was about seventy and in so-called retirement after years and years of being a pastor, then was called to an interim position. He decided to try something he had never tried before: he invited about ten people from the congregation to meet with him on a Sunday afternoon. He exegeted the text for the next Sunday, and they engaged in discussion about it. After about six or eight weeks, four or five members rotated out, new ones came in, and they continued the process. I can still see his face as he said, "After seven or eight months I could go into the pulpit, and I could look out and see sixty or seventy people who had some notion of what goes into the preparation of a sermon, and how to listen to it." He said that it was the richest sense of dialogical communication that he had ever experienced. And it didn't happen to him until he was seventy. So let them evaluate your sermon!

I want to encourage you to use first-person biblical character sermons. I remember a man who came to a clinic in which I kept talking about first-person biblical characters. He came to me afterward: he had been preaching about twenty-five years, and he wasn't sure about this at all. But about a year later he called me and said, "Guess what? At Advent, I took four of the main characters from the Christmas story, and did first-person biblical characters for each of them. My people kept telling me they had never listened to me like they did then; they had never heard sermons that reached them in that fashion!" He was elated.

Reading the Bible from the underside, from a liberation perspective, can release even more of these stories for us. This is the kind of thing that Robert McAfee Brown did, what occurs in *The Cotton Patch Parables of Liberation,* and in books coming out of Central America that tell of peasants, uneducated people, who encounter the very personal reality of Jesus and the Bible because they respond to and identify with the text.

A Hermeneutic of Suspicion and Openness to New Learning

A sixth assumption: that part of our incarnational, relational, dialogical, and transformational responsibility as preachers is to exercise a hermeneutic of suspicion. That means that we must ask the text the hard questions. Who is left out of this? Who doesn't get to say a word in this story? Who is not even named? Ask the text why the narrative is recorded the way it is. What was the culture in which these stories were told and retold, and how were they shaped for that which we've come to call the canon? We may even be able to admit that most of us have a kind of private canon, sections that we preach with great conviction and connection, and sections we avoid altogether because we cannot bring the interpretative tools to bear that will yield a liberation understanding. This leads to a seventh assumption: that the person who is truly committed to preaching as an incarnational and artistic medium will voluntarily open him- or herself to new experiences, new ways of seeing, new possibilities for growth and interaction, new ways of reading the Scripture, and a deeper, broader vision of the links between the spiritual life and the creative life.

I want to say, Don't be afraid of your imagination and where it will take you. Because as the creative imagination functions to help us invent metaphors and images, it offers us an intuitive way of gathering images and restructuring material. It can simplify, or it can intensify; it can develop the narrative for purposes of suspense, or to shock. Imagination invents new ways of doing things; it orders chaotic images. The scientist invents and the poet produces a poem, and each enables us to appreciate something, to experience beauty and awe, and to move toward wholeness. Certainly there are dangers in the use of imagination, which has the potential to obscure rather than reveal. It has the potential for deception: you may latch onto something in your imaginative reading of the text that is so far out that it has nothing to do with the reality of proper exegesis. There is even the danger that we will love the imaginings themselves, and never move toward realization. There is the danger of attempting to be creative just for the sake of creativity, the products of which may have no substance whatsoever, but rather be undisciplined and uprooted. That too is why it's good to work in collaboration with other people.

My final assumption is that a sense of fun, an attitude of excitement, a willingness to submit to Scripture — letting it become our own, letting us belong to Scripture — and a love of discovery, will do a great deal to bring joy to our journey as preachers, and can give us more excitement about preaching, more positive anticipation going into the pulpit, than we have ever experienced.

Preaching Rhetorically:
Thanks, Aristotle and Apostles

MARTIN E. MARTY

2001

For the message about Christ's death on the cross is nonsense to those who are being lost; but for us who are being saved it is God's power. The scripture says, "I will destroy the wisdom of the wise and set aside the understanding of the scholars." So then, where does that leave the wise? or the scholars? or the skillful debaters of this world? God has shown that this world's wisdom is foolishness! For God in his wisdom made it impossible for people to know him by means of their own wisdom. Instead, by means of the so-called "foolish" message we preach, God decided to save those who believe. Jews want miracles for proof, and Greeks look for wisdom. As for us, we proclaim the crucified Christ, a message that is offensive to the Jews and nonsense to the Gentiles; but for those whom God has called, both Jews and Gentiles, this message is Christ, who is the power of God and the wisdom of God. For what seems to be God's fool-

Professor Marty kindly granted permission for the transcription and editing of his lectures, but declined the opportunity to participate in the editorial process due to conflicting commitments. This abridgement (previously published online in the *McMaster Journal of Theology and Ministry;* http://www.mcmaster.ca/mjtm/) seeks to capture the vitality, imagination, and intellectual acuity of the original presentations. [*ed.*]

ishness is wiser than human wisdom, and what seems to be God's weakness is stronger than human strength. Now, remember what you were, my friends, when God called you. From the human point of view few of you were wise or powerful or of high social standing. God purposely chose what the world considers nonsense in order to shame the wise, and he chose what the world considers weak in order to shame the powerful. He chose what the world looks down on and despises and thinks is nothing in order to destroy what the world thinks is important. . . . God has brought you into union with Christ Jesus, and God has made Christ to be our wisdom. By him we are put right with God; we become God's holy people and are set free. So then, as the scripture says: "Whoever wants to boast must boast of what the Lord has done." (1 Corinthians 1:18-31, GNT)

Paul's text is a complete refutation of everything that I intend to say.

When I was a student at the University of Chicago, all of forty-five years ago, the greatest gospel singer there's ever been, Mahalia Jackson, was in her prime. We had her sing once among the wise of the world in Mandel Hall, jammed with University College students and professors. There were two professors on stage, Alfred Korzybski, who was head of the semantics movement and S. I. Hayakawa, later a U.S. senator. With the piano playing, Mahalia would thump her foot a while and then sing these wonderful gospel songs. Then she had to step back and these two men would get up and say, "Now what Miss Jackson was doing here, was the semiotics of this, which fit with the symbolism of that, which ran over against the sign of that." And she was sort of nonplussed by it all. "No, no, no," she said. "That's not what it's about!" "Well, what was it about?" they asked. "Play it again!" And she sang it again.

Rhetoric has a bad name. A lot of people say, "O, that was just rhetoric!" Rhetoric really means "speech or writing designed to persuade." Fifty years ago, when I was a theological student, Krister Stendahl, later the dean of Harvard Divinity School and Archbishop of Stockholm, now retired, was a very young traveler for the World Council of Churches. When he came to our seminary, he said, "It's really interesting, but they mix the modes. In the chapel they act as if everybody knows all this stuff and they just have to repeat and expound it. In the classroom it's as if we have to convince everybody." He said, "It really should be the other way around: in the classroom you have to analyze and take it apart and so on, but in the sermon you are engaged in persuasion."

Surely the same person can do both. Edward Levi, the former President of the University of Chicago, whose grandfather had been a rabbi, invited me to speak at the last of the graduation commencements when he was President. Later I was invited to give the convocation sermon, which was the Sunday before. At the post-commencement party at his home, he said, "Marty, why do you sound so different on two different days?"

"What do you mean?"

"Well, there you were in the same room both days, same pulpit, same building, same microphone, same everything, but it was so different. Well, the one was like what your grandpa would do: teaching, but in the form of a sermon. In the commencement address — highly pluralistic, highly diverse, all disciplines, no common assumptions except the celebration of learning and relief that it is over with — there's a very different intention."

I told him: "A theological lecture describes God, a sermon offers God." It doesn't mean that the theological lecture is not heavily committed or persuasive or whatever, but the task is in a sense to walk around and see the footprints and take the traces and look at the text; whereas in the sermon, something is really happening. The Gideon Bible in your hotel room may have the same words as you just heard expounded from the book of Acts, but in a very different context. So if you're involved in chaplaincy, in counseling, in pastoral calling, in preaching, in administering the congregation, you are in the persuasion business.

I think it is very useful for us from time to time to ask ourselves what goes on under the category of rhetoric, which is how Aristotle keeps coming back in. Think about how important it is in your own lives. When I'm to speak on a campus, I will often stay at a large hotel somewhere. I will be walking down the hall past the rooms where some large firm is meeting. It's 1:30 in the afternoon, a lethal time. In one room there's somebody reading off a chart: "This is our new product, 104C32 which plugs in . . ." And everybody's gone. Next room: "And this our new . . . now if you'll watch the pointer here . . ." Again, everybody's gone. But in the next room, someone who really believes in what she's doing is holding forth. Everybody's leaning forward to listen. It's rhetoric: she's out to persuade.

Aristotle's Rhetoric: Analytic and Dialectic

For Aristotle there are two kinds of rhetoric: *analytic,* which concerns first principles, and *dialectic.* In the Christian church, the "analytic" would come closer to doctrine or dogma, or creed or confession, being expounded. That's what should go on in the classroom: "How do you get this aspect of our witness to God to correlate to that one?" "How has this changed in the Middle Ages and Reformation and the modern world?" And so on.

Father William O'Malley, a high school teacher, recently wrote in *America* magazine his story of how he teaches young Catholics.[1] He said that all of them come from parochial schools. You don't go to a Catholic high school unless you've been through confirmation and the parochial school system. But he writes — to paraphrase his argument — "What strikes me is that nobody knows anything. Nothing! I can't say 'Incarnation,' and think they understand. They're not dumb, but nothing they've been told matches their experience. What do I have to do? I have to back up to get into story and experience. After they've known what it is to be reconciled, *then* I can teach reconciliation."

After you've had the experience, after you've been through it, *then* you do the analytic. But for Aristotle, much closer to what we do as preachers is "dialectic," which doesn't demand closure, doesn't demand your having the answers to everything. What is a sermon but a bidding of people to a way of life they would not otherwise have entertained? That's dialectic.

Our sometime colleague at Chicago, Paul Ricoeur, said that there are three things you do with a text:

1. *Treat the world **behind** the text.* That's what we historians do, that's what biblical critics do when they try to analyze. That's what Luke/Acts

---

1. William J. O'Malley, "Plow Before You Plant," *America* 183, no. 7 (Sept. 16, 2000): 5, 15.

is out to do, or the student of it is out to do. You're out to ask what Mars Hill might represent; you're out to ask how Luke put these narratives together. That's really important, but it has very little to do with faith. You didn't get your faith through historical accuracy, just as you're not going to lose your faith through historical accuracy. The Jesus Seminar people run up and down the country telling all these things and there's never one more or one fewer believer in the world. I've outlived eight such final, all-purpose explanations of what Jesus was "nothing but." One year he was nothing but a zealot: Jesus had a knife that he was going to pull some day, I don't know on whom. One year Jesus was the head of a mushroom-munching cult that was into hallucinogenics. One year it was a Passover plot. But there's always another year. All these people are doing something legitimate; they're all trying to get at the world behind the text. But it has very little to do with what goes on in persuasion.

2. *Treat the world **of** the text.* Again, this is extremely important. It's extremely important to know the difference between a parable and a psalm and a historical line and a vision. Think of how much trouble the churches, or parts of the churches get into because Ezekiel, Daniel, and Revelation, which call themselves visions but are actually weird dreams, are treated literally. You can get into trouble there. If you had dreams last night I don't even want to hear about them — if you take them literally. It's really important to know the difference, but again it has very little to do with being persuaded, or with living out the consequences of faith.

3. *Treat the world **in front** of the text, the "not yet."* This is what Aristotle means by "dialectic": dealing with common opinions that haven't yet found closure. You're open to new insights. Michael Oakeshott, the great British philosopher; David Tracy, a great American Catholic theologian; and Martin Marty who borrows from the other two, make a distinction between argument and conversation. Argument (as I have learned from these two and Aristotle) is guided by the answer, and conversation by the question. Argument fits with analytic better than it fits with dialectic. In argument, put two people on stage: pro-life, pro-choice; pro-gay, anti-gay; pro-nuke, anti-nuke, or whatever. Each has a position to defend and their object is to defeat the other, convince the other, embarrass the other, convert the other. But *conversation* is guided by the question, "What are we going to do about such and such a situa-

tion?" It's still open: it's dialectic; it's a bid that gets answered back. You never hurt somebody and come home saying, "I sure won *that* conversation." You *learn* from a conversation.

Aristotle's Persuasion: Three Modes

Rhetoric is the counterpart of dialectic: it is a persuasion that involves the persuader who herself, himself is not a finished product. By contrast, the people who believe that you come to faith by historical accuracy put a lot of investment in the Shroud of Turin. They make tests of one little corner for carbon dating and they do various kinds of analysis, and they have endless debates. Their assumption always is that if we can prove its origin, then everyone will believe in the resurrection. You could have that cloth and it could say, "Bought at Sam's Linen Shop on 13th of Nissan, 29 AD," but it wouldn't do anything about proving the resurrection. If it would, don't you think the disciples would have run around Asia Minor saying, "Here, look at this rag, it proves that he is risen"? But what did they do? They sent Barnabas to Antioch, the first place where they're called "Christians," and because he was a good person, full of the Holy Spirit, many believed. Barnabas types are persuaders, and this is one of the modes of Christian discourse that we should pay attention to.

According to Aristotle, persuasion first involves the faculty of *discovering* the available means of persuasion in the particular case. That's what conversation does. It opens entirely different things. When you say, "God the Father," it means one thing to one kind of child and something else to another. Victimizers and victimized have different hearings, oppressed and unoppressed, in every circumstance. You must discover! I love that word. I once spoke at the funeral of Charles Huggins, the father of chemotherapy and a Nobel Prize winner. A little while later his daughter came to me with a beautifully framed Chinese calligraphy from San Francisco. It had hung on his office wall for forty years, and translates, "Discovery is our business." I think that is so for theology. A lot of people think that there is nothing new to discover. But in every situation or particular case, you're busy employing the faculty of discovery to find the available means of persuasion. Paul tried it that day at the Areopagus: "One of your own poets has said" (Acts 17:28). It didn't connect, but at least he was trying: he was seeking to discover.

The second thing is style. Here there are three features of persuasive language. Any of you who have ever read Aristotle's *Rhetoric* will have this down cold: the three key words are "Pathos," "Ethos," and "Logos." "Pathos" has to do with the audience or congregation. "Ethos" has to do with the character of the speaker, and "Logos" is their interrelation, what you actually talk about. In all cases it has to do with persuasion-producing effect. For example, God said, "Let there be light," and there was light. In the Hebrew Scriptures the authority of God is constantly connected to the persuasive character of the Law, and why one should love it. Place it on the doorpost, teach the children, await the day when a covenant will be written on the heart: the authority of God. In the New Testament it becomes the transferred authority of Jesus, of Paul, of Peter, of James, of disciples, of apostles who have a derived authority. But if they don't make it their own, you might as well have stayed home and read the Gideon Bible, which can be persuasive but it's persuasive mainly because whoever takes it up is predisposed to it.

Martin Luther said, "The gospel is not so much to be *schreiben* as to be *schreien*"; not so much to be written as to be shouted. "The church is not a *feder* house but a *mund* house"; not a quill-pen feather house, but a "mouth" house. Faith is an acoustical affair, faith comes by hearing. Why? Because it is transported in the light of pathos, ethos, and logos. It's really fun to see how Paul adapts in the versions stylized by Luke/Acts. Check him out in Acts 26 and Acts 22, and see how differently he speaks in front of Agrippa, or in front of the Jews. In both cases he is trying to reach through, to defend himself, to meet them where they are. The technical word for this is *Horizont Verschmelzung* — Hans-Georg Gadamer's concept that translates as "fusion of horizons." Every one of you brings a horizon to your encounter with each other. I bring a horizon conditioned by things like the travail of getting here and you by the travail of getting here, and the anxiety of yesterday. Our horizons meet: the horizon of that abused young woman I was talking to; the horizon of somebody facing cancer; the horizon of somebody who is a parent of a new child; somebody who got an award. All these things are there, and you bring the horizons together through rhetoric.

I've been so interested in the concept of "horizon" because it is both there and not there at the same time. That is, it is visible, but you don't know how far it goes. That sums up a lot of the mystery of faith, which brings us to a horizon where you have the incidents of Bethlehem and Calvary, but they're pointing beyond the text to a yet-unknown world, and the people who take us there tend to be the apostles, the prophets, the men and women whom we call "saints," the unknowns who led us to this place by their word and their example.

Pathos

For Aristotle, "Putting the hearer into an appropriate frame of mind, persuasion occurs when [hearers] are aroused to pathos [emotion] by the speech, for the judgments we deliver are not the same when we are influenced by joy or sorrow, love or hate." Aristotle is exactly to the point of what goes on in a sermon. It doesn't mean you have to overdo emotion; you don't have to always whip everybody up that way. You have to be aware of the situation, of what could be a problem, and what you can do to address it. The object of rhetoric is judgment, he says. And for that, we have to develop and understand the audience. How do we learn this, how do we learn audiences? Through listening, through a great deal of attentiveness, and — in any spare moments — through our apprehension of culture.

My favorite archbishop, which means that he will never be cardinal, is Rembert Weakland of Milwaukee. He got his Ph.D. at age 68 on Ambrosian Chant, during a one-year sabbatical, is a concert-level pianist, and in 1994 celebrated the one hundredth anniversary of the papal social teachings. We were at a conference in San Francisco and he was there in his T-shirt and sweatshirt hanging around all week. One day we were on a fake cable-car tourism thing going around San Francisco, so I had him for a couple of hours and I said, "What are you going to do this summer?" Earlier we had talked about why he was always going to be an Archbishop of Milwaukee and not Cardinal of Chicago. He said, "Rome doesn't have one word against me. They've never heard a word from me that violates Catholic teaching. I'm in trouble because I listen to women." He has groups in which women speak of their experiences. Rome wasn't interested in hearing what women thought about child-bearing and birth control and so on. He said, "But that's not all I do. I also want to know how profound articulators of the culture do it. So, this summer is my Muriel Sparks summer. A couple of years ago was my Flannery O'Connor summer, my Margaret Atwood summer, my whatever. Every summer I read the entire corpus of a woman author because artists see some things that we don't normally see."

That's an example of how we learn about *pathos,* through the gifted people of our day. If you look at preachers like Desmond Tutu, Dietrich Bonhoeffer, Martin Luther King; always there's that sense of *pathos.* In 1961, I was the morning lecturer in front of five or six hundred African American pastors at the Hampton Institute of Virginia, and Martin Luther King came and preached in the afternoons. When I spoke, everybody would be taking notes. But when King spoke there were no note-takers at all, because they were already in it. He sensed that he was dealing with leaders of people who were on a move toward civil rights, leadership, and so on. I was in South Africa the year before the change came, and preached in the cathedral. It was packed. I had been told that the cathedral, with its well-off people, was an old symbol of the imperial establishment; that Desmond Tutu lived in luxury. It was the year of martial law and detention, and on the prayer list as I walked in were the names of two hundred people being detained from that congregation alone. Eight-year-old children: no one knew where they were, detained. You have to know the pathos of it. If I had gotten up and assumed it was the old imperial cathedral I would have missed them entirely. You can never know too much about the situation; you can't assume you're really inside it, but every attempt we make at listening with attentiveness can add to pathos.

Ethos

The second of the three is *ethos,* the character of the one who persuades. This is really tricky because, according to Paul, we have this treasure in earthen vessels; not many wise were called, and so on. Two years ago I gave a commencement address at McCormick Theological Seminary called "Welcome to the Goldfish Bowl," because I'd heard some students say, "In ministry, my spouse and I will be in the goldfish bowl . . ." I said, "I don't envy you at all when the day comes that you're not in the goldfish bowl; when nobody cares about the character of the people who are presenting the gospel." Not that you're perfect, not that you're above other people, but there must be some effort to have a congruence between the *logos* and the *pathos* and you as the connector, the *ethos*.

For Aristotle, the question is, "Why should I believe this particular person? What are the warrants?" The technical term for it is the "hermeneutics of testimony." A lot of people were Mormon because they knew that Joseph Smith knew he was going to be killed, and he was. A lot of people found King compelling because they knew that there were knives aimed at his back all the time and you never knew what might happen. Dietrich Bonhoeffer was in that circumstance. But you don't have to be in those circumstances to have an authenticity with which people can identify enough to get you through. This is the trickiest of all the things I'm saying, because it might sound as if you have to be somehow perfect and exemplary in order to be heard. People will tolerate an awful lot in our faults, but you have to remember, as Aristotle says, that the stories we tell are always presented through our experience and then we have to connect them with our listeners.

Some years ago in the *Christian Century*, we had an article we didn't want to publish, that we didn't like at all, but we found that it resonated and we knew it said something important. From a little Episcopal church in Indiana, the writer said, "We always have evangelism committees; we get rector after rector and they all like to grow and get new members and so on and we never get any. We never make house calls and we never invite. Does it ever occur to him that we don't want anybody new?" And why not? (Then she got much more tender, or we wouldn't have printed it at all!) She said, "Well, for example, on the missal stand for the prayer book are the names of nine men from this congregation who were killed in World War II. Will a new rector find that meaningful at all? By today's standards, they are long gone. Those names don't mean now what they meant then, in 1960, fifteen years after the fact when their memories were still very alive. Will he do that?"

Yes, a good one will. You learn the history, you learn what the names are, but you have to connect with them along the way. Aristotle assumes that you need common stories for this to take place, but a real problem in our culture is that we increasingly lack common stories. We still have a head start but, as Father O'Malley says, "People don't know an awful lot." Where are they going to get it? Not much at schools, none on television, not much from playmates, not much from parents if they're just whooshing by the fast-food place and not sitting around the dinner table in the evening. How could they know? But I think we have to work to get these basic, basic stories that unite us, before us. And then, how do you develop that *ethos*? You develop it in company. The French novelist Stendhal said, "One can acquire everything in solitude — except character." Only character produces character.

You may have heard about the big Marty family, four sons and then we adopted two more. We had five sons running cross-country and we were spared drugs and all that. Why? Because they hung out with fellow cross-country runners who wouldn't mess up their lives. A few years earlier, with a different crowd, and I have a hunch our family biography would have been very different, because parents who cared just like we cared had kids who hung out with druggies . . . I have a hunch our autobiographies in this room would tell us a lot of that. The luck of whom your kids hang out with. So, only character begets character.

Logos

Then finally, *logos,* "Word." Now what did Paul do in the words I read at the beginning? He distanced himself from Aristotelean rhetoric, from the language of Athens. Why? Because its pursuit of wisdom suggested that when you exhausted it, you would find ultimate and absolute truth, God or whatever. Paul says, "That's not the way God, our God, comes to us. Our God comes in weakness, in the tracks left in history. Our God comes in the foolishness of the cross."

What has Paul done? He has restored a *different* logos, but one that's just as compelling. One point eight billion people in the world today are called by the name of the Christ of this Logos. You don't have quite that many Aristoteleans or Athenians running around. When somebody has to ask, "Shall we pull the plug on Grandma in the hospital?" clinical ethicists at the University of Chicago report that they have never had a phone call saying, "Send over one Aristotelean, two pragmatists, and three post-deconstructionists." They ask, "What does that good nurse say; what does my good doctor say; what does my good aunt say; what does my good pastor say?" What these people are doing is presuming upon persuasive language with people who are going to be there with them as they live through the consequences.

If you take Aristotelean ethics in Med school, you learn about "justice," "autonomy," "benefits," and "non-malfeasance." Four things down cold; wonderful for debating allocation of resources, making them available to people; for making basic decisions. But in the end, when you get to the *pathos* of the individual, your decision is going to be prismed through the experience of someone who has actually been there, and so you're more likely to use the kind of *logos* that Paul uses.

Paul is playing a little trick on us, because he's against rhetoric for the sake of rhetoric. He's against Aristotle's way of persuasion in order to make room for the persuasion of God in the pattern of the cross. Words are very important, but Aristotle's kinds of words don't do it. At the risk of sounding uncharitable, I am going to suggest that within orthodox Christianity we often have the trouble of using the wrong mode at the wrong time. A little illustration of this was some years ago when Carl Henry, the major theologian of the neo-evangelical movement, wrote six volumes on propositional theology. All Christian revelation is reduced to propositions: all words, words, words. It was a heavy blast against existentialism and experientialism and therapy and all that, because they're going to soften it and water it down and so it was words, words, words. A colleague at Fuller Seminary reviewed the book and said, "This is a wonderful series of books, these six books, but this attack on experience and so on and the assertion that nothing but words count is refuted in the dedication to Volume One: 'To Helga, my wife, who means far more to me than words could ever say.'"

Well, when Dr. Henry preaches, he is doing what preachers should do, but what I'm getting at here is that the language of the proposition is not what brings people to faith. Propositions are part of Aristotle's argumentation and analysis, but the task of commending the faith — persuasive, preached rhetoric — is of a very different character. So to summarize, I hope nobody will go home and say, "I'm going to preach 'Aristotelean'; I'm going to use rhetoric." You're allowed to use the word "persuade," and you don't ever need to use the words "ethos," "pathos," or "logos," but if you think of them as character, as identifying the situation of the people, and coming in with the different word that matches human experience, you will come closer to what Aristotle and Paul were both after.

"Grace Sufficient":
The Theology of Preaching

Biblical Preaching in the Modern World

⁓

John R. W. Stott

1996

I begin with three introductory points that I do not want to omit. The first is a personal one. In daring to speak to you about preaching, I am assuming neither that you are novices nor that I am an expert. There is always something anomalous about one preacher speaking to other preachers about preaching and I sense that anomaly as I begin. I can honestly say that when I am in the pulpit I am not infrequently seized with what I can only describe as a communication frustration, because I am burning with something I want to say and sense the difficulty with communicating it. When I come down from the pulpit, I constantly need to cry to God for forgiveness and for grace to do better next time. So I hope this puts us on a level. All I can really do is to share with you some of my convictions and experiences. That is a personal word.

Secondly, I have a social or cultural point to make, namely that, on the whole, contemporary society is unfriendly to preaching. It seems to many an outdated medium of communication, what somebody has

---

A previous version of this address appears as "Expounding the Word," in John Stott, *The Contemporary Christian: Applying God's Word to Today's World* (Downers Grove, Ill.: InterVarsity, 1992), pp. 207-18.

called "an echo from an abandoned past."[1] Who wants to listen to sermons nowadays? People are drugged by television. They are hostile to authority. They are weary and wary of words. So when the sermon begins they quickly grow impatient, fidgety, and bored. "No one but a preaching clergyman," wrote Anthony Trollope, "has . . . the power of compelling an audience to sit silent, and be tormented."[2] If that was true in nineteenth-century England, it is even more true at the end of the twentieth century in Canada, and in North America, and in Europe. So that is my second, social or cultural point.

My third is a pastoral point. In spite of the problems — of which there are many — we must persevere with our preaching because the health of the church depends upon it. If what Jesus said, quoting Deuteronomy, is true of individuals, "that a human being does not live by bread only but by every word that comes out of the mouth of God" (Matt. 4:4), then we must persevere. For it is equally true of churches. Churches live and grow and flourish by the word of God, and they languish and die without it. This is the lesson of history. Dr. Martyn Lloyd-Jones, a well-known evangelical leader in the Fifties and early Sixties, in lectures on preaching that he gave at Westminster Theological Seminary and published under the title *Preaching and Preachers,* said that the decadent eras and periods of the church's history have always been those in which preaching has declined.[3] The low level of Christian living in many parts of the world today is due to the low level of Christian preaching. So these are the three points that I want to make by way of introduction.

I offer, for your reflection, a definition of preaching in twenty-one words. To preach is *to open up the inspired text with such faithfulness and sensitivity that God's voice is heard and his people obey him.* This definition of preaching contains six implications: two convictions about the biblical text, two obligations in expounding it, and two expectations as a result. We begin first with the two convictions about the biblical text.

1. Clement Welsh, *Preaching in a New Key: Studies in the Psychology of Thinking and Listening* (Philadelphia: Pilgrim, 1974), p. 32.

2. Anthony Trollope, *Barchester Towers* (London: Longman, Brown, Green, Longmans and Roberts, 1857), I.86.

3. D. Martyn Lloyd-Jones, *Preaching and Preachers* (Grand Rapids: Zondervan, 1971), p. 24.

Two Convictions

The biblical text is an *inspired text;* to preach is to open up the inspired text of Scripture. So a high view of the biblical text, that it is unlike any other text, unique in its origin, its nature, and its authority, is indispensable to authentic Christian preaching. Nothing undermines preaching more than skepticism about Scripture. This is not the place to develop a sustained defense of that statement and of the authority of Scripture, but I hope I may carry you with me in three words that belong together in our doctrine of the Bible, namely revelation, inspiration, and providence.

Revelation describes the initiative that God has taken to disclose or unveil himself. Revelation is a very humbling word, because to speak of divine revelation is to imply that we would know nothing of God if he had not taken the initiative to make himself known. Without revelation we wouldn't be Christians at all; we would be Athenians, like those whose altar Paul discovered outside Athens, inscribed "To an unknown god" (Acts 17:23). Without revelation he would be to us an unknown god. But we believe that God has revealed himself, not only in the ordered loveliness of the created universe, but supremely in his Son Jesus Christ, and in the totality of the biblical witness to Christ. Without that revelation expressed in speaking — human speech is the model that God has chosen to indicate what is meant by revelation — without it we would know nothing of him. We can't even read each other's thoughts if we don't speak. So if we can't read each other's minds, how much less can we read the mind of God? The mind of God is inaccessible to us; there is no ladder by which this little finite and fallen mind can climb up into the infinite mind of God. Revelation is indispensable. Do not be ashamed of the doctrine of revelation, which is essentially reasonable.

The second word, *inspiration,* describes the process by which God chose to reveal himself, namely by speaking to and through the biblical authors. It was emphatically not a dictation process, which would have demeaned the authors into being mere machines. On the contrary, it was a process that treated them as persons in full possession of their faculties, as the phenomena of Scripture make clear. For example, a very large percentage of the Old and New Testaments is history. We do not imagine that all that history was supernaturally revealed to the human authors of Scripture. On the contrary, within Ezra or Nehemiah, for example, come several imperial edicts from Persia. But we don't imagine that the texts of those edicts were supernaturally revealed to the biblical writers. No, they discovered those edicts for themselves. Thus divine inspiration is not incompatible with historical research. Luke tells us as much in the prologue to his gospel, in the painstaking trouble he had taken in order to investigate the things that had occurred in his day.

We could go beyond historical research to theological emphasis — as appropriate to the personality, background, and temperament of each biblical author — and not only to theological emphasis but also to literary style. Divine inspiration did not iron out those things; divine inspiration did not smother the God-given personality of the human authors. Nevertheless, God spoke to them and through them in such a way that their words were simultaneously his words and his words were simultaneously their words. This is the double authorship of Scripture. To say it is the word of God alone might be heretical, because that is only part of the truth. The truth is that Scripture is the word of God *through* the words of men, and we must not emphasize the humanity of Scripture in such a way as to deny its divinity or its divinity in such a way as to deny its humanity any more than we may in the person of our Lord Jesus Christ. The human and the divine are together in Scripture as they are also in Christ.

The third word is *providence*. We believe in the loving provision by which God arranged for the words that he had spoken to be written down to form what would become Scripture and then preserved across the centuries so as to be available to all people in all places at all times. Scripture is "God's word written." That is an Anglican definition of Scripture, according to Article 20 of the Thirty-Nine Anglican "Articles of Religion." It is God's self-disclosure in speech and in writing, the product of his revelation, inspiration, and providence.

"Well," you say, "what on earth has that got to do with preaching?" It has a great deal to do with preaching. This first conviction is indispensable to preachers. If God had not spoken, we would not dare to speak. We would have nothing to say except our own threadbare speculations. But since God has spoken we too must speak, communicating to others what he has communicated through his word. Indeed I hope we may be able to say that we refuse to be silenced. As Amos put it,

"The Lord God has spoken. Who can but prophesy?" (Amos 3:8). So I pity the preachers who enter the pulpit with no Bible in their hands or with a Bible that is more rags and tatters than the word of God. They cannot expound Scripture because they have no Scripture to expound, and they cannot speak because they have nothing worth saying. Instead we must enter the pulpit with the confidence that God has spoken, that he has caused what he has spoken to be written, and that we have this inspired text in our hands. Why, then the head begins to spin, the heart to beat, the blood to flow, and the eyes to sparkle, with the sheer glory of having God's word in our hands and on our lips. That's the first thing: the biblical text is an inspired text.

Now we move on to the second conviction, which is that the inspired text is a partially closed text. If to preach is to open up the inspired text, then it must be partially closed or it would not need to be opened up. At once I see your Protestant hackles rising! What do you mean that Scripture is a partially closed text? Don't you believe with the sixteenth-century Reformers in the perspicuity of Scripture, that Scripture has a see-through quality, a transparent quality? Cannot even the simplest and uneducated read it and understand it for themselves? Is not the Holy Spirit our God-given teacher? With the Word and the Spirit must we not say that we need no ecclesiastical magisterium to instruct us? Well, yes. Thank you for asking those questions. I am able to respond to all of them with a resounding "yes." You are quite correct in all those things. But what you are rightly saying also needs to be qualified.

The Reformers' insistence on the perspicuity of Scripture refers only to its central message of salvation through Christ by grace and through faith. That is as plain as day in the Bible. But they didn't claim that everything in Scripture was equally plain. How could they, when Peter said that there were some things in Paul's letters that were hard to understand (2 Pet. 3:16)? If one apostle didn't always understand another apostle, it would hardly be modest for us to claim that we can. No, the church needs pastors and teachers and preachers to expound or open up this partially closed text, and the ascended Christ continues to give these gifts to his church. You remember the story of the Ethiopian eunuch on his way back to Ethiopia, to the upper Nile, after being in Jerusalem (Acts 8:26-38). You will recall that he had open on his knees in the chariot the scroll of the prophet Isaiah. Philip was sent to join him, and one man sat beside another man talking about Isaiah 53.

Philip asked, "Do you understand what you are reading?" "Why, of course," said the Ethiopian. "Don't you believe in the perspicuity of Scripture?" No. He replied, "How can I understand unless somebody teaches me?" (Acts 8:30-31). Calvin, in his marvelous commentary on the Acts comments on the Ethiopian's humility and contrasts with it those whom he calls "swollen-headed with confidence in [their] own abilities." Calvin goes on to say that this "is also why the reading of Scripture bears fruit with such a few people today, because scarcely one in a hundred is to be found who gladly submits himself to teaching."[4]

Here, then, is the biblical case for biblical exposition. It consists of two fundamental convictions, namely that God has given us in Scripture a text that is on the one hand inspired, having a divine origin and authority, and on the other hand is to some degree closed and difficult to understand. Therefore, in addition to giving us the text, God gives us teachers to interpret and apply the text, explaining it and making it relevant for people in the contemporary world. These are very strong convictions that have grown with me through the years; I hope I will never lose them or ever lose their strength or power.

Two Obligations

Now we move from our two convictions to our two obligations in expounding the text. Granted that these inspired texts need to be expounded, how shall it be done? Before I answer this question, let us address ourselves to one of the major reasons why the biblical text is partially closed and difficult. It concerns the cultural gulf or canyon that yawns between the biblical text and the modern world: two thousand years of cultural change between the ancient world in which God spoke his word and the contemporary world in which we listen to it. When we pick up the Bible and read it, even in Today's English or another modern version, we step back two millennia, beyond the microchip revolution, beyond the electronic revolution, the scientific revolution, the industrial revolution. We go back in history into a world that

---

4. John Calvin, *The Acts of the Apostles 1-13*, trans. John W. Fraser and W. J. G. McDonald, ed. David W. Torrance and Thomas F. Torrance (Grand Rapids: Eerdmans, 1965), pp. 246-47.

has long ago ceased to exist. So when we read the Scripture, even in a modern version, it feels odd, it sounds archaic, it looks obsolete, and it smells musty. And we say to ourselves, what has that old book got to say to us today?

I take the liberty of telling a story that also appears in *I Believe in Preaching*, or *Between Two Worlds* (its title in the United States).[5] I was talking in the early seventies with two young men who were brothers. They had been brought up in a very conservative Christian home and like many of us they had absorbed and assimilated the faith of their parents during their childhood and their boyhood. But now they were students. One was at Edinburgh University, the other at Oxford University, and they told me they were busy repudiating the faith of their parents. They no longer believed. One said he was an agnostic; the other said he was an atheist. So I pricked up my ears and I began to question them.

I said, "Tell me about it. What has happened to you? Is it that you no longer believe that Christianity is true?"

"No," they said. "That's not our problem. Even if you could persuade us that Christianity is true, we are not at all sure that we could embrace it."

"Oh," I said, with mounting surprise. "Then what is your problem?"

"Our problem is not whether Christianity is true but whether Christianity is relevant, and frankly we can't see how it can be."

These are their exact words: "Christianity is a primitive Palestinian religion. It arose in a primitive Palestinian culture. So what on earth does it have to say to us who live in this exciting modern world?" They were all turned on by modernity. They said that with men on the moon in the seventies, there should be men on Mars in the eighties (they were a little optimistic!). They said that with transplant surgery today, there should be genetic engineering tomorrow. And then, with a sneer, almost a leer, on their faces they said, "What has your primitive Palestinian religion got to say to us? It's irrelevant."

I'm not going to tell you how I replied because I did very badly, but I have often thanked God for that conversation because it challenged me more than I had been challenged thus far concerning the task of the

---

5. John R. W. Stott, *Between Two Worlds: The Art of Preaching in the Twentieth Century* (Grand Rapids: Eerdmans, 1982), pp. 138-39.

Christian communicator. That task is not, of course, to *make* Jesus Christ and the gospel relevant but rather to *demonstrate* their relevance to the modern world.

So imagine, for a moment, a flat piece of territory, a plateau of some kind that is deeply divided by a canyon. On this side of the canyon is the biblical world, the ancient world. On the other side is the modern world, and the canyon between the two represents two thousand years of changing culture. Those of us who are conservative or evangelical Christians live on this side of the divide. We read the Bible. We believe in the Bible. We love the Bible. We are Bible people. We find our security in the biblical world. But we don't feel so comfortable on the other side, in the modern world. We read a book like Alvin Toffler's *Future Shock,*[6] and we actually go into shock! So how should I depict our preaching? It all comes from the Bible; we wouldn't dream of preaching from anywhere else. Then it rises up in the air — but it never quite lands on the other side. It isn't earthed in contemporary reality. This is the characteristic fault in the preaching of evangelical, conservative preachers. We are biblical but we are not contemporary.

Then those who like to call themselves "liberal" are on the other side. They live in the modern world. They read Alvin Toffler. He doesn't shock them because they have built-in shock absorbers, and they are moving with the moving times. They read modern philosophy, modern psychology, modern poetry: they go to the theater and the movies, they watch television, and they are modern men and women. That is why people listen to them. They resonate with the modern world. But the problem is that they have lost the biblical revelation. So how shall I depict their preaching? It is fully earthed in contemporary reality, but where it comes from, heaven alone knows! It does not come out of the Scripture. I know that this is an oversimplification, a caricature if you like. But I believe that my image of the canyon expresses one of the greatest tragedies of the Christian church today: that evangelical people are biblical but not contemporary, while liberal people are contemporary but not biblical, and almost nobody is building bridges and relating the ancient word to the modern world in such a way that is faithful to the Word and sensitive to the world.

We must not resent the cultural gap between the ancient word and

6. Alvin Toffler, *Future Shock* (New York: Random House, 1970).

the modern world simply because it causes us problems. It is one of the glories of divine revelation that when God decided to speak to human beings, he did not speak in his own language, if he has one, because the people of the ancient world wouldn't have understood it if he had. Instead, God condescended to speak in their languages, especially in classical Hebrew and Koine Greek. Moreover, in speaking their languages he reflected their cultures: the Ancient Near East in the case of the Old Testament, Palestinian Judaism in the case of the Gospels, and the Greco-Roman world in the case of the Epistles. No word of God was spoken in a cultural vacuum; every word of God was spoken in a cultural context. It is this cultural chasm between the biblical world and the modern world which determines the task of the biblical expositor, and which lays down our two major obligations.

The first is *faithfulness to the ancient word*. We have to accept the discipline of exegesis, of thinking ourselves back into the situation of the biblical authors, their history, geography, culture, and language. This is what used to be called grammatico-historical exegesis. To neglect this task or to do it in a half-hearted way is inexcusable because it expresses contempt for the way God chose to speak. If he chose to speak in particular languages, particular contexts, and particular cultures, we cannot — we dare not — neglect those cultures within which he chose to speak. The worst blunder we can commit is that of eisegesis, which is to read back our twentieth-century thoughts into the minds of the biblical authors, and to manipulate what they said in order to make it conform to our opinions, to what we want them to say. To claim their patronage for our opinions is both sick and inexcusable.

Calvin, perhaps the greatest exegete that God has given the church at least until his own day, perhaps even until now, wrote in the preface to his commentary on Romans that the first business of an interpreter is to let his author say what he does say and not force him to say what he does not say.[7] At the beginning of the last century, Charles Simeon of Cambridge (who remains one of my heroes) said it also: "My

---

7. John Calvin, *The Epistles of Paul the Apostle to the Romans and to the Thessalonians,* trans. Ross MacKenzie, ed. David W. Torrance and Thomas F. Torrance (Grand Rapids: Eerdmans, 1960), p. 1: "Since it is almost [the interpreter's] only task to unfold the mind of the writer whom he has undertaken to expound, he misses his mark, or at least strays outside his limits, by the extent to which he leads his readers away from the meaning of his author."

endeavour is *to bring out of Scripture what is there, and not to thrust in what I think might be there. I have a great jealousy on this head.*"[8] So in order to do this — to expound to the congregation the things that are there in the text and not twist or manipulate the Scripture to make it mean what we want it to mean — that requires courage because without any doubt it will involve us in proclaiming doctrines and ethics which are not politically correct. They are not popular; they are not fashionable; and we need courage.

If you have read the great lectures on preaching by Bishop Phillips Brooks, you may recall this quotation:

> Courage . . . is the indispensable requisite of any true ministry. . . . If you are afraid of men and a slave to their opinion, go and do something else. Go and make shoes to fit them. Go even and paint pictures which you know are bad but which suit their bad taste. But do not keep on all your life preaching sermons which shall say not what God sent you to declare, but what they hire you to say. Be courageous. Be independent.[9]

So we need that courageous faithfulness to the biblical text.

Our second major obligation is that we need *sensitivity to the modern world.* Because although God spoke to the ancient world in its own languages and its own cultures, he intended his word, we believe, to be for people of all languages and all cultures, including us at the end of the twentieth century. So the expositor is more than an exegete. The exegete explains the original meaning of the text, but the expositor goes further and applies it to the modern reality. So we have to struggle to understand the rapidly changing world in which we live. We have to listen to its many discordant voices, the cries and the sighs of the oppressed. We need to listen to the questions of the questioner and the loneliness of those who have lost the way. We need to feel the disorientation and despair of the world around us. It's all part of our Christian sensitivity. So

8. Charles Simeon (1759-1836), from a letter of 1832 to his publisher, cited in William Carus, ed., *Memoirs of the Life of the Rev. Charles Simeon, M.A., with a Selection from His Writings and Correspondence* (London: Hatchard; Cambridge: Deightons and Macmillan, 1847), 2.703 (emphasis original).

9. Phillips Brooks, *Lectures on Preaching, Delivered Before the Divinity School of Yale College* (New York: Dutton, [1877] 1893), p. 59.

this is our double obligation, the obligation of biblical expositors: we are to open up the inspired text of Scripture with faithfulness to the ancient word and sensitivity to the modern world. That means that we are neither to falsify the word in order to secure a phony relevance nor are we to ignore the world in order to secure a phony faithfulness. We are not to fulfill either obligation at the expense of the other.

That leads us to what I like to call "double listening." It seems to me that double listening is the task of every Christian communicator. In the first case we listen to the word of God. We listen with great deference, great humility, to what God has said and is saying through his word. But we also listen to the voices of the modern world. Of course we don't listen to those with the same degree of respect with which we listen to the voice of God. We listen to the word of God in order to believe it and to obey it. But we don't listen to the world uncritically, in order to believe it and obey it: we listen in order to understand, so that when we relate the word to the world we may do so sensitively.

This combination of faithfulness and sensitivity really makes the authentic expositor. Being difficult, it is also rare, and in practice as we start at the text we need to ask ourselves two questions in the right order. The first question is, "What did it mean?" Or you could say, "What *does* it mean?" — because the actual meaning of the text does not change with the changing years. In his book, *Validity in Interpretation*, E. D. Hirsch says that "a text means what its author meant."[10] That is in clear contradiction to the whole spirit of postmodernity, but Hirsch is right: a text means what its author meant. The meaning of a text cannot float free of the words that constitute the text, and the person who has established the meaning of the text is the author of the text, not the reader of the text. That is where we part company with Bultmann and with all Christian existentialists. Rudolf Bultmann, of course, said that a text means what it means to me, but what it means for every other reader may be totally different. In postmodernity, a text is "infinitely interpretable." No, it is infinitely *applicable* but it is not infinitely interpretable. Every text has its own meaning and that meaning has been established by its author. So we have to ask, "What *did* it mean?" and "What *does* it mean?" And that leads us into the careful study of language and context.

10. E. D. Hirsch, *Validity in Interpretation* (New Haven: Yale University, 1967), p. 1.

The second question is, "What does it *say?*" That is, we turn from its meaning to its message. Some of us are so eager to get on to the message that we don't give ourselves to the discipline of discovering what it meant in the first place. Let me put it like this: if we grasp the original meaning of a text without going on to its contemporary application, we have surrendered to antiquarianism, which is unrelated to the real world in which we live. But if we make the opposite mistake — if we start with the message, "What can this say to my congregation next Sunday?" — without first asking the disciplined question of what it originally meant and means, we have surrendered to existentialism, which is unrelated to past revelation. We have to bring the past and the present together, the revelation of the past and the reality of the present. Faithfulness to the one and sensitivity to the other. We have to ask both questions in the right order, first being faithful in working at the meaning of the original text and then being sensitive at discerning its message for today. In order to do that, we have to study.

It is important to establish that our study must be on both sides of the cultural chasm. It is not enough to study the Bible and Christian theology and ethics and church history and so on. We also have to study the modern world. We have to go to the movies and watch television and read books and find out what are the cult books that are being read by students at university. Otherwise, we can never relate the word to the world in a way that is equally faithful and sensitive. Nothing has helped me more in this second task than bringing into being a reading group. I started it with some young graduate friends about fifteen to twenty years ago, and it is still going on today. We meet somewhere between four to six times a year and agree at the end of our previous meeting what book we are going to read next. I let them choose it. They choose all kinds of books I would never have heard of. I remember reading *Zen and the Art of Motorcycle Maintenance*,[11] Toffler's *Future Shock*, many other modern classics such as those by Sartre and Camus, and more recent works as well. We have to soak ourselves in this culture in order to be able with understanding and sensitivity to declare the relevance of the eternal gospel of Jesus Christ.

---

11. Robert M. Pirsig, *Zen and the Art of Motorcycle Maintenance* (Toronto: Bantam, 1974).

Two Expectations

We have looked at two convictions about the text, and two obligations in expounding it. We come now to two expectations as a result. The first expectation is that God's voice will be heard, because if we believe that God has spoken through the biblical authors, we also believe that he continues to speak through what he has spoken. This was the conviction of the apostles in relation to Old Testament Scripture. You will remember that they constantly introduce their quotations from the Old Testament with one of two formulae, either, "Because it stands written," or, "Because it speaks." If you compare these formulae, it is not only that one is written and the other spoken, but that one is in the perfect tense and the other in the present. It was written centuries ago; it stands written in the text today; there it is. So that was the conviction of the apostles and it must be understood in the same way today.

But such an expectation — that as we read and expound the ancient word, God will speak again — is at a very low ebb today. The late Langmead Casserley, an American Episcopalian scholar, once wrote, "We have devised a way of reading the word of God through which no word from God ever comes because we are not expecting it." So, when the sermon arrives, the people close their eyes, and clasp their hands with a fine show of piety, and sit back in the pew for their customary doze, which the preacher encourages by his somnolent voice and manner. But how different it is when preacher and people are actually expecting the living word of God to meet with his people and address and confront them through the Scripture. Why, the whole atmosphere becomes electric as the people sit on the edge of their seat or pew with the Bible open in front of them, waiting eagerly for what the Lord God has to say. That is what Cornelius said when Peter arrived in his household. He said, "Now we are all here in the presence of God to hear what the Lord God has to tell us" (Acts 10:33). So let's take trouble to recover this sense of expectancy that God will speak. I think preaching is a dead art unless it is a response to this eagerness of some to listen.

So then the second expectation is that God's people will hear and obey him. The word of God always demands a response of obedience. We are not to be forgetful hearers but obedient doers of God's Word (James 1:22). Throughout the Old Testament we hear God's lament: "O that you would listen to my word." I am sure that God's lament is still heard today, and the epitaph engraved on Israel's tomb is that they refused to listen. God spoke but nobody listened. It is the same today.

So how should people respond? What kind of obedience is required? Well, the nature of the response expected varies according to the content of the word that is spoken. What we do in response to God's Word depends on what he says to us through it. If in and through the text, God speaks about himself and his own glorious greatness, and we are given a fresh glimpse of the majesty, holiness, and love of God, then we respond by humbling ourselves in worship, for worship is the only form of response that is appropriate if God has disclosed more of himself. Or if God speaks in the passage about us instead of about himself, about our waywardness, our foolishness, our rebellion, and our fickleness, then we respond with repentance and confession. If God speaks in the text about Jesus Christ who died to bear our sin and was raised from death to prove it and has been exalted to glory, then we respond in faith. We lay hold of this heaven-sent Savior. Or if God speaks about his promises, then we determine to inherit them. If about his commandments, we determine to keep them. If he speaks about the outside world and its colossal spiritual and material need, then we determine to do something about it. We respond in obedience and action. Or if God speaks to us about the future, about the coming of Christ and the glory that will follow, then our hope is kindled and we determine to be holy and busy until he comes.

So the conclusion. Here is the definition of biblical exposition or preaching which I have ventured to offer you. It consists of two convictions: that the biblical text is an inspired text that yet needs to be opened up; two obligations: that we must open up the Scripture with faithfulness to the text and sensitivity to the contemporary context; and two expectations: that through the reading and the exposition of the word God himself will speak and his people will respond in obedience. It is an enormous privilege to be a biblical expositor, to stand in the pulpit with God's Word in our hands and in our minds, with God's Spirit in our hearts, and God's people before our eyes, waiting expectantly for God's voice to be heard and obeyed.

Power Through Weakness

(1 Corinthians 1:17–2:5)

JOHN R. W. STOTT

1996

We live in a society that positively worships power. Of course that is not new, because the lust for power has always been a characteristic of the human story. It was this that led to the fall of Adam and Eve when they were offered power in exchange for disobedience. Still today there are three major human ambitions, all of which amount to a concealed longing for power: the pursuit of money, the pursuit of fame, and the pursuit of influence. We see this lust for power everywhere. We see it in politics and in public life, in big business and in industry: we see it in the professions because professional expertise gives people power over the powerless. And unfortunately we also see it in the church in top-level ecclesiastical power struggles, in denominational disputes and rivalries, in some local churches in which the local clergy hold all the power in their hands and refuse to share it with the lay people, let alone the young people. We see it in parachurch organizations that dream of expanding into world empires. And we see it in the pulpit, which is a very dangerous place for any child of Adam to occupy. Power: it is more intoxicating than liquor and more addictive than drugs.

A later version of this address appears in *Basic Christian Leadership: Biblical Models of Church, Gospel, and Ministry* (Downers Grove, Ill.: InterVarsity, 2002), pp. 31-52.

Probably we have all have heard the well-known quotation by Lord Acton, who said that "power tends to corrupt, and absolute power corrupts absolutely." I wonder if you know the context of that particular saying. Lord Acton was a British politician in the middle of the nineteenth century, a close friend of Prime Minister William Gladstone. He was very disturbed to see democracy being undermined by power struggles. As a Roman Catholic, Lord Acton was concerned about the First Vatican Council in 1870, and in particular with the decision of that council to attribute infallibility to the Pope. He saw it, he said, as "power corrupting the church."[1]

To be frank, I am myself very worried about the evangelical lust for power that I see all around me, even the quest for the power of the Holy Spirit. Why do we want to receive power? Is it honestly for witness, for humble service, and power for holiness? Or is it in reality personal ambition — the boosting of our own ego, ministering to our own self-importance, extending our influence, wanting to impress, to dominate, to manipulate? All these things lie buried in our fallen human nature and, I fear, break out too often. Is it an exaggeration to say that even some evangelism is a disguised form of imperialism, because it sometimes builds human empires rather than the kingdom of God? There is only one imperialism that is truly Christian, and that is our concern for his imperial majesty, our Lord Jesus Christ, and for his glory.

Jesus warned us against this lust for power, especially among Christian leaders. We know well that passage in Mark 10, where the new style of servant leadership that he introduced into the world is described: "In the world they exercise power and authority; they lord it over people, they boss people around in the secular community, but it shall not be so among you" (Mark 10:42). The Christian community operates on a different principle from the lust for power. "Whoever wants to be great among you must be your servant and whoever wants to be first must be your slave. Even the Son of Man did not come to wield power, but to renounce it" (Mark 10:43-45). That is to say, he did not come to be served but to serve, and to give himself as a ransom for many. All

---

1. John Dalberg-Acton, First Baron Acton (1834-1902), letter of April 3, 1887, to the Rt. Rev. Mandell Creighton, Bishop of Peterborough, published in Louise Creighton, *Life and Letters of Mandell Creighton, D. D., Oxon. and Cam., Sometime Bishop of London* (London: Longmans, Green, 1905), I.371-72.

this is introductory, but I venture to say that at no point does the Christian mind come into such violent collision with the secular mind as in its insistence on the weakness of humility. The wisdom of the world values power, not humility. We have drunk in more than we realize of the power philosophy of the German philosopher Friedrich Nietzsche (1844-1900). Nietzsche dreamed of the rise of what he called a daring ruler-race that would be brash, tough, masculine, overbearing, and oppressive. Nietzsche worshiped power and despised Jesus for his weakness. The ideal of Nietzsche was the *übermensch,* the "superman," but the ideal of Jesus was the little child. There is no possibility of compromise between those two models: we have to choose.

With this introduction I come to First Corinthians, because the central theme of the Corinthian correspondence is not actually power, as you might think at first sight, but rather is "power through weakness," divine power manifest in human weakness. That is the major theme of the whole Corinthian correspondence, and of 1 Corinthians 1:17–2:5 in particular, where the apostle gives three illustrations of this principle. First, in 1:17-25, we see power through weakness in the gospel itself: the weakness of the cross which is the power of God. Second, in 1:26-31, we see power through weakness in the converts who accept and embrace the gospel: "God chose the weak in order to shame the strong" (1:27). Then, thirdly, in 2:1-5 we see power through weakness in the preacher of the gospel, in Paul himself: "I was with you in weakness," he says (2:3). So the gospel, the converts, and the preachers — or, if you like, the evangel, the evangelized, and the evangelists — all exhibit the same truth, that God's power operates best in our weakness, and that weakness is the arena in which God can best manifest his power. It is a very unpopular subject. We don't like to talk about weakness because of our worship of and our lust for power. I pray that God will convince us by his Spirit operating in our minds, hearts, consciences, and wills, that this is an inflexible principle that we cannot escape. Now we turn to Paul's three illustrations in greater detail.

Power Through Weakness in the Gospel

First, power through weakness in the gospel itself (1 Cor. 1:17-25). In this section, the apostle repeats the same thesis twice. I hope we have learned the need for repetition. It is very difficult to hammer a nail into wood with one almighty blow. The better way to do it is by repeated little hammer blows. The same is true in teaching. So in both paragraphs the apostle begins with a reference to the cross (vv. 18, 23), and he points out that people's perspectives, understandings, and reactions to the cross are very different from one another. In verses 18-21, the first time he develops his thesis, the word or message of the cross is said to be "foolishness to those who are perishing, but to us who are being saved it is the power of God." Verse 21 is a particularly beautiful, chiseled sentence, an antithesis: "For as the world failed through its own wisdom to know God, it pleased God through the foolishness of the gospel to save believers."

The second exposition of this theme comes in verses 22-25, with an elaboration of the same thesis of wisdom through the folly of the cross and power through the weakness of the cross. Here the apostle subdivides the human race into three categories: Jews, Greeks or Gentiles, and Christians. Each has a different perspective on the cross.

First, he says, Jews demand signs — miraculous signs (1:22a). The Jews were expecting a political messiah who would drive the Roman legions into the Mediterranean Sea, one who would re-establish the lost national sovereignty of Israel. So for every revolutionary claiming to be the Messiah, of whom there were many at that time, they demanded appropriate evidence. They demanded signs of power that would give plausibility to their messianic claim. That is why they kept saying to Jesus: "What signs do you do that we may believe in you?" The Jews sought signs of power.

Then the Greeks looked for wisdom (1:22b). Greece had a very long tradition of brilliant philosophy, and the Greeks believed, much like the later Enlightenment, in the autonomy of the human mind. They listened eagerly to every new idea, every speculation, so long as it seemed reasonable. "But we preach Christ crucified" (1:23). This obviously promotes different reactions from the other two groups.

To the Jews, the cross was a stumbling block. They were looking for this powerful, military messiah riding on a warhorse at the head of an army. What were they offered instead? A pathetic, crucified weakling. It was an insult to their national pride. How could God's Messiah end his life under the condemnation of his own people and under the Deuteronomic curse of God against one who hangs on a tree (Deut.

21:23)? The cross was an absolute stumbling block to those who worshiped power.

Then secondly, to the Greeks the cross was foolishness. Crucifixion was not only a public execution, it was deliberately a public humiliation. It was reserved for slaves and criminals. No free man was ever crucified. And it was inconceivable to the Greek mind that the Son of God could end his days on a cross. You may be familiar with the oft-quoted phrase of Cicero that the cross was to be absent not only from the body of the Roman citizen, but also from their minds, their eyes, and their ears.[2] Not only would they not be crucified themselves, they wouldn't look upon a crucifixion, talk to someone about one, or even imagine one in their minds, so abhorrent was crucifixion to the Greek and the Roman, the Gentile mind.

Yet thirdly, to those who were being called, whether Jews or Greeks (in other words Christians), Christ crucified was "the power of God and the wisdom of God" (1 Cor. 1:24). Because "the foolishness of God is wiser than human wisdom, and the weakness of God is stronger than human strength" (1 Cor. 1:25). This whole text seems to me particularly embarrassing in its relevance to us. There are, of course, no first-century Jews today, and there are no first-century Greeks, but there are many modern representatives of both groups.

So, first, the cross is still a stumbling block to those who, like Nietzsche, worship power. It is a stumbling block to those who are confident in their own power and in their own ability to save themselves — or at least if they cannot save themselves, to contribute substantially to their own salvation. When they are told that salvation is a totally non-contributory gift of God they are profoundly offended. The human heart wants to strut around heaven like a peacock, imagining that it has got there by its own beauty or power. William Temple, the greatest Archbishop of Canterbury this century, once said, "The only thing of my very own which I can contribute to my own redemption is the sin from which I need to be redeemed."[3] Otherwise, it is an absolutely free, non-contributory gift, and the human heart hates this.

---

2. Cicero (106-43 BCE), *Pro C. Rabiro Perd.* 5.16, quoted in full by Martin Hengel, *Crucifixion in the Ancient World and the Folly of the Message of the Cross,* trans. John Bowden (Philadelphia: Fortress, 1977), p. 42.

3. A. E. Baker, *William Temple and His Message; Selections from His Writings* (Harmondsworth: Penguin, [1946]), p. 100.

I remember very well when I first went up to Cambridge University as an undergraduate. I was trying to win another student for Christ, a very smooth, very proud, upper-class aristocratic student, very full of himself. I was trying to tell him that if he wanted to receive eternal life, he had to receive it as a free gift. I shall never forget how suddenly he broke into the conversation and shouted three times: "Horrible, horrible, horrible!" I didn't think I'd said anything particularly horrible, but I've often thanked God for that experience because he'd given me a glimpse into the human heart, into its pride and its hatred of the gospel.

Like the Jews of Paul's day, there are those who are going about trying to establish their own righteousness, believing they can accumulate merit and put God in their debt. Such people either have a very low view of God or a very exaggerated view of themselves, or probably both, whereas those who have caught even a momentary glimpse of the majesty and holiness of God have not been able to bear the sight. Like Moses, they have shrunk away from him, covering their faces, because they are afraid to look upon God. In his great book, *The Mediator,* Brunner tells us that all other religions save us from the ultimate humiliation of being stripped naked and, I think we could add, being declared bankrupt before God.[4] So the cross is a stumbling block to those who are morally proud.

The cross is also foolishness to those who are intellectually proud. I haven't found any modern example of this better than some sentences from A. J. Ayer. Professor Sir Alfred Ayer (1910-1989), professor of philosophy in the University of Oxford, a well-known logical positivist and author of a little book called *Language, Truth and Logic,* had a great antipathy to Christianity.[5] Here is A. J. Ayer: "Of all the historic religions there are good reasons for regarding Christianity as the worst. Why? Because it rests on the allied doctrines of original sin and vicarious atonement, which are intellectually contemptible and morally outrageous."[6] The cross is foolishness to the philosophers of this world, but to those whom God calls the cross is not weakness, for we see in it the power of God. Again, to those who are called the cross is not folly but the wisdom of God. It is the exact opposite of the secular mind. The

---

4. Emil Brunner, *The Mediator* (London: Lutterworth, 1934), p. 474.

5. A. J. Ayer, *Language, Truth and Logic* (London: Victor Gollancz, [1936] 1946).

6. Alfred Ayer, *Guardian Weekly,* August 30, 1979.

cross is the power of God because through it God saves those who believe, and transforms them. The cross is the wisdom of God because through it God has not only solved our problem, the problem of sin and guilt, but reverently we say that God has solved his own problem.

Although P. T. Forsyth wrote that "there is nothing in the Bible about the strife of attributes,"[7] yet it is not wrong to speak of the divine "problem" or "dilemma." It arises from God's character of holy love. For God is not just love; at least he is not one kind of love that is sentimental love. The love that God is is holy love. Therefore he can only find a solution to his problem and ours if he is true to his character of holy love. The one thing the Scripture says that God cannot do, because he will not, is to contradict his own nature of holy love. His problem was how he could express his holiness in judging sinners as they deserve without compromising his love or frustrating it, or how he could express his love in forgiving sinners as he longed to do without compromising his holiness or justice. How could he be at one and the same time a just God and a Savior? His answer was the cross, for on the cross God in Christ took our place, bore our sin, and died our death. So, as we read in Romans, God demonstrated on the cross both his justice (Rom. 3:25) and his love (Rom. 5:8). In the cross you do not know which is clearer, the love or the justice of God. The holiness of his great love is revealed in the cross of Christ. So it is not only the power of God, but also the wisdom of God that is seen in the cross. I pray that we will never stray from that essence of the gospel. It is very easy because it is very unpopular. A. J. Ayer is by no means the only person who has spoken of it in such terms. It requires courage for us to stand firm as preachers of the cross.

Power Through Weakness in the Converted

Secondly, we see power through weakness in the converts. The apostle has been inviting the Corinthians to reflect on the gospel and on its weakness. He now invites them to reflect upon themselves and their own weakness, because what is common to the gospel and to the converts is the same thesis of power through weakness. The situation in

7. P. T. Forsyth, *The Work of Christ* (London: Independent, 1938), p. 118.

Corinth is described in verses 26-28: not many wise by human standards were chosen, and not many who were powerful, influential, or noble in social terms. In other words, wisdom and power were not conspicuous in the Corinthian converts. On the contrary, the opposite had been the case: "God chose the *foolish* things of the world to shame the wise, and the *weak* things of the world to shame the strong" (1:27).

We cannot fail to notice this continuing theme of wisdom through folly and power through weakness. So in verses 29-31, the apostle tells us the purpose of this providential arrangement by God: It was so that nobody might boast before God (v. 29), because the credit for salvation belongs to God (v. 30). It is because of God that we are in Christ Jesus, who has become for us, on the one hand, the wisdom of God, and, on the other hand, we might say, the power of God. The three tenses of salvation — justification, sanctification, glorification — are all there. And Christ has been made all of these to us. He is not only the wisdom of God, he is the power of God in these three tenses or phases of salvation. Therefore — verse 31 — as it is written in Jeremiah 9:24, "Let him who boasts boast in the Lord," for all other boasting is excluded by the gospel.

I think it is evident from this section that most of the Corinthian converts were drawn from the lower ranks of society. Most of them were not the city's influential rulers; they were not its intelligentsia or its aristocrats. On the whole they were the uneducated, the poor, the social outcasts, and probably slaves. The fact that the gospel reached, saved, and changed them was another illustration of God's power through human weakness.

What about the situation today? Paul is not saying — as is sometimes alleged — that God never saves people who are clever or wealthy or influential or middle-class or upper-class or however you would like to describe them. Saul of Tarsus, for instance, had a massive intellect. Luke tells us in Acts 18 that Crispus, the ruler of the Jewish synagogue in Corinth, was converted in the course of Paul's ministry there (Acts 18:8). In Romans 16:23 — written from Corinth — Paul sends greetings from Gaius the Corinthian, who was wealthy enough to give hospitality to the whole church. He sends greetings also from Erastus, the city's director of public works. So have we liberty to conclude from this passage that it is wrong to take the gospel to students, or to graduates, or to the wealthy or influential? No! What Paul was saying was that there are not many among such categories who were saved. It was Origen in the middle of the third century, who in his defense of Christianity against Celsus — and especially against Celsus' sneer that Christianity was for the uneducated — first pointed out that Paul did not say "not any" but "not many."[8] The same is true of the famous Countess of Huntingdon, the eighteenth-century aristocrat who was a personal friend of Wesley and Whitefield, who sought to win the British upper classes for Christ. She thanked God for the letter "m" in "many."[9]

So how do we apply this to ourselves? I think what Paul means is that God's power operates only in the salvation of the weak. Therefore, if the strong want to be saved, they've got to become weak or acknowledge their weakness in order to be saved. It is almost exactly as Jesus said when he declared, "The Kingdom of God belongs to little children and if you adults want to get into the Kingdom you've got to become like little children, because the only people in the Kingdom of God are the children and the childlike" (Matt. 18:1-6). I think Paul is saying the same thing here. Luther expresses it well when he says, "Only the prisoner shall be free, only the poor shall be rich, only the weak strong, only the humble exalted, only the empty filled; only nothing shall be something."[10]

Power Through Weakness in the Proclaimers

Having discussed power through weakness in the gospel and power through weakness in the converts, now thirdly we examine power through weakness in the evangelists or in the preachers. The weakness that Paul expresses here was very different from the condition of those he called the "super-apostles," his rivals. They were proud, arrogant, and vain, very confident in their own influence, power, and so on. What Paul tells us here is that he has made a double renunciation: hu-

---

8. See Origen, *Contra Celsum* 3.44, 48-49, trans. H. Chadwick (Cambridge: Cambridge University, 1953), pp. 158, 161-62.

9. Selina Shirley, Countess of Huntingdon (1707-1791), quoted by F. F. Bruce, *1 and 2 Corinthians* (NCB; London: Marshall, Morgan, and Scott; Grand Rapids: Eerdmans, 1971), p. 36.

10. Karl Barth, *The Epistle to the Romans,* trans. Edwyn C. Hoskyns (Oxford: University Press, 1933), p. 42, referring to Luther, "Epistola ad Romanos," *D. Martin Luthers Werke; kritische Gesamtausgabe* (Weimar: Hermann Böhlaus Nachfolger, 1938), 56.218.

man philosophy on the one hand, the wisdom of the world in favor of the cross of Christ, and Greek oratory or rhetoric on the other, in favor of his own personal weakness and trust in the Holy Spirit. That was his double renunciation. In place of philosophy, the cross; in place of rhetoric, the Holy Spirit.

I am afraid that these words of Paul, "When I came to you I came in weakness and in fear and in much trembling" (1 Cor. 2:4) — "I was nervous and rather shaky," says J. B. Phillips[11] — would not be an accurate description of many evangelical preachers today. Weakness is not an obvious characteristic of theirs. Homiletics classes aim to inculcate self-confidence in nervous students. If Paul had enrolled as a student in one of our seminaries, we would have regarded him as exceedingly unpromising material. And since he was supposed to be a mature Christian, we might even have rebuked him and said, "Paul, you've got no business to feel afraid and weak. Don't you know what it is to be filled with the Holy Spirit? You ought to be strong and confident and bold." But Paul was of a different opinion. He was not afraid to admit that he was afraid. True, he had a massive intellect and a strong personality, but he was physically frail, as we know, and he was emotionally vulnerable.

Second-century tradition in the apocryphal *Acts of Paul and Thecla* tells us that he was an unattractive fellow, small, and even ugly, with a bald head, bandy legs, beetle brows, and a hooked nose. His critics said that his bodily presence was weak and his speech contemptible (2 Cor. 10:10). So he was nothing much to look at and nothing much to listen to. Consequently, in his human weakness he relied on the power of God. He called it a "demonstration of the Spirit's power." If you ask what he meant, it does not seem to be miracles; it just seems to be conversions. Gordon Fee, one of the best modern commentators on First Corinthians, belonging himself to the charismatic and Pentecostal traditions, writes of this verse: "It is possible, but not probable given the context of 'weakness,' that it reflects the 'signs and wonders' of 2 Cor 12:12. More likely it refers to their actual conversion."[12] I agree with that because every conversion involves a power encounter between Christ

---

11. *The New Testament in Modern English* (New York: Macmillan, 1958), p. 352.

12. Gordon D. Fee, *The First Epistle to the Corinthians* (NICNT; Grand Rapids: Eerdmans, 1987), p. 95.

and the Devil in which the superior power of Jesus Christ is seen. The Holy Spirit takes our human words, spoken in great human weakness and frailty, and he carries them home with power to the mind, the heart, the conscience, and the will of the hearers in such a way that they see and believe.

This is not an invitation for us to suppress our personality. It is not an invitation to pretend that we feel weak when we don't. It is not an invitation to cultivate a fake frailty. Nor is it a renunciation of rational arguments since, as Luke tells us in Acts 18, Paul continued to argue the gospel when he came to Corinth. No, it is rather an honest acknowledgment that we cannot save souls by ourselves, whether by our own personality, our own persuasion, or our own rhetoric. Only the power of God can give sight to the blind, hearing to the deaf, and life to the dead, and he does it through the gospel of Christ crucified, proclaimed in the power of the Holy Spirit. So the power in every power encounter is not in us; it is in the cross and in the Spirit.

Although I am very hesitant to talk about myself, I thought that I would share with you now an incident that was very influential in my experience along these lines. It was long ago in 1958, when I was in Australia leading a university mission at Sydney University. I shall never forget it because I got news during it of the death of my father in England. It was not easy to go straight from the news of his death to preaching the gospel in the university. But we'd come to the final day in the great hall of the university. That afternoon I had lost my voice; I couldn't speak. It was already late afternoon within a few hours of the final meeting of the mission, so I didn't feel I could back away at that time. I went to the great hall and asked a few students to gather round me. I asked one of them to read 2 Corinthians 12:9-10: "I will gladly rejoice in my infirmities that the power of Christ may rest upon me . . . for when I am weak, then I am strong." Christ said to Paul, "'My grace is sufficient for you, for my strength is made perfect in weakness'" (2 Cor. 2:8-9). A student read these verses and then I asked them to lay their hands on me to identify the person they were praying for, and to pray that those verses might be true in my own experience.

When the time came for me to give my address I preached on the two ways, the narrow way that leads to life and the broad road that leads to destruction (Matt. 7:13-14). I had to get within half an inch of the microphone and I croaked the gospel like a raven. I couldn't exert my personality. I couldn't move. I couldn't use any inflections in my voice. I croaked the gospel in a monotone. Then when the time came to give the invitation, there was an immediate response, larger than in any other meeting during the mission, as students came flocking forward. The reason I tell you this is that I've been back to Australia about ten times since 1958, and on every occasion somebody has come up to me and said, "Do you remember that final meeting in the university in the great hall?" "I jolly well do," I reply. "Well," they will say, "I was converted that night."

Conclusion

So let me sum up what I've been trying to say: the central theme of Paul's Corinthian correspondence is power through weakness. We have a weak message, Christ crucified, which is proclaimed by weak preachers who are full of fear and trembling, and is received by weak hearers who are socially despised by the world. God chose a weak instrument (Paul) to bring a weak message (the cross) to weak people (the Corinthian working classes), but through that triple weakness he demonstrated his almighty power.

Above all we see this principle in Christ and the cross, that he who is in very nature God from eternity did not think equality with God a prize or privilege to be selfishly enjoyed, but laid aside his glory, divested himself of his glory, and humbled himself to serve (Phil. 2:6-7). In the Judean desert the Devil offered him power, but he declined the offer. Instead he set his face to go to Jerusalem, gave himself voluntarily to the ultimate weakness and humiliation of the cross, and therefore God has highly exalted him and given him the name above every name, the rank beyond every rank, the dignity beyond every dignity, that at the name, the rank, the dignity of Jesus, every knee should bow and every tongue confess that he is Lord (Phil. 2:9-11).

So today, as is revealed in chapters 4 through 7 of the Book of Revelation, at the very center of God's throne, which is a symbol of power, is a slain lamb, which is a symbol of weakness. In other words, power through weakness, dramatized by God on the cross or the lamb on the throne, lies at the very heart of ultimate reality and even of God himself.

So I pray that this mind may be in us which was and still is in Christ Jesus. The Christian leaders and preachers needed in the world today are those who have seen the slain lamb on the throne and who follow him wherever he goes because they know that God's power will be revealed and demonstrated in their acknowledged weakness.

Preaching for a Church in Conflict

(1 Corinthians 1:1-17)

STEPHEN C. FARRIS

2002

Conflict in the Christian Church

No one can say with certainty how many of our churches are in conflict. This is partly because it would be very difficult to define "conflict" precisely. What is the difference between conflict, on the one hand, and the ordinary day-to-day friction that occurs in any organization primarily made up of human beings? Surely the number of churches in conflict is distressingly large, however. In my own denomination, the Presbyterian Church in Canada, there must appear in the "Acts and Proceedings of the General Assembly" a report of all cases in which a presbytery has "severed the pastoral tie," that is, removed a minister from his or her charge. One of my students discovered that in a recent four-year span, extreme action had been taken in 3 percent of the pastoral charges of the denomination. In the majority of cases that action had been taken because of irreconcilable differences within the charge. In still others, the lengthy process required to remove a minister had itself engendered conflict.

A previous version of this address was published online in the *McMaster Journal of Theology and Ministry;* http://www.mcmaster.ca/mjtm/.

It cannot reasonably be argued that my own denomination is unusually quarrelsome or that church conflict is a purely local phenomenon. Nor can it be suggested that conflict is limited to those charges in which such drastic action has been taken. The number of cases in which a minister has departed voluntarily or is seeking a change, or in which the conflict does not center on the person of the minister or priest, must be many times larger. My own guess would be ten times larger — or 30 percent — and that accords well with the guesses of others. Even if a congregation does not suffer conflict, it lives within a wider church that is riven by conflict. Denominations are torn by bitter debates over the interpretation of Scripture, human sexuality, language for God, the role of women, and scores of other bitterly divisive issues. And if we are not fighting about these issues we are quite capable of fighting over the color of the new carpet in the church parlor. Conflict is an ever-present possibility for the church.

A very considerable body of literature has arisen in response to the reality of church conflict: many books, articles, and other resources address the question of conflict resolution in troubled churches. The issue is commonly dealt with in terms of the insights of other disciplines. So, for example, in *Church Conflicts: The Hidden Systems Behind Church Fights,* Cosgrove and Hatfield draw on family systems therapy.[1] Hugh Halverstadt, in *Managing Church Conflict,* draws on various principles of organizational dynamics based on power relationships.[2] But such studies do not treat church conflict primarily as a theological issue. Nor do they make extensive use in their reflections of that resource which the church has primarily used to shape its identity and determine its path, namely the study of Scripture. I do not question the usefulness of these approaches and others like them, particularly in the short term and as a response to crisis. There is, however, considerable anecdotal evidence that troubled churches begin to heal when the ordinary activities of ministry are carried out faithfully and well. Notable among those activities is preaching. To the best of my knowledge, however, there ex-

1. Charles H. Cosgrove and Dennis D. Hatfield, *Church Conflicts: The Hidden Systems Behind Church Fights* (Nashville: Abingdon, 1994).

2. Hugh Halverstadt, *Managing Church Conflict* (Louisville: Westminster/John Knox, 1991).

ists but one rather general book on preaching in situations of church conflict.[3]

So while the church may be *like* a family, it *is* the church. It may display interrelationships also characteristic of secular organizations, but it *is* the body of Christ. There may be many short-term tactics that will increase its well-being, but its nature is not defined by any of them. For the church is what it is because of the gospel. And the primary witness to the gospel lies in Scripture alone.

A Crisis of Identity

The portion of Scripture that most clearly addresses a divided church is Paul's Corinthian correspondence. Several passages in First Corinthians provide a resource for reflecting theologically on the problem of church conflict, for even a cursory reading of the letter will indicate that Corinth is a church in crisis. At heart the crisis in Corinth is neither organizational nor financial in nature. Nor is it primarily a crisis in relationships. For Paul does not look at the church in Corinth either as an organization or as an extended family, but as a spiritual and theological entity. When considered theologically, it looks as if the church in Corinth is suffering from a spiritual identity crisis, but one with very practical consequences. It has been said that Paul's ethics can be summarized in the simple sentence, "Be what you are." The Corinthians, it appears, need to be reminded of who they are. Then, perhaps, they can become what they were meant to be. So Paul tells them, again and again, who they are in Christ. Just so, although the many crises and conflicts within churches today may have a range of different surface causes, perhaps behind those surface causes lies a root cause, namely the loss of Christian identity. And it is that root cause that the Apostle Paul can help us address in our preaching to the church in conflict.

The preacher's point is not simply to replicate in the pulpit what Paul does in his epistles. A sermon is a very different genre from a letter, with each serving a different purpose. A letter can specifically address particular problems and can issue very definite directions. Paul

3. William Willimon, *Preaching About Conflict in the Local Church* (Philadelphia: Westminster, 1987).

does just that in the middle chapters of First Corinthians. The only limit on this function is in the willingness of the receivers to accept the authority of the sender. But, once again, preaching is different. Some things preaching does poorly. It does not function well when the preacher attempts to use the pulpit to give specific directions to a congregation. It does not deal effectively with the details of complicated organizational issues. Most importantly, preachers lose their effectiveness when they try to tell people what they should or should not do. Certainly that is true in a time when all authority figures are questioned, and it is particularly true in situations of conflict where the authority of clergy is in dispute. But preaching *can* be good at helping the church find its identity.

Defining Identity: Narratives, Doctrines, and Practices

Group identity is defined in several different ways. It is defined when a community shares a constitutive narrative, a story that gives later generations a sense of belonging, a history to which they refer for guidance. In truth, we are what our stories tell us we are. The Bible as a whole is certainly the constitutive narrative for the Christian church, and preaching that recounts this story in whole or in part, linking that story to contemporary reality, provides the church its identity. This mode of creating or reinforcing identity is present to some degree in First Corinthians. Paul reminds his readers of the crucifixion (the latter half of chapter 1) and the resurrection (chapter 15). He also links the present experience of the Corinthians to the story of Israel (chapter 10). But it must be said that Paul makes less extensive use of this means of strengthening identity in First Corinthians than we might expect. The three instances mentioned exhaust the list.

The idea of retelling our story to create identity is fashionable, perhaps even trendy, in contemporary homiletics. What is less fashionable is the notion that Christian doctrine also creates identity. That doctrine can have this capacity should hardly surprise us since many of our denominations are formally defined with respect to a particular statement of Christian doctrine. Think, for example, of Lutherans and the Augsburg Confession, or of Presbyterians and the Westminster Confession of Faith. In our churches statements of faith are often queried, re-

143

written, radically reinterpreted or, in practice, simply abandoned. The mere fact that bodies of doctrine are now questioned should not, however, obscure the fact that for many centuries our denominations have found their identity in them. Paul is not a systematic theologian in the modern sense of the word. It would be a gross anachronism to apply to him that fuzzy and trendy phrase "postmodern." It may be, however, that theologians in a postmodern period may be more sympathetic in our time to Paul than were our immediate forerunners. We might find a theology that grows in the interactions with very particular issues more compelling than a systematic one. Christian belief that intersects with Christian life is for Paul the true mark of Christian identity. We also are what we believe. Preaching in a situation of church conflict may rightly declare this core theology that provides the church its identity and explores the relevance of that identity to the present crisis.

This leads naturally to a third mode of identity, identity that is shaped by a set of practices. Once again, we can recognize this in our own collective pasts. We're Roman Catholic: we don't eat fish on Friday. We're Lutheran: we sing chorales. And so on. Of course, something more serious is at stake in the Corinthian letters. The kinds of Christian practice that Paul addresses in First Corinthians are for the most part far more weighty than these small matters. But the principle remains intact: we are what we do. Preaching amidst conflict may rightly address the practices that are necessary for the life of a healthy Christian community.

As we turn to Paul's text, we will bear in mind these three modes of identity and the preaching strategies they imply.

Who Are We? Reclaiming Christian Identity

Paul's policy in writing to the troubled church in Corinth is instructive. He does not begin with the problems in the church; he tells the Corinthians who they are in Christ. He does not, in the beginning, tell them what to do or what not to do. That comes later. Rather, he gives thanks for them. But notice that he does not give thanks for the Christians as they are according to the standards of the world. He gives thanks for them as they are *in Christ*. It is a question of identity, which Paul defines theologically and, more specifically, christologically. The identity of the Corinthians is shaped by what they believe.

If preaching does well when it addresses identity, it may even do more: it may create identity. For churches are shaped by what they hear preached Sunday after Sunday. It could almost be said that Christian churches are what they hear preached. If they hear "tedious moralizing discourses"[4] week after week, they become, almost inevitably, tedious moralists. But if they hear grace, there is at least the possibility that they will become grace-full. Paul seems to think that reminding the Corinthians of their true identity is a vital step towards the end of the destructive conflict that so marks their life together. It is almost as if he thinks that if the Christian church hears what it really is, it will become what it already is in Christ. Perhaps Paul is onto something. Perhaps preaching in a situation of church conflict is not primarily a matter of telling people what to do but of reminding them who they are. We may be tempted to tell our people what they ought to be doing and what, by heaven, they ought not to be doing. To give in to this temptation, however, would be a mistake. We ought not to address conflict directly without first laying the theological groundwork for our preaching. And we need to be instructed by the way in which Paul goes about that task.

First Corinthians 1:1-17: Giving Thanks for the Church

The letter is from "Paul, called to be an apostle of Christ Jesus by the will of God, and our brother Sosthenes." It is addressed to "the church of God that is in Corinth, to those who are sanctified in Christ Jesus, called to be saints" (1:2). This is in one way nothing more than the formula that begins all ancient letters, which states the identity of the writer and of the receivers of the letter, then addresses a word of salutation.[5] But identity is always a theological issue for Paul, because the identity both of the apostles and of the Corinthians is defined by their relationship to God and to Christ Jesus the Savior. And note: that identity is a present reality. In our English translations we read that the Co-

4. This is the second definition of the word "homily" given in the *Concise Oxford English Dictionary*.

5. See Hans Conzelmann, *1 Corinthians: A Commentary on the First Epistle to the Corinthians* (Hermeneia; Philadelphia: Fortress, 1975), p. 19, indicating that the three parts of the formula are the *superscriptio, adscriptio,* and *salutatio.*

rinthians are "called to be saints," or something very similar. This suggests that God wants the Corinthians to become saints, but leaves the matter of whether they will actually achieve that status very much up in the air. Their "sainthood" appears to be a matter of possibility rather than one of present reality. But notice also that Paul uses exactly the same formula about himself: he is "called to be an apostle." What would Paul have said to anybody who even hinted that he was not an apostle already? The letter to the Galatians, where just such a charge is voiced, indicates that his response would be forceful, to say the least. Paul is already an apostle and the Corinthians are already saints. There is, in fact, no form of the verb "to be" in the Greek of these verses. A strictly accurate translation would be, "Paul, the called apostle . . . to the called saints." Notice also that the Corinthians are "those who are sanctified," made holy, *made into* saints. There is a play on words here, since in Greek (as in English) the words "sanctified" and "saints" come from the same root: the letter is written "to those who are sainted in Christ Jesus, to the called saints."

Yet the contrast between the theological identity of "those who are sanctified in Christ Jesus, called to be saints" and the recent report, says Paul, "that there are quarrels among you" (1:11) is striking, and provides a possible homiletical entry into the text. The mention of quarrels, moreover, anticipates discussion of all the other troubles in the church at Corinth: the fornication, the lawsuits, the disputes over basic Christian doctrine, and drunkenness at the Lord's Table. But while the Corinthians are, humanly speaking, drunks and sex fiends and argumentative troublemakers, to Paul they're still saints. This observation would be of no particular interest if it did not also touch on a reality that affects all present-day churches. As Fred Craddock writes, "Corinth and the Christian community within it are not very far away or long ago."[6] This contrast from Corinth is only a particularly arresting instance of the gap that troubles every church between what we want to be and what we fear we really are. As such, the contrast itself can be the starting point for a powerful sermon. For contrasts, gaps, and inconsistencies are themselves homiletically useful, sometimes opening the door for the gospel to squeeze through and take us by surprise.

6. Fred B. Craddock, "Preaching to Corinthians," *Interpretation* 44 (1990): 161.

We can easily be led astray here by the word "saint," since in our society the word carries the connotation of spiritual superstardom. Even Protestants are influenced by the use of the word in Roman Catholic piety. In that context one becomes a saint by a process of testing and election somewhat analogous to election to a sports hall of fame. The process is rigorous and the result genuinely useful to pious Catholics. It is clear, however, that here the word "saint" means something entirely different, as a result of which many translations prefer the word "holy" in this verse. After all, the sorry band of quarrelsome Corinthians is not made up of spiritual superstars. The point, of course, that the same kind of contrast can be noted in our own churches: retaining rather than abandoning the word "saints" might help listeners become aware of this contrast.

It is also important to notice where all this "saintedness" comes from, for it derives from the same source as Paul's own call to be an apostle, namely the will of God. The church belongs to God, says Paul, and its saints are sanctified *by* God. Note the passive voice of the verb. Sanctity is indeed a spiritual achievement, but it is *God's* achievement — not ours. This echoes the first word Paul says about the Corinthians: collectively they are, with all their faults, "the church of God." All this makes it clear that the holiness of the church rests not on the achievements of Christians but on the "call" of God. In the second half of the chapter Paul will change his language slightly: there the corresponding verb is "choose" (1:26, 27). But both verbs bear witness to the primacy of God's initiative in the matter of Christian identity.

Paul then adds something that seems quite odd. The address concludes with the phrase, "together with all those who in every place call on the name of our Lord Jesus Christ, both their Lord and ours." Paul wants to remind the Corinthians that Christian identity is a shared identity. We are never alone either in our joys or in our conflicts. Troubled churches, on the other hand, tend to focus inward on their own conflicts and difficulties. A reminder that we share our Christian identity with a wider fellowship may be healthy in itself. Stories of the struggles and — where realistic — the triumphs of the wider church can lift the focus of the congregation beyond itself. What links the Corinthians to other Christians, including ourselves, is that we "in every place call on the name of our Lord Jesus Christ, both their Lord and ours." Ours is an identity shared in Jesus Christ. Once again it is clear that Paul refuses to define Christian identity other than theologically and, indeed, christologically.

This theme continues in the salutation to the Corinthians. Paul does not merely send them his personal "best wishes." Even his greeting is theologically loaded, as he greets them with "grace" and "peace." Both gifts, the undeserved favor of God and complete wholeness, come from "God our Father and the Lord Jesus Christ" (1:3).

Paul then thanks God for the Corinthians. A thanksgiving for those to whom Paul is writing is a regular feature of his correspondence. One should not, however, assume that this is simply a meaningless courtesy on his part. We should not even think of it merely as a good rhetorical tactic to state the positive before the negative. This is more than a clever appreciation of human nature, for we must note that Paul is thanking God for the church, *as it is*. He is speaking not of some ideal society or of the church invisible, but of a particular and particularly troubled group of Christians with all kinds of spiritual warts. Something very important is at stake here. The church belongs neither to the clergy (even an apostle), nor to the people who make it up: it belongs to God. Because it belongs to God it is in essence good, and thanks can be given for it. This has enormous psychological and spiritual consequences, not least for the preacher.

Along the same lines, John Calvin makes an interesting observation regarding Paul's identification of the Corinthians as "the church of God" in verse 2:

> We should give close attention to this verse, however, lest we should expect in this world a church without spot or wrinkle, or immediately withhold this title from any gathering whatever, in which everything does not satisfy our standards. For it is a dangerous temptation to think that there is no church where perfect purity is lacking [*i.e., that the church does not exist*]. The point is that anyone who is obsessed with that idea must cut himself off from everybody else, and appear to himself to be the only saint in the world, or he must set up a sect of his own along with other hypocrites.[7]

---

7. John Calvin, *The First Epistle of Paul the Apostle to the Corinthians,* trans. John W. Fraser (Grand Rapids: Eerdmans, 1989), p. 17.

Our present-day temptation with respect to churches "in which every-thing does not meet our standards" may be different from those that Calvin identified. Our own temptation may be to think of our congregation primarily as a "problem." Such an identification immediately distances us from our hearers, placing preachers on a higher spiritual plane than the people. As a contemporary analog to the spiritual superiority that Calvin identifies, this is irritating to our listeners and spiritually dangerous to ourselves.

One often hears the phrase, "That person needs an attitude adjustment." The same is probably also true with respect to churches in conflict. Troubles arise from bad attitudes, and bad attitudes arise out of a faulty sense of identity. But the converse is equally true: identity shapes attitudes and theologically healthy attitudes can contribute to healing. Of course, the first attitude that needs adjustment may well be the preacher's own, so giving thanks for the church is an effective exercise in attitude adjustment for the preacher. It is, after all, practically impossible to think demeaningly of people for whom one has genuinely given thanks.

I remember having difficulty with a particular leader in my first congregation. He consistently opposed my plans for the congregation, plans that I was sure were wise and far-sighted. I was well on my way to thinking him a "thorn in the flesh" and little more. Then, just before Christmas, word came that a lovely thirteen-year-old girl in our congregation had been diagnosed with an acute and fast-acting form of leukemia. At our small midnight Christmas Eve communion service I prayed long and hard for her and her family. When I opened my eyes, I saw tears coursing down the lined cheeks of this same leader, and at that moment realized that there was something deeply good about this "thorn in the flesh." There was a depth of caring in the man that I had refused to see prior to that prayer. I never spoke to him about what I had witnessed, and he would have been embarrassed if I had. But our relationship changed, because thereafter I saw him with different eyes.

While Paul thanks God for the Corinthians, he is neither sentimental nor unrealistic about their failings. He is not thanking God for their faults and flaws, but for the grace of God that has been given to them. They have been enriched in speech and knowledge and they possess every spiritual gift (1:5-8). As we see later in the letter, these same gifts, when wrongly used, are also the source of many of the conflicts they

149

experience. The Corinthians esteem clever speech too highly and fight over the relative value of their spiritual gifts. Nonetheless, fine speech and spiritual gifts are good in themselves. This presents an interesting thought to the pastor of a church in conflict. Is it possible that the sources of conflict in a congregation are actually mis-used blessings? Can the same characteristics or qualities that lead to conflict, if put to good use, actually serve the gospel? If so, it would be happy news for the preacher, since it is obviously far easier to put a church's character-istics to a different use than it is to suppress or to change those charac-teristics altogether.

All this suggests three related points. First, a preacher can look for the signs of grace in a church so that he or she can thank God for that grace. This exercise will likely change the preacher's own attitude for the better. Second, human nature is such that publicly recognizing what is good in the people will prepare them to listen to the one who offers such recognition. After all, who wants to hear a steady flow of criticism, even from an apostle? As such, giving thanks for what is good in a church is indeed a wise rhetorical tactic. But, third, looking for signs of grace in order to give thanks may already point to those strengths which, if put to proper use, can serve the gospel in that place.

Still, we must not forget that the prayer of thanksgiving is centered not on the church but on God. The gifts for which Paul thanks God come *from* God. They have been given "in Christ Jesus," one of Paul's fa-vorite phrases (1:4). "The testimony of Christ has been strengthened" among the Corinthians (1:6). The intended result of all this is that they may be "blameless on the day of our Lord Jesus Christ" (1:8). In the end, Paul does not speak of the faithfulness of the Christians in Corinth. No, he says, "God is faithful; by *him* you were called into the fellowship of his Son, Jesus Christ our Lord" (1:9).

Finally, the phrase "the day of the Lord" in verse 8 reminds us of the strong eschatological emphasis in all of Paul's thought. This too is a use-ful reminder to a church in conflict. When Christian identity is set "in a cosmic frame of reference that points toward the final triumph of God's righteousness, the setting right of all things in Christ Jesus," our little di-visions seem petty indeed.[8] In light of this ultimate concern, their true insignificance appears and the troubles themselves can be cast away.

---

8. Richard B. Hays, *First Corinthians* (Louisville: Westminster/John Knox, 1997), p. 20.

Divisions in the Church

"Now I appeal to you, brothers and sisters, by the name of our Lord Jesus Christ, that all of you be in agreement and that there be no divisions among you" (1:10). This is what rhetoricians called the *propositio* of Paul's letter:

> In Greco-Roman rhetoric the *propositio* is the thesis statement of the discourse. In a deliberative discourse it is the main advice the rhetor wants his hearers to heed.[9]

In more contemporary language, at this point Paul gets to the "presenting problem" in Corinth. The Corinthians are divided among themselves. Chloe's people, apparently an identifiable group within the church, perhaps a house fellowship, report as much (1:11). If we have been involved with a church in conflict we can imagine what the rest of the Corinthian congregation thought about Chloe's people when they heard that these folks had informed on them. But it appears that Chloe's people were quite correct in their report. The fabric of the church had been "rent," a possible reading of the Greek word *schismata*, all in the name of favorite ministers.

We can only guess at the situation in Corinth and ought not to speak too confidently about it.[10] Some, it appears, admired Paul (1:12). This is entirely understandable, for Paul had been the founding minister of their congregation. Others swore by Cephas, the apostle Peter. This too is understandable, for he had been the Lord Jesus' closest companion. Of course Christians ought to respect him.[11] It may even be that the presence of people who owed allegiance to an apostle with whom Paul had differed, and who had been close to the earthly Jesus, partly explains Paul's strange silence concerning the life of Jesus. Still

---

9. Ben Witherington III, *Conflict and Community in Corinth: A Socio-Rhetorical Commentary on 1 and 2 Corinthians* (Grand Rapids: Eerdmans, 1995), p. 94.

10. See the commendable caution of Gordon Fee, *The First Epistle to the Corinthians* (Grand Rapids: Eerdmans, 1987), pp. 55-59.

11. It is a "moot point" whether Peter had ever been in Corinth (Conzelmann, *1 Corinthians*, p. 33). 1 Corinthians 9:5 implies that the Corinthians know that other apostles, perhaps including Peter, travel about with their wives. This might or might not suggest that a visit has taken place (Fee, *The First Epistle to the Corinthians*, pp. 57-58).

others favored Apollos, who had followed Paul in ministry in Corinth (1 Cor. 3:6). According to Acts 18:24-26, Apollos was a noted preacher, and it appears that Paul respected, perhaps even envied his eloquence. It was equally natural that this man should attract a following. Still others claimed, "I belong to Christ."[12] There is nothing seriously wrong with admiring ministers and there is something positively right about saying, "I belong to Christ." It accords with the identity "in Christ" that Paul has been so eager to establish. But in a situation of church conflict, *being right is not enough*. Paul does not explain himself at this point: the answer is not given until chapter 13. Being right is never enough, if it is not accompanied by Christian love (1 Cor. 13:2).

Paul then demonstrates the absurdity of these artificial and insignificant divisions, using his own party as the negative example (1:13). This contrasts with the attitude of many clergy in conflict situations. Again and again these clergy say, "The spiritually mature people in the church are on my side," or "The *real* Christians support me," or, "Only a few fringe people are against me." Paul knows that his supporters too, insofar as they derive their identity from Paul rather than from Jesus, are part of the problem. Such an attitude is both refreshing and wise: it is also worth emulating when one ministers to a church in conflict.

Again, we notice how Paul repeatedly emphasizes that Christian identity is identity *in Christ*. That is the point of the series of rhetorical questions he poses. Some congregants, perhaps influenced by mystery religions, may have supposed that the act of baptism establishes a mystical bond between baptizer and baptizee.[13] In fact, so insignificant is this relationship that Paul can barely remember just who he has baptized (1:14-16). This, by the way, is *not* a ministerial characteristic to be imitated! The only bond that really matters is the bond with Christ. Paul then concludes this section of his letter by introducing the contrasting realities of human wisdom and the cross of Jesus Christ, to which we will turn in the next lecture.

12. It is possible that Paul is here speaking in his own voice as if to say, "You follow Paul or Cephas or Apollos, but I follow Christ." However, this seems an unlikely interpretation. In the Greek the four "party" statements are parallel in form, which suggests that they are also parallel in meaning. Moreover, this latter interpretation is much more homiletically interesting, a genuine consideration in a study such as this.

13. On this point see Conzelmann, *1 Corinthians*, p. 35.

Preaching I Corinthians 1:1-17

There is enough material in these verses for many sermons. Yet in preaching, less is often more: it is better to say a few things well rather than many things poorly. While any number of sermons might derive from these verses, the issue of identity shaped by the call and choice of God in Christ is crucial. Specifically, the contrast between the identity of the Corinthians implied by their conduct and their true identity in Christ provides a fitting point of departure for the sermon. One other observation bears repeating: the troubles mentioned in these verses anticipate the troubles described later in the epistle. But, as we have seen, a renewed understanding of our theological identity in Christ is part of the answer to these difficulties also, so it is appropriate to recall them here. For this reason, a "stand-alone" sermon on these verses can serve as an introduction to the letter as a whole, and to a consideration of concerns that remain relevant for the church in our day.[14]

14. Dr. Farris's own sermon on these verses, "And He Has . . . ," appears in the concluding section of this volume. [*ed.*]

A Wise Sort of Foolishness

(1 Corinthians 1:18-31)

STEPHEN C. FARRIS

2002

The church in Corinth was divided, for the Christians there quarreled over many issues: basic Christian doctrine like the resurrection, speaking in tongues, and favorite preachers. But the real problem in First Church, Corinth, was not any of those things. The real problem was that they had forgotten who they were and — even more important — *whose* they were. They were experiencing a theological and spiritual identity crisis. So before Paul deals with most of their specific problems (the lawsuits, the embarrassing sexual behavior, the drunkenness at the Lord's Table), the apostle must remind them who they are and what is the basis of their faith. Specifically, here as elsewhere in his epistles, Paul offers his listeners a Christ-shaped identity. To be even more specific: he offers them a *cross*-shaped identity. To people who far too often are merely cross, Paul offers a way of being that is cruciform. Or to put it very bluntly indeed, to these argumentative troublemakers Paul offers neither organizational dynamics nor family systems therapy. Rather, he says, "We preach Christ crucified." Here is a very simple idea. In a situation of church conflict our main strategy remains to

Previously published online in the *McMaster Journal of Theology and Ministry;* http://www.mcmaster.ca/mjtm/.

preach Christ crucified so that our listeners may grow towards a Christ-shaped identity. Everything else in this address develops or illustrates the homiletical outworking of that single idea.

Christian identity is a matter of shared *doctrine,* even as it is marked by shared *practices.* Here, however, our focus is on identity shaped by a shared *story.* In 1 Corinthians 1:18-31, this kind of identity obviously depends on familiarity with the story of "Christ crucified." Narrative is highly valued, indeed fashionable, in contemporary homiletics. At first sight, by contrast, the letters of Paul seem uninviting to the narrative preacher. Paul does many things in his epistles but avoids telling stories. In fact, however, Paul does something in 1 Corinthians that may be a far more telling testimony to the power of the story of Christ crucified. He simply alludes to the story, and that is enough: "We preach Christ crucified."

As an aside, let me tell you a story of my own. One Sunday last winter I was scheduled to preach at a church north of Toronto. It was a cold, icy morning and I did not quite leave enough time for a comfortable journey to my destination. Near my house there is a large intersection, six lanes by four lanes, very much exposed to the weather. As is always the case when we are in a hurry, all the lights, including that one, turned red. An older gentleman crossed the intersection in front of me, limping noticeably on his cane. The light turned orange for him as he neared the opposite sidewalk, so he quickened his pace. In his hurry he planted his cane on a patch of ice and fell heavily to the ground.

Everything else happened in the moment of time that it took me to put the transmission into "Park" and reach for the door handle. I thought, "Oh no, he may be hurt. I'll have to stop and see if he is all right. I may even have to take him to the emergency room." We all know, of course, how long you might have to wait in an emergency room these days. "I'll be terribly late for church. I might not even make it." I could picture the ushers checking their watches, the organist playing the prelude . . . for the third time, the elders, heads together, drawing straws to determine who would be stuck conducting the service in my absence. In the midst of these unexpressed grumbles, however, a phrase from a story came to my mind, a story that was first told me as a small child and repeated many times over the years. It's a well-known story — you've heard it too — so you all recognize the phrase: "And he passed by on the other side" (Luke 10:31).

I don't have to say anything more than that phrase. Because it is a life-shaping story, all I have to say to you is, "And he passed by on the other side." That is the way it is with life-shaping stories: an allusion is enough. The whole story comes to your mind and you understand the connection to my little tale. Partly because I have heard that story so many times, from Bible stories read by my mother, from Sunday School lessons, from sermon after sermon, I am the person I am. I could not "pass by on the other side" and be the person I am.

Far more importantly, I knew with confidence that this story would also come to the minds of the people in that congregation. As the kind of story that comes automatically to mind, it had also shaped who they were. If I phoned from the emergency room and explained my situation, they would understand my absence. The organist would not say, "He ought to be here!" She would begin a congregational hymn-sing. The elders would choose someone to pray, someone to read the lessons and perhaps even to reflect on them. No one would say, "He ought to have passed by on the other side." Who were they? They were the kind of people who knew the story of the Good Samaritan and let it shape their actions and attitudes. They could not expect their Sunday preacher to pass by on the other side and still be the people they were. These people were collectively a church.

By the way, before I had fully opened the door, the old gentleman had staggered to his feet. He glared at me as if daring me to take notice of his tumble, and stumped away. I drove on and even made it to church on time.

For Christians, the story of "Christ crucified" is even more an identity-shaping narrative than the Good Samaritan. Sometimes with this story also, an allusion is enough. In the midst of all the thorny troubles of the church, Paul reminds the Corinthians, "We preach Christ crucified" (1 Cor. 1:23). Everything in the church in Corinth must be done in the light of that story. It is no different in our day. The task of the preacher in situations of church conflict — indeed before situations of church conflict ever arise — is to preach Christ crucified, so that this may become the story that shapes the identity and thus the actions of the church.

Please note, however, that those who receive the letter are Christians already; Paul writes "to the called saints" (my translation of the phrase in 1 Cor. 1:2). Paul can assume a certain basic familiarity with the gospel. They have heard him "preach Christ crucified"; they already know, though doubtless they do not fully understand, some of the implications of the statement. His strategy, therefore, may be to remind them of what they already know rather than to inform them of something new. James Thompson has noted that this is a typical part of Paul's strategy when writing to the churches in which he has preached.[1]

Much the same could be said of many of our listeners. They too are Christians and have some familiarity with the core of the gospel. Preaching in our churches can also take the form of reminding the listeners of what they already know. We preachers are sometimes desperately eager to discover new techniques, new insights, new styles, as if novelty in itself guarantees success. We live in a society that values innovation and has a horror of "the same old thing." As a result, we preachers often feel pressured to "say something new" or at least to say the old thing in a new way. (Incidentally, homileticians ought not to complain about this phenomenon. It helps keep us in business.) There can, however, be a real tyranny in this constant demand for innovation. In the early church, by contrast, innovation was not considered a positive value but rather a sign of unfaithfulness. Perhaps, in our time, we need to reclaim the sense of the early church that the first duty of the preacher is faithfulness. New techniques, new insights, and new styles may indeed be useful . . . but only if through them Christ crucified is still preached.

But back to Corinth. It was not an easy task for Paul to preach Christ crucified because, in a Greek society that loved wisdom, much of what he had to say sounded like sheer foolishness. It was the Greeks, after all, who coined a word for the love of wisdom: *philosophia*. The Greeks loved wisdom, Jews wanted a miracle, and everyone, in an empire built on power, respected power (1 Cor. 1:22). But Paul was offering not a fine sounding *philosophia*, not a miracle, not a tale of power and success, just "Christ crucified"! This, we need hardly be reminded, is nothing but the story of a carpenter rabbi from Nazareth who managed to get himself executed by the Romans in a particularly unpleas-

---

1. James Thompson, *Preaching Like Paul: Homiletical Wisdom for Today* (Louisville: Westminster/John Knox, 2001), pp. 54-55. At this point Thompson is speaking primarily of Paul's custom of reminding the churches of what they already know about Paul and his ministry with them. This strategy is even more obvious with respect to the work of Christ (p. 145).

ant manner. Humanly speaking it must have seemed weakness. Paul knows full well that to many in Corinth it must have seemed sheer foolishness. But while it is foolishness to many (Paul is quite blunt: "to those who are perishing"), "to us who *are being saved* it is the power of God" (1 Cor. 1:18).

From time to time I am asked by some earnest soul, "Are you saved?" There is a biblically correct answer to this question: "I have been saved. I am being saved, and I will be saved." It would be a useful but not particularly difficult exercise for an adult or teen Bible study group to investigate the past, present, and future aspects of salvation.

Quite often, however, the correct answer seems a little long and pretentious, so I simply respond, "Yes!" Perhaps it says something unfortunate about my character or reputation that my questioner generally seems astounded by my reply. "But when?" she will ask in an unbelieving tone of voice. What this question really means is actually quite clear. The questioner wants to ask, "When did you commit your life to the Lord Jesus as your personal Savior?" She wants to know the particular point, at a crusade or a summer camp, for example, at which I made a decision for Christ. In fact, I could give a perfectly respectable answer to this question also: "When I was sixteen at the Scott Mission Camp." I am not convinced, however, that this answer, though certainly vital for me, is the most important one.

It is said that Karl Barth was once asked this question also. His reported response was, "On a Friday afternoon, in the spring, outside the city of Jerusalem, in or about the year 30 AD." A good Calvinist might even echo the letter to the Ephesians and say, "Before the foundation of the world," in the will and purpose of God (cf. Eph. 1:4). These answers suppose, rightly, that salvation is not primarily our work or the consequence of our own choices, important though those choices doubtless are. Our choice of God is made only in response to God's choice of us.

In many of our churches there are both people who might ask, "Are you saved?" and others who cannot understand why anyone would even bother asking it. The difference between these sorts of people is frequently a cause of conflict. As is the case with many other forms of conflict, this issue can and must be answered theologically. One group must be convinced from Scripture that "being saved" is a process rather than a point. (The words "being saved" in themselves imply both a past and a future dimension to the reality.) The other group may need to be convinced that being "saved" is necessary in the first place, not merely tediously old-fashioned, indeed little more than embarrassing church talk.

There are many such people both within and without the church. It is still not an easy task to preach Christ crucified to such people. We ought not to suppose, however, that it was easy in Paul's time. Paul could not assume that the Corinthians would fully understand the gospel he preached. They were in many ways still "infants" in Christ. It cannot be assumed that the gospel as Paul preached it would have been well received in Corinth. Nor can it be assumed that preaching Paul's gospel will be well received by all our listeners today. At the very least, in an age that loves narrative, he is out of fashion.[2] More seriously, Paul may be accused of turning the simple and pure gospel of Jesus into lifeless dogma, sexism, and an unhealthy attitude to the body. It cannot be presumed in many churches that a sermon from a text in Paul will meet with unqualified approval.

Paul says, "*We* preach Christ crucified," presumably in contrast to others who preach a different gospel. But presumably he also means to say that this gospel is not declared by him alone, but by preachers of the early church as a whole. The gospel of Christ crucified is not Paul's possession alone. It belongs to the church as a whole to preach Christ crucified. To do so is to claim that God has in Christ done for us what we were and are incapable of doing for ourselves. Our salvation rests not on our own wisdom, our own power, or anything else we might hope to possess or achieve. It rests on the work of another, much as it cuts against the grain in our society to accept that we depend on the strength of another. Such recognition would demand that we acknowledge that in this respect we ourselves are helpless. Far more acceptable would be a different gospel. In our time that would likely be some version of the quintessential North American creed, "The Lord helps them that help themselves."

We belong to a society that believes fervently in self-help. We preachers may be tempted to preach self-help because our society is so in love with the idea. Think, for example of all the self-help books you have seen. If you read them,

---

2. Thompson, *Preaching Like Paul*, pp. 14-16.

You're going to *Do Less and Have More* (in five easy steps), *Whip Your Career into Submission* and *Organize Your House from the Inside Out*. After you *Heal from the Heart* and *Find Mr. Right*, you'll unravel the secret to *Hot Sex* and discover why you shouldn't *Sweat the Small Stuff in Love*. Then you'll *Make the Connection* to a better body (while writing it all down in your *Journal of Daily Renewal*), begin to *Eat Right for Your Type, Learn the Seven Habits of Highly Effective People* and *Retire Wealthy in the 21st Century*.[3]

These are all, of course, titles of bestsellers. A leader in the Canadian publishing industry puts it simply: "Self-help blows fiction out of the water."[4]

It's quite possible to verify this interest in self-help writing. An interesting exercise to undertake and then describe in the pulpit is to look at cover articles in the magazine rack of the corner store. A huge percentage of the titles will have to do with self-help. Most of the titles will tell you how to get fit, lose weight, or earn more money. "Learn to be a more effective negotiator," they'll tell us. "Get the most out of your computer," or "Have a Spring/Summer/Fall/Winter makeover." My favorite title when I tried this exercise was, "Fifteen Ways to Fake Fabulous Skin!"

The church also is tempted to proclaim this comfortable gospel. On a church sign near my home appears a weekly "gospel." The sign recently read "Improvement begins with 'I'"! I believe Paul would call that sign "a different gospel." The contagion has also spread to official committees of the church. Our core theology is often enshrined in our hymns and in such a climate we begin to change the words to hymns, not just to become inclusive but to reflect the gospel we live by. A hymnbook committee, left unnamed here to protect the guilty, once changed the words of a beloved children's hymn. No longer were we to sing:

Jesus loves me! This I know,
For the Bible tells me so.

---

3. Alexandra Gill, "Note to Self: Change Life Now," *The Toronto Globe and Mail*, January 1, 2000 (note the date!).
4. Gill, "Note to Self."

Little ones to Him belong,
They are weak, but He is strong.[5]

Now we were directed to sing: "In his love we will be strong."

In a world that wants to turn us into the spiritual equivalents of personal trainers, "We preach Christ crucified" will still sound like foolishness. It may be a stumbling block to the Jews, foolishness to the Greeks, and terminally old-fashioned to the Canadians. It might even be — horror of horrors — damaging to our self-esteem. Frankly, a lot of people will prefer to hear tales of power and success — dressed up, to be sure, with a few spiritual trimmings. Do not imagine that preaching Christ crucified will be easier in Canada than in Corinth.

It will still often seem foolish. It's still a reasonably respectable thing to be Christian in our society, but even so there are times when what we believe and do must seem foolish. It sometimes happens to me when I visit a hospital. I walk through those imposing doors, as imposing as if they were the portals of the temple of a new religion. I watch the doctors and nurses garbed as the priests of that new religion. I hear them speak a language I barely understand. I peek through half-opened doors and glimpse complicated scientific equipment the purpose of which I certainly do not understand. They do such marvelous things, these people and these machines. By contrast I have nothing but some words translated from ancient tongues that no one speaks anymore, just a little box with some bread and wine. Sometimes I feel like a witch doctor. It seems such foolishness.

I suspect that there are times when you too feel foolish. Perhaps it happens when you consider the magnitude of the problems of the world, the hunger and disease and hatred, and you compare with those plagues the slenderness of our resources and the paucity of our response. Perhaps it happens when you compare the power of the mighty forces of the nations of this world and consider how small is our strength. The dictator Stalin was once warned that the Pope would disapprove of some action he was contemplating. "How many divisions does the Pope have?" sneered Stalin. Why none, of course, just some Swiss guards in ridiculous medieval costumes, and we Protestants don't even have that! It seems such foolishness.

---

5. "Jesus Loves Me, This I Know" (1860), by Anna Bartlett Warner (1820-1915).

But the truth is that it has always been this way.

Consider Jesus himself. He went about the roads and villages of Palestine, healing the sick; he lifted up the poor and resisted the rich. He taught with an authority beyond that of the religious leaders of his day and gathered to himself fishermen and tax collectors and some generous women. And where did it get him, all this teaching and healing and genuine goodness? It took him to death on a Roman cross, the excruciatingly painful death of slaves and outcasts and enemies of the state. They mocked him as he hung there, saying, "He saved others; himself he cannot save! If you are the Son of God, come down from the cross" (cf. Matt. 27:40-41).

But he didn't; he just . . . died.

And to the mockers, it seemed such foolishness. This is just what it is, says Paul. It is foolishness . . . but it's *God's* foolishness.

And what about Paul himself? He had so many advantages in life: born a Roman citizen, educated under the great rabbi Gamaliel, becoming a respected leader among his own people. He gave it all up to become a wandering preacher of the new way of the Messiah Jesus. He was rejected by all but a minority within a minority; was shipwrecked, jailed many times, beaten until near death. In the end he was taken prisoner and sent to trial in far-off Rome. Tradition says, almost certainly truly, that he was convicted by the mad emperor Nero and beheaded.

It seemed such foolishness.

But now we call our sons Paul and our dogs Caesar. It's foolishness, but it's *God's* foolishness.

There's still quite a bit of this foolishness around. Once there was a young woman from Albania, the poorest and most backward country in Europe. Though her country did not educate women or respect their achievements, she was foolish enough to want to give her life to Christ. She traveled to India. At first she did not even know the language of the people: the problems that confronted her there were so overwhelming and her resources so very slender. But she decided, foolishly, of course, that she could at least give some last comfort to the dying on the streets of the great city of Calcutta. And so she did.

Others followed her example and, in due time, the world noticed. But even when the world noticed, it still seemed only foolishness to some. They invited her to Stockholm to receive the Nobel Prize. In Stockholm, a young reporter cast scorn on her efforts, comparing them belittlingly to the enormity of the problems that still plague India. She replied, "Young man, I do what I can, where I am, with what I have." When Mother Teresa died, the world wept.

It is foolishness, but it's *God's* foolishness.

Sometimes, whole groups of people become foolish. Faced with the might of the Soviet Empire, some Christians in a church in Leipzig, East Germany, agreed to meet once a week for prayer for peace and freedom. Such foolishness to pray in the face of the Soviet divisions! They prayed and they kept on praying, though some of them died without seeing an answer to their prayers. Then in the summer of 1989, for some reason, people began to gather in the square outside the church when they prayed and there they stayed. People from other parts of East Germany came in their smoking, fuming Trabants. The authorities didn't know what to do with all these people so they opened the borders to disperse them. And soon the wall, the WALL, came tumbling down.

It's foolishness, but it's *God's* foolishness!

I attended the twenty-third World Alliance of Reformed Churches General Council in Debrecen, Hungary, in August of 1997. On our first Sunday it was announced that the sermon in what is called the Little Church of Debrecen would be translated into English. Accordingly, delegates from around the world whose first or second or third language was English gathered there. Between the delegates and the Hungarian congregation there were, I suppose, nearly a thousand people.

A choir from the Ukraine was there to sing. The choir director was an older woman, quite fierce looking, as if determined that everything should go well on this day of days. The preacher was an older minister, also from the Ukraine. I later found out that, as a young minister in 1946, he had been arrested by the KGB for corrupting youth . . . by preparing them for confirmation. The KGB had sneaked a camera into the church and had photographed him confirming these young people.

He was arrested, confronted with the photos and asked, "Who is doing this?" Life was all ahead of him — he had recently become engaged — but he did not deny his role. "Who else would it be?" he replied. He was sentenced to ten years hard labor in a Siberian prison camp, the Gulag. Did his Christian faith seem foolish those long years in the Gulag? Was there any point in standing up against these forces?

In 1953 the dictator Stalin died, and as a result of an amnesty the minister was released. He went home to the Ukraine. His fiancée had waited for him. She was the choir director. No wonder she wanted things to go right!

When the choir sang, they sang in Hungarian an old hymn about Jesus walking on the water. In the hymn the disciples complain to the master, "Do you not care, Master?" And Jesus responds, "Peace. Be still. Do you not know that even the winds and the waves obey me?" The Hungarians, who could understand the words and had lived through the long night of oppression, wept.

It's foolishness, but it's *God's* foolishness.

One Christmas eve between services, a certain minister goes with that little box to the home of a woman dying of cancer. Her daughter is there. She has wandered the world and done hard things, and between mother and daughter there has been . . . a coldness.

The minister takes the bread and says, "This is my body given for you." He takes the cup and says, "This cup is the new covenant in my blood shed for the forgiveness of sins . . ."

Mother and daughter embrace, and they cry. There is no cure, but there is a healing.

The minister is called to the hospital, a heart attack. He's too late — he's not a very good minister, and he's often too late. The family is gathered in a little room off to the side. Perhaps in your time you've sat in that room. The doctor is just leaving. They're grateful to him, as they ought to be, for he has done everything that medical science can do. But the family looks beyond the doctor to the minister, not because he's a good minister, but because he has those words translated from an ancient tongue:

Yea, though I walk through the valley of the shadow of death,
Thy rod and thy staff are with me.
They comfort me.

It's such foolishness but it's *God's* foolishness. Call these stories foolish but call them cruciform stories also and telling cruciform stories is still our best preaching strategy for churches in conflict. If our listeners are truly grasped by this cross-shaped foolishness they might be shaped into a new identity. And they might just not bother to fight anymore.

For there is still power to the story of Christ crucified. A recent graduate of the college where I teach became minister of the Presbyterian church in a small Ontario town of about two thousand people. He was blessed in his ministry by the presence in this little church of a man who had a passionate interest in children and youth, and a gift for reaching out to them. Together they began a youth program that turned out to be amazingly successful. Soon they were drawing seventy-five or eighty kids to their program. You will understand from these numbers that they were attracting kids from beyond their own congregation and indeed from beyond any congregation in their small town. Some of these kids knew startlingly little about the Christian faith. When he first came into the church, one of them, Marty, looked at the ornate chairs arrayed at the front and asked, "Which chair does God sit in?" If we suppose even for a minute that Canada remains a Christian nation, think of the implications of that question. Marty might be a forerunner of many in our society for whom the story we tell will not be familiar.

Pete, the leader of the group, was a gifted storyteller. Sometimes they would build a campfire and Pete would dress up as a shepherd and tell Bible stories. One night Marty was present when Pete was telling the story of the death and resurrection of Christ. As Pete told the old, old story, the kids followed Jesus to Jerusalem. They watched him heal the sick and give sight to the blind. They listened as the rulers plotted to destroy and heard the tinkle of thirty pieces of silver. They sat with Jesus at table in an upper room and followed him to the garden where he was betrayed with a kiss. They witnessed the trial, saw Peter deny Jesus, and heard the lash of the Roman scourge. They stood by the foot of the cross and in deepest silence watched him die. Marty was transfixed. When Jesus, betrayed and abandoned, drew his last shuddering breath, Marty could take it no more. "Oh, mannn!" he cried out in sorrow.

A child from the church, someone who already knew the story, was sitting next to Marty. He gently placed his hand on Marty's arm and said, "That's all right, Marty. The story isn't over yet."

No, the story isn't over, even for churches in conflict.

"Grace Sufficient":
Sermons

Quid Pro Quo:
Our Sins for Christ's Righteousness

(2 Corinthians 5:20–6:2)

DAVID G. BUTTRICK

1993

Therefore, we are ambassadors for Christ, God appealing through us; for Christ's sake, we beg you, Be reconciled to God. Someone who didn't know sin, [God] made sin for us, so that in him we can become the righteousness of God. So, in partnership with God, we also appeal to you, don't receive the grace of God in vain. For [God] says:

At the right time I heard you, and
On the day of salvation I helped you.

Look, now is a very right time! Look, now is a day of salvation!
(2 Corinthians 5:20-6:2)

Latin may be a "dead" language, but actually it's still alive. There are more Latin words in English than from any other source. Some words we use and don't even realize they are Latin — doctor, index, ego. Lawyers speak of *Amicus Curiae* and doctors scribble *Quantum Placet* on prescriptions. Well, there's a Latin phrase for Christians, here and now. *Quid Pro Quo.* Literally, *Quid Pro Quo* means "something for something." Nowadays we'd say, "tit for tat," or perhaps talk about a "trade-off." Listen: the Bible records a great Quid Pro Quo: our sins for Christ's righteousness. A trade-off? Hardly. In the Bible, all God's trades add up to grace.

I

Quid Pro Quo. Christ was made sin for us. "Made sin" — what an odd phrase. Made sin? All you have to do is look at the story of Jesus and you understand. Sin. He was arrested in the garden like a common crook. Stood trial before the Sanhedrin where bony fingers pointed like bayonets: "Do we need to hear any more from this blasphemer?" And he was hauled into Pilate's court while the crowd outside began to chant, "Crucify him!" Sin. He was sin to the soldiers who slapped him silly. Sin to the crowd that laughed at his genitals while he died naked, nailed on the cross. Sin. Remember the great scene in Graham Greene's *The Power and the Glory,* when a drunk priest is tossed into a dark, common jail with the curses and catcalls, the copulation and urine stink? "You don't belong here," said a voice in the dark. But he, for a moment recalling Christ's passion, answered, "I am not a good man."[1] But Christ *was* a "good man." How does the Bible put it? "Someone who didn't know sin, God made sin." Quid Pro Quo. God made Christ into sin for us.

Of course, be honest, we can't pretend we weren't involved. "Were you there when they crucified the Lord?" Answer: Yes, we were there. Look, Jesus Christ was not crucified by villains. No, Jesus Christ was killed off by dedicated people, people like us. Was Caiaphas a pariah? No, he was a loyal man trying to protect religion in a time of change; he probably had an inerrant Bible tucked under his arm. And Pilate, Pilate was a loyal patriot, ready to compromise, but committed to Rome. Can you see a yellow ribbon tied around a pillar in the Praetorium? As for the crowd, well, in nearby Indiana, law and order people have been known to gather outside prisons to cheer when the switch is thrown for an execution. There were no villains around the cross; there were our kind of people. So look, if you want to picture the crucifixion, do not forget symbols of loyalty. You can paint in a clerical collar, a VFW cap, a judicial robe and, perhaps, a Kiwanis Club sign. Were we there when they crucified the Lord? Yes, our faces, our values, our loyalties.

---

1. Graham Greene, *The Power and the Glory* (New York: Viking, 1940), chapter 3.

II

Now, stand back and hear the good news: Christ the Lord is risen. How do we sing it on Easter morning? "Jesus Christ is risen today." Well, he is. The man we branded a heretic is a member of the Godhead now. The revolutionary we got rid of has been appointed Lord of Lords. Wasn't it Reinhold Niebuhr who described Christianity as a "revaluation of values"? The phrase is much too tame; Christianity turns our world upside down. Every once in a while the fundamentalists publish a winner: a few years ago there was a pamphlet with a picture of Jesus on the cover. He was drawn wearing prison stripes, with a number stenciled on his shirt, staring out through a barred prison window. Under the picture was a single word: "Risen." Well, that's the real picture. Jesus Christ, whom we condemned for all the "right reasons," God has raised up. God has declared Christ innocent: He's acquitted, and all our right reasons are suspect now — our religion, our family values, our patriotism. Christ is risen and stands innocent before the throne of God.

III

So, guess what? Now we can run around the world handing out mercy. "Now," sings St. Paul, "*now* is the right time. *Now* is the day of salvation!" For Christianity is good news of God's mercy. Christianity *is* forgiveness. Oh, yes, it's a personal salvation; God knows we need to be forgiven sins that stare from the dark shadows of our lives, what Harry Emerson Fosdick called "The harm I done by being me." But Christianity is much more than personal. Forgiveness is as big as the whole wide world. We fought a Gulf War two years ago and, in a "turkey shoot," killed off around 170,000 Iraqis to our 150 dead. Well, in the midst of divine tears, God has forgiven us. We've been playing competitive religion in North America of late. So Methodists bumper-sticker their cars with "Catch the Spirit," and Presbyterians are busy boosting something they call "The Reformed Tradition," and Baptists are trying to revise a slogan, "A million more in '94." In the name of competitive Christianity we gleefully dismember Jesus Christ. Choking back divine sadness, God forgives us. No wonder St. Paul can shout, "Be reconciled to God." For God has forgiven us all. Now is the day of salvation.

A question: How do we know we are forgiven? How can we be sure of Mercy? Simple: We know we are forgiven because Jesus Christ the righteous has joined himself to the human race. He became one with us. Down in the swirling waters of the Jordan he was baptized hand in hand with repenting sinners. And later, in some Capernaum roadhouse, there he was hoisting a few with a table full of sinners. And then, on the cross, we see him strung up between a couple of crooks, cut-throat terrorists to be exact. Oh, we preachers try to play it down; we picture Jesus on a missionary expedition. He didn't really want to hoist that cup, we say; he'd much rather have been passing a macaroni casserole in some church basement dinner. But no. Evidently Jesus enjoyed the company of sinners. You picture him with his head thrown back, laughing at the jokes, or perhaps with his arm around their shoulders in a kind of comradery. He was one with sinners, joined to sinners — so we have hope.

Let's try a vision on for size. See Christ standing before the mercy seat hand in hand with the whole human race. See the brightness, soft as sunrise. Hear a voice that shouts in silence. Hear a wordless word of absolution that seems to dress us in light. Over the violence and the proud loyalties, over the sold-out-ness and the cruel indifference, there is light reclothing us in a kind of strange innocence. Amazing grace hand in hand with Jesus Christ the Lord.

IV

A personal plea: *Do not receive the grace of God in vain.* Do not let God's grace be null and void — at least not in your lives. Look, we preachers preach to ourselves not just on Sundays but every day. So we know we are sinners. Down deep we all feel inadequate before God. Oh, it's easy to tabulate sins of omission and then move on to motives. Look, along with all humankind, we have stood hand in hand with Jesus Christ and been loved innocent. So now, forgiven — how hard that is for preachers to accept — forgiven, we can be free. We don't have to justify ourselves any more. We don't need status. We don't have to be "professional," a whiz-bang counselor or a shrewd church executive. No, we can be preachers handing mercy to sinners, hoisting a few with riff-raff, repenting with the repentant. A few years ago a wonderful old tobacco-spitting preacher died in north Michigan. He had served a parish of fewer than seventy people for nearly fifty years, paying his way by sign-painting on the side. Well, people testified at his funeral. "Eccentric," sniffed one lady. "He was different alright," said a church officer. Finally one of the members summed it all up: "Maybe we're trying to say that he wasn't afraid to be Christian." There it is: Do not let the grace of God be in vain. Be Christian and freewheeling Christian too, free in the grace of our Lord Jesus Christ.

*   *   *

What an odd phrase. Christ was made sin so we can become the righteousness of God. A trade-off. Good heavens, no! Grace, all grace, spelled out in capital letters. Grace beyond amazing. Forgiven, Free, and Reconciled. Therefore, my dear friends in Christ, be reconciled to God.

The Only Time You Have Is Now

(2 Corinthians 6:2)

JOHN N. GLADSTONE

1993

In a very dark and depressing time in the nineteenth century, Ralph Waldo Emerson wrote to a friend, "Everyone is criticizing and belittling the times. Yet I think that our times, like all times, are very good times, if only we know what to do with them." It would be very easy for us to criticize and belittle the times in which we live. Some people, of course, criticize and belittle everything and everyone, and they will be critical even when they get to heaven itself. There was one critical lady who got to heaven, and when asked how she was getting on, she said, "Well, the harp you gave me is out of tune, my halo is too tight, and the cloud that I'm sitting on is damp." Some people are like that, and other people criticize only some of the time — and that's most of us. These are days in which we find it very easy to be critical — it is very easy to be critical of the times in which we live. Yet Emerson said, "I think that our times, like all times, are very good times" — and I too believe that this is true.

When Lowell Thomas, the famous newsman, died in 1981, Walter Cronkite gave a tribute to him on CBS. He said that Lowell Thomas had lived a very full and exciting life, and at the end of his program, *The Best Years of Our Lives,* when someone asked him, "What were the best years of *your* life?" he answered, "All of them." Walter Cronkite said that Thomas kept on his desk a plaque that read, "This is the day which the Lord has made; let us rejoice and be glad in it" (Ps. 118:24). For notice what Emerson said: "I believe that our times, like all times, are very good times, if only we knew what to do with them." I believe that we had better find out what to do with the times in which we live, for this reason: the only time you have is now, this present moment. I think Robert Frost captures it best in one of his most beautiful poems, "A Prayer in Spring":

> Oh, give us pleasure in the flowers to-day;
> And give us not to think so far away
> As the uncertain harvest; keep us here
> All simply in the springing of the year.[1]

The only time you have is now: "Now is the accepted time" is the biblical injunction (2 Cor. 6:2).

How can we live in the "here and now"? How can we live today as men and women who really believe that today is God's gift, and today is the only gift that we can be sure of? Let me make four suggestions. Begin with this: Don't allow the past to haunt you. When I am traveling on an aircraft alone, I always hope and pray that the person sitting next to me will perhaps be unable to speak English, or very tired, or very antisocial. Because the trouble is that if you get next to one of those chatty people, eventually they ask you the deadly question, "What do you do for a living?" And if you admit that you are any kind of preacher, immediately they will pick an argument. They will hold you responsible for two thousand years of persecution, the Pope's views on abortion and contraception, to say nothing of the eccentricities of their local minister. So what I usually say, following the advice of a friend of mine is, "I'm in insurance, fire insurance" — and that usually keeps them very quiet. But one day, traveling to North Carolina, I sat next to a girl who was using a laptop word processor. Eventually, when the meal came, she put it away, turned to me, and asked, "What do you do for a living?" She looked harmless, so I said, "Well, I'm a Baptist preacher." "Of course," she said, "I don't go to church; I'm not a bit religious. My parents were very religious; they went to church every Sunday and I had to go every Sunday. They rammed religion down my

---

1. Robert Frost, "A Prayer in Spring," lines 1-4, from *A Boy's Will* (New York: Henry Holt, 1915), p. 23.

throat, so I never go near it now. You understand, don't you?" So I said, "I'm afraid I don't understand. Because, you see, that was when you were a child. Your parents may have been misguided, they may have been quite wrong, but you're grown up now. You're an adult now: don't you ever give serious attention to the spiritual life? Don't you wonder about the impact of Christianity over the centuries? Don't you ever explore the idea of God and what it may mean to you? When are you going to stop living in the past and start living in the present?"

There are many people like that: they allow the past to haunt them, and to control the present. One American minister whom I greatly admire went to a prison one Christmas to interview some of the prisoners, and spoke to some twenty of them. Not one prisoner complained that he had been unjustly sentenced. One man spoke for all them when he said, "It wasn't my father; it wasn't my mother; it wasn't my teacher: I made a damn fool of myself and I'm doing the best to see that my son doesn't make the same mistake." He accepted responsibility for himself, without allowing the past to haunt him or complaints to stifle him.

There are other people, Christian people, who allow the past to haunt them. Oh, they believe in the forgiveness of sins; they repeat it in church; they accept the fact that God in Christ has forgiven us, but they've never really forgiven themselves. And so they are haunted by past sins and blunders and failures. When I was growing up in England, there used to be a movement called the "Moral Rearmament." Part of their practice was to sit around in drawing rooms, hold hands, and rehearse their sins and lusts of the past — a kind of orgy of reliving the past. Leslie Weatherhead went to one of these sessions, and wrote a very amusing article about it. He said that he had discovered eleven new temptations and six new sins! Now, this kind of thing is dishonoring to the God of the gospel. The God of the gospel is a God who "as far as the East is from the West" has removed our transgressions from us, a God who forgives us in Christ and expects us to live in the light of that forgiveness with the liberty of the children of God. Don't allow the past to haunt you: remember to forget it if you have repented and received the forgiveness of God. I think one of John Bunyan's most eloquent passages is that passage where he describes Christian at the cross:

> So I saw in my Dream, that just as Christian came up with the
> Cross, his burden loosed from off his Shoulders, and fell from

off his back; and began to tumble; and so continued to do, till it came to the mouth of the Sepulcher, where it fell in, and I saw it no more.

Then was Christian glad and lightsome, and said with a merry heart, "He hath given me rest, by his sorrow; and life, by his death."[2]

Don't allow the past to haunt you. Forgiven, forgotten, forever.

Here's the second suggestion: keep the future in true perspective. In no sense would I denigrate the future in your life and mine, but how many people there are who live in the future, and forget that the future is not yet ours to claim. In 1919, the American Lincoln Steffens went to Russia and looked at the Marxist experiment. He was so enamored of it, so excited by it, that he became a Marxist and proclaimed the message, "I have seen the future and it works!" I wonder what he would feel like seventy-three years after, when the whole thing has collapsed and been seen for the monstrous fraud that it was? One Russian intellectual, mocking Lincoln Steffens, said, "I have *been* the future, and it stinks." If the stench of Marxist deeds could reach higher and better worlds than this, the very angels must have been nauseated over and over again. You can't see the future, and you can't claim the future, yet so many of us are dominated by it. Remember how Charlie Brown says in one of his cartoons, "I only dread one day at a time." A lot of us are like that. Some ministers are never in the church they are in, but always in the church that is to come. But the future is not yet ours to claim. Albert Camus put it like this: "Real generosity towards the future lies in giving all to today."

The only time you have is now, and to give your utmost now is the best preparation for what may yet come.

Here's the third suggestion: commit yourself to a worthy cause. Macneile Dixon in those scintillating lectures of his, *The Human Situation*, says this: "If you would make human beings happy, give them a task and a cause, and the harder the better."[3] When Albert Schweitzer

2. John Bunyan, *The Pilgrim's Progress*, ed. W. R. Owens (Oxford: Oxford University, 2003), p. 37.

3. William Macneile Dixon, *The Human Situation: The Gifford Lectures Delivered in the University of Glasgow, 1935-1937* (London: Edward Arnold, 1950 [1937]).

was addressing the graduating class of Eton College, England's most famous public school, he said to them, "I do not know what your destiny will be. Some of you may be actors, politicians, teachers, doctors, surgeons, but I do know this: the only ones among you who will be really happy are those who have sought and found how to serve." And when they talked to Schweitzer about his sacrifices, he dismissed it and said, "It's not a matter of sacrifice, it's a matter of happiness, actually: happiness consists in service, in giving yourself here and now to that which is worthy and above your own self-interests."

Commit yourself to a worthy cause. You may say, "I don't know what the needs of Canada will be in the year 2000. I don't know what the needs of this university will be or of your particular church, but I know what they are now, and I know that I am called to serve here and now in this present time and to be a committed man or woman giving my utmost to the demands of the present."

First, don't allow the past to haunt you; second, keep the future in true perspective; third, commit yourself to a worthy cause. Here's the fourth suggestion: believe that God will give you adequate strength for every strain. What is it that overshadows the present for people like you and me? Is it not this: we wonder if we can cope with that which may yet come. What if a serious illness comes to me or to my spouse? What if I lose my power to do this? What if I get this disease or that? What if this tragedy comes to my family? What if, what if, what if? Can we cope? To use biblical language, how shall we do "in the swelling of the Jordan"?

There is a marvelous text in the book of Deuteronomy that you may take away with you: "*As* your days, *so* will your strength be," underlining "as" and underlining "so" (Deut. 33:25). A student in Scotland went to church years ago one Sunday. He was desperate. He wondered if he would have adequate financial resources. He wondered if he would have the mental equipment to pass his exams, to obtain his degree, and he was a confused motley of emotional difficulties. He went to church, and the great biblical expositor George Adam Smith was preaching. This was his text: "As your days, so will your strength be." Smith paraphrased it memorably: "With strain will come the strength, not before but with it."

Sometimes when in my pulpit I have talked about the great heroes of the Christian faith — someone like Dietrich Bonhoeffer — somebody has come up to me afterwards and asked, "Could you die for your faith?" I say, "I don't know, I don't know — I've never had to do it. All I need at the moment is strength to *live* for it, and to be a good minister of Jesus Christ." If the time came when I had to die for my faith, I believe the strength would come to do it. "As your days, so will your strength be." Will you believe that? That whatever comes to you, God will be there to strengthen you with the needed grace and strength for that particular moment.

Here's my last word. Richard Selzer, a surgeon, has written in his memoirs of a young wife who came to him with a cancerous tumor on her face. He operated on it, and in doing so he had to sever the nerve that controlled the muscles of her mouth. Her mouth drooped badly. She looked in the mirror, and saw this droop, and she turned to him and said, "Will my mouth always be like this?" He said, "Yes, it will." Then her young husband bent down and said, "I like it this way" — and he kissed her. Richard Selzer lowered his gaze because, he says, "One is not bold in an encounter with a god. . . . I remember that the gods appeared in ancient Greece as mortals, and I hold my breath and let the wonder in."[4] For he was indeed in the presence of God.

God will give you adequate strength for every strain, when the strain comes. And so you can live now.

Not for one single day
Can I discern my way,
   But this I surely know, —
He who gives the day
Will show the way,
   So I securely go.[5]

---

4. Richard Selzer, *Mortal Lessons: Notes on the Art of Surgery* (New York: Simon and Schuster, 1976), pp. 45-46.

5. John Oxenham, "The Day — The Way," from *Bees in Amber: A Little Book of Thoughtful Verse* (London: Methuen, 1913).

All Things Are Yours

(1 Corinthians 3:21-23)

CHARLES G. ADAMS

1994

In First Corinthians, the third chapter, the twenty-first through twenty-third verses, we find these words:

> Therefore let no man glory in men. For all things are yours, whether Paul, or Apollos, or Cephas, or the world or life or death or things present or things to come. All are yours, and you are Christ's, and Christ is God's.

When we evaluate our lives, the saddest thing in the world is to see narrowness, insularity, and poverty of spirit. Too often, life for us is so meager, when it might have been so magnificent. So sorry, when it might have been so significant, so feeble when it might have been so full, so paltry when it might have been so powerful, so little when it might have been so luxuriant. If it be that our faith is a clear witness to the freedom of God, the vast resources of the grace of God, and the rich endowments that the love of God has poured on all humankind, then we are challenged to cross-register broadly in the opulent university called life. "All things are yours." Claim everything; miss nothing; care for everything; abuse nothing. We are here confronted with a tremendous opportunity to take both responsibility for and possession of every life, every idea, every race, every nation, every institution. We may join Emerson in saying,

I am owner of the sphere,
Of the seven stars and the solar year,
Of Cæsar's hand, and Plato's brain,
Of Lord Christ's heart, and Shakespeare's strain.[1]

"All things are yours." If it strikes you as absurd and cavalier to be told that all things are yours, how nonsensical it must have sounded to that very small group of First Corinthian Christians who were very ordinary people. Not many intellectuals, no royalty, no aristocracy, no political leaders, no social stars, no persons with pedigrees, poor people every one of them. If any one of them had gone to the First National Bank of Corinth to take out a loan, the banker would have said to him or her, "You don't have any collateral. You don't have a good reference. You need a co-signer. You cannot possibly take the lead in the revitalization of Corinth. You can't possibly turn urban blight into benefits for human beings." But Paul looked at those same people, and read to them from a different balance sheet: "All things are yours. I am yours. Apollos is yours. Cephas is yours. This world is yours. Life is yours. Death is yours. The present is yours, the future is yours, all things are yours."

Is this nonsense? Try it. Try getting that message across in Somalia, where I went twice to feed the hungry. Look at those poor, hopeless, homeless refugees of East Africa, whose bellies are bloated in the last stage of starvation when the body sends all of its fluids to the abdomen so that the body actually begins to feed on itself. Look them square in the face and tell them, "All things are yours." Go to Detroit, one of the most troubled cities in the United States, where the per capita income is the lowest of any large city in the United States. Where the unemployment rate is near the highest in the nation; where the schools are failing, and citizens wage war against state taxes for education; where hospitals are closing and jails are expanding. Tell them, "All things are yours." You might have a hard time convincing the authorities that you should not be committed.

And yet we may proclaim to everybody everywhere, to the haves and to the have-nots, "All things are yours." Yours, not by theft but by legiti-

1. Ralph Waldo Emerson (1803-1882), from "History," *Essays: First Series* (Boston: Monroe, 1841).

mate acquisition; yours, because the King of kings has assigned them to your inventory; yours, because the redeemer of human life has written them on the ledger; yours, because it has been certified in blood and sealed by the resurrection; yours, if not by natural birth then by legal inheritance. For the children are the heirs of God, and joint-heirs with Christ. Yours. Not by ownership, but by possession. Now be careful. Those two words must be distinguished, lest they be taken to mean the same thing. To own is not necessarily to possess, and to possess is not necessarily to own. You may possess peace of mind, but can you own it? You may possess happiness, intelligence, and the respect of your peers, but can you own those benefits? Do you have the ability to borrow, stash, or market them? Do you have any exclusive title on the things of the mind? By diligent and protracted study, you may possess English literature, German philosophy, or African history. But to be sure, you may not monopolize, dominate, control, or restrict these fields by any means. Sometimes, in haughtiness of pride, we *think* we can, as if recognition in a certain field gives us at least partial ownership over the field in which we have been recognized. Then along comes a Reinhold Niebuhr without a Ph.D., and scholars are forced to move over and make room for him while he leads the whole field of Christian social ethics. Then comes along a W. E. B. DuBois, and the white fraternity of the learned is no longer all white. Then come the Jews, and it's no longer all Christians. Then come the women, and the fraternity becomes a "frasority."

The amazing grace of God gives everybody possession, but nobody ownership. Professor George Lyman Kittredge of Harvard had only a lowly bachelor's degree, and yet he was the greatest scholar on Shakespeare that the world has ever known. And when a prude asked him, "Why don't you have a Ph.D.?" he said, "It's only because I can't find anyone who knows enough to examine me." You may possess the Holy Ghost, but can you own it? Can we who are Christian own Jesus Christ? Sometimes we think we do, as we lustily sing, "Blessed assurance, Jesus is *mine.*" And then along comes a Mahatma Gandhi, whose morally demonstrated possession of Christ can be far superior to our vaunted claims of orthodox ownership. Or then there is Elie Wiesel, whose movement for world peace and justice is closer to the mind of Christ than the social ethics of Pat Robertson. Jesus told Nicodemus, "God is *free.* The wind blows where it wills, and you hear the sound of it. But you do not know whence it comes or whither it goes. So it is with everyone who is born of the Spirit" (John 3:8).

Nobody can own God. Everybody can possess God. The government has no monopoly on justice; the university has no exclusive on truth; the military has no copyright on power; and the church has no patent on God. By the same token, there are certain things that you may own, but never possess. You may own property, and never take possession of it, never even see it. You may own a bank account and never use it, a car and never drive it, a great library and never possess it in the sense of reading and enjoying its many volumes. You may own valuable works of African and European art, and never possess them, unless you understand and appreciate them. You may own fifty Bibles, but you will not possess one of them unless you open it, read it, and try to live by it. You may own an insurance policy on your life, but I am afraid that you will never live to possess its full benefits.

So now that we have reviewed the difference between ownership and possession, we are free in the freedom of God to possess without owning the blue crystal lake, the vast gorgeous sky, the majesty of mountains, the mystery of sunrise, the evening star, the music of the birds, the green of trees, the fragrance of flowers, the power of Beethoven's Ninth, the mind of Shakespeare, the heritage of Harvard, the mission of McMaster, the wisdom of Solomon, the music of David, the scholarship of DuBois, the genius of Paul Robeson, the understanding of Einstein, the determination of Tubman, the moral might of Mandela, the faith of Abraham, the courage of Jomo Kenyatta, the spirit of Martin Luther King Jr., the love of God, the grace of Jesus Christ, the universal fellowship of the Holy Spirit, and the moral strength of the Word of God. All these you can never own, but you may possess. All things are yours, in the freedom of God.

In the application and enjoyment of this vast freedom, be it resolved that we will never become narrow, bigoted, judgmental, or prejudiced in our theology or practice of religion. For nobody wholly possesses the whole truth of God. Nobody sees perfectly the whole revelation of the divine. No church, denomination, or doctrine can contain all there is of ultimate reality. And our affirmations of what we see and know must never be asserted by disparaging the equally valid certainties and experiences of others. Is the opulence of the grace of God to be measured by the narrow inventory of *my* experience? Is the great faith of twenty centuries to be reduced to any particular national, racial, or cultural dimension? Are the arching lines of the divinely possible to be pulled down to fit the narrow scope of my own peculiar compass?

The occasion of the text was bigotry in the church of Corinth. The church was divided into factions, parties, and cliques, based upon what they erroneously perceived to be competition between the pastors. One faction said, "We are followers of Paul." Another group said, "We believe in Apollos, the silver-tongued orator." Another group said, "We believe in Peter, an eye-witness to Jesus Christ." But Paul said, "Stop this wrangling. Why must *your* experience be used to put down the religious experiences of others? If Apollos can teach anything, learn it. If Paul can contribute anything, take it. If Cephas can explain anything, listen to it. Do not oversimplify. Do not be a reductionist. Do not cut down to a single, simple, canonized way the enormous variety of ways that the Holy Spirit can accomplish the incredible work of amazing grace."

"There's a wideness in God's mercy like the wideness of the sea,/ . . . For the love of God is broader than the measure of man's mind."[2] God is free. Grace is wonderful. Salvation in Christ is not a narrow, exclusive Christian possession. It is not a negative put-down of other religions and races, but it is a positive assurance and a gleeful celebration of Christ's cosmic presence, ubiquitous influence, and universal redemption. The creation is not a drab monotony of sickening sameness, but a wonderful variety of amazing differences. If we look hard, we will see and celebrate a living Christ in all churches, all religions, all races, and all nations. For no one has an exclusive on God. And if we are wise, we will claim everything and everyone. Though the United Methodists claim John Wesley and the Presbyterians claim John Calvin, the Lutherans claim Martin Luther and the Baptists claim Roger Williams, the Church of God in Christ claims Charles Mason, the Episcopalians claim William Tyndale, the African Methodist Episcopal Church claims Richard Allen, the Adventists claim Ellen White, the Roman Catholics claim Saint Peter, the Orthodox Church claims Saint John, the Jews claim Abraham and Moses, the Muslims claim Mohammed,

---

2. From the hymn, "Souls of Men! Why Will Ye Scatter" (1862), by Frederick William Faber (1814-1863).

white folks claim George Washington, black folks claim Martin Luther King Jr., Republicans claim Abraham Lincoln, and Democrats claim Franklin Roosevelt, I claim all of them in Christ. For I want everything in Christ: every perspective of truth, every contribution to humanity, every enhancement of life. I want the wisdom of Lincoln *and* the compassion of Roosevelt; I want the heritage of Washington and the legacy of King; I want the social ministries of the Methodists and the strict theology of the Presbyterians; I want the pioneering protests of the Lutherans and the defining spirit of Richard Allen; I want the kingdom keys of Saint Peter and the glorious liberty of the non-Conformists; I want the gorgeous liturgy of the Episcopalians and the intellectual honesty of the Unitarians; I want the family consciousness and cohesiveness of the Jews and the daily disciplines of the Muslims and the spiritual fervor of the Pentecostals and the startling stewardship of the Adventists and the wonderful freedoms of the Baptists. There is no place for narrowness, bigotry, and competition in the church of Jesus Christ. We are all in one and one in all. The divine mystery cannot be sung in a solo, but only in a choir. It is not a restricted monologue but an expanding dialogue. It does not look like a clear glass, but resembles an opulent and opaque stained-glass image extravagantly drawn in interdependent contours, configurations, and colors.

In the history and heritage of black churches is to be found a great love for all kinds of music. It is very un-black for a black person to say, "I don't like anthems," or "I refuse to sing a gospel." We have composed all kinds of music, from symphonies to shouts, and we can sing anything that anybody has written, or conveniently left unwritten. We can sing grand opera, oratorios, and anthems, with precision and power. And I enjoy hearing us sing anthems, because we can put in them a certain fire and soul power that makes them come alive. There are times when I want to hear us sing J. S. Bach's "Sheep May Safely Graze," Beethoven's "The Heavens Are Telling," Haydn's "Creation," Brahms's "Requiem," and Handel's "Messiah." But we can go on from there and sing the standard White Protestant hymns, like "Lead On, O King Eternal," "A Mighty Fortress Is Our God," and "Come, Thou Almighty King." But we can go on from there and sing the White missionary gospel hymns of personal religion, like "What a Friend We Have in Jesus," "Blessed Assurance, Jesus Is Mine," and "Love Lifted Me." But we can go on from there and sing the soul-reviving hymns of black composers like "Hold to God's Unchanging Hand," "We'll Understand It Better By and By," and "Beams of Heaven As I Go." But we can go on from there and sing those beautiful antebellum black spirituals like, "Were You There?," "Swing Low, Sweet Chariot," and "Lord, I Want to Be a Christian." And we can go on from there and sing the short-meter, common-meter, and long-meter hymns in our own tunes and without accompaniment. And we can go on from there and sing the hard rock, jazzy gospels like, "I Really Love the Lord." Now wouldn't it be a shame for us to allow anyone to attempt to reduce and squeeze all of that rich variety to fit the straightjacket of someone's narrow sense of what is liturgically correct?

But the text is not limited to a preachment against musical or religious bigotry. It's against *all* bigotry. Paul does not simply say that all spiritual values are yours, all things are yours, the world is yours. Now, unless this be mistaken as a holy call to military occupation, colonial expansion, and political domination, we ought to hear it as a moral appeal, to be both intelligent and responsible in our appreciation and our appropriation of the whole world. We are called upon to claim everything and to liberate everybody in the freedom of God. I do not understand any Bible-believing Christian who feels that he or she has no stake in this world, no mandate to claim its responsibilities, discover its mysteries, solve its problems, or meet its needs. Or those who feel that because they have romance they don't need finance. Or those who feel that because God is on their side they may be excused from the moral struggle to improve and enhance our common life. Or those who think that because they have Jesus, that's enough. Jesus never said it was enough. But he did say, "Get your priorities lined up, and seek ye first the kingdom of God and his righteousness, and *all these things* will be added unto you" (Matt. 6:33). That's not just "Pie in the sky by and by as you fly when you die": it's something "Sound on the ground by the pound to be found while you're still around."

The world is yours. There is no conflict between faith and science. No antagonism between evolution and creation: the one is a theory of empirical development and the other is a declaration of divine purpose and meaning. It's not a matter of being exclusive; it's the truth of interdependence. The world with all of its problems belongs to you who are being prepared here to solve human problems and meet human needs. So go into all of the world. Take the energy of your mind and the light of your faith, the power of your knowledge and the strength of your convictions. Go to Bosnia-Herzegovina, where old feuds have opened fiercely into tragic hostilities. Go to Lebanon, where all sides are frustrated and confused. Go to Israel, where a great nation-state is wrestling with its consciousness of prophetic vision. Go to South Africa, where twenty-three million people are being crucified daily, and political freedom will mean nothing without economic equity. Go to Ireland, where the blood is still flowing in the streets. Go to England, where there is a need for imaginative leadership. Go to Central America, where the tentacles of corporate greed are tightening around the necks of the poor. Go to the cities of the United States, where there is endemic unemployment, inadequate educational opportunity, substandard housing, absentee landlords, desolation and blight, lack of social services, the destruction of the family, unrelieved poverty, unmitigated despair. This world is your world, and all people are your people. Their problems are your opportunities to turn night into day, despair into hope, and the trampled-down into the upward-bound. All things are yours.

The past is yours: learn from it. The present is yours: fulfill it. The future is yours: preserve it. The Bible is yours: believe it. Science is yours: master it. The gospel is yours: preach it. Cancer is yours: cure it. The church is yours: claim it. Jesus is yours: expect him. Injustice is yours: correct it. The Holy Ghost is yours: receive it. Sickness is yours: heal it. America is yours: improve it. Canada is yours: make it greater. Violence is yours: stop it. Hope is yours: affirm it. The world is yours: share it. The environment is yours: cleanse it. Time is yours: use it. Life is yours: extend it. Death is yours: prevent it, delay it, overcome it. Eternal life is yours: receive it now. African American life and history and soul and mind belong to everybody. Just as there is no baseball without Cecil Fielder and no football without Emmitt Smith, and no basketball without Michael Jordan, no music without Jessye Norman, no South without the souls of black people; and there is no world, no earth, no heaven, without everybody. Nobody has a monopoly on anything. Show me a George Washington and I'll show you a Crispus Attucks; show me a William Lloyd Garrison and I'll show you a David Walker; show me a Joan of Arc, I'll show you a Harriet Tubman; show me an Abraham Lincoln, I'll show you a Frederick Douglass; show me an Albert Einstein, I'll show you a Benjamin Banneker; show me a Theodore

Roosevelt, I'll show you a Booker T. Washington; show me a Franklin Roosevelt, I'll show you a Mary McLeod Bethune; show me a Dwight D. Eisenhower, I'll show you an Adam Clayton Powell Jr.; show me a John Fitzgerald Kennedy, I'll show you a Martin Luther King Jr.; show me a Lyndon Baines Johnson, I'll show you a Thurgood Marshall; show me a Jimmy Carter, I'll show you a Coleman Young; show me a Harry Emerson Fosdick, I'll show you a Gardner Taylor.

So we will not be intimidated by diversity; we will be enriched by diversity. We will not be blinded or disheartened by the times or discouraged by the system; we will face it and challenge it and change it and correct it. Because all things are ours. Never be discouraged; never claim that you do not have what you already possess. If you have a hard way to go, just keep walking by faith; if you have a mean problem, work with it till you work through it; if you have a misunderstanding, settle it; if you have a grudge against anybody, drop it; if you have hatred or resentment, shake it off; if you have a high mountain, move it by prayer or climb it by work. If you have a battle, fight it; if you have a handicap, rise above it; if you have prejudice, overcome it; if you have a temptation, conquer it; if you have evil, destroy it; if you have a challenge, face it; if you have trouble, take it; if you have a cross, bear it. If they knock you down, get up; if they push you against the ropes, come out reaching; if they hate you, keep loving; if they laugh, you keep smiling, and if they kill you, rise up again. For all things are yours. And you are Christ's. And Christ is God's.

Glorying in the Cross Alone

(Galatians 6:14)

JOHN R. W. STOTT

1996

I invite you to reflect with me on one of the most extraordinary statements ever made by the apostle Paul, which is claiming a good deal. You will find it in Galatians 6:14: "God forbid that I should glory in anything except in the cross of our Lord Jesus Christ, by which the world has been crucified unto me and I have been crucified unto the world." You may know that there is no exact equivalent in English of this Greek verb, *kauchasthai*. It means "to boast in, to trust in, to glory it, to revel in, to live for." In a word, our glory is our obsession. It dominates our minds, fills our horizons, and engrosses our attention. For the apostle Paul this was the cross. The cross of Christ was the center of his faith, of his life, and of his ministry; and it should be the center of ours. Let other people be obsessed with fame, power, sex, and money; we who claim to follow Jesus should be obsessed with the cross like the apostle Paul.

This was not a peculiarity of Paul's, however. I think we might say that the cross was central to the mind of Paul only because it had been central to the mind of Christ. Did Jesus not repeatedly predict the ne-

---

A later version of this sermon appears as "The Cross of Christ," in John Stott, *Evangelical Truth: A Personal Plea for Unity, Integrity, and Faithfulness* (Downers Grove, Ill.: InterVarsity, 1999), pp. 67-84.

cessity of his sufferings, saying that the Son of Man must suffer many things? Did he not speak of his death as the hour for which he had come into the world, which kept delaying until finally he could say that the hour had come? Did he not give instructions for his own memorial service, telling the apostles to take bread and eat it, and to drink wine, so that it was by his death more than anything else that he wanted to be remembered? So the church has been right in its choice of symbol for the Christian faith.

Mind you, there were many options. The church could well have chosen the crib, the symbol of the incarnation, in which the baby Jesus lay. It could have chosen the carpenter's bench in Nazareth, by which he dignified honest manual labor. It could have chosen the boat from which he taught the people at the Sea of Galilee, or the towel or apron which he wrapped round himself before getting on his hands and knees to wash their feet, a symbol of servitude. It could have chosen the tomb in which his body was laid and from which he rose from the dead. It could have chosen the throne he occupies at the right hand of the Father today. It could have chosen the wind, the fire, or the dove, which are emblems of the Holy Spirit. There could have been many different emblems or symbols of Christianity, but the church with unerring vision chose the cross. We see it everywhere within Christendom. We see it in the medieval cathedrals of Europe, which were deliberately built on a cruciform ground plan so that the nave and the transepts form a cross. Many of us wear a cross on our lapel or a necklace. It is in this faith of Christ crucified that we were baptized and when we're dead, as likely as not, our family and friends will erect a cross over our grave. So the Christian faith is the faith of Christ crucified, and in it we are called to live, to serve, to suffer, and to die.

This centrality of the cross has been recognized by many people, from whom I choose just two quotations. From the great Congregational theologian P. T. Forsyth:

Christ is to us just what his cross is. All that Christ was in heaven or on earth was put into what he did there. . . . You do not understand Christ until you understand his cross.[1]

1. P. T. Forsyth, *The Cruciality of the Cross* (London: Hodder and Stoughton, 1909), pp. 44-45.

And here is Bishop J. C. Ryle, the evangelical bishop of Liverpool in the north of England at the end of the last century. He wrote, with characteristic vigor,

> If you have not yet found out that Christ crucified is the foundation of the whole volume, you have read your Bible hitherto to very little profit. Your religion is a heaven without a sun, an arch without a keystone, a compass without a needle, a clock without spring or weights, a lamp without oil. . . . Beware, I say again, of a religion without the cross.[2]

So the question before us now is, why did Paul glory only in the cross, especially when in the Greco-Roman world the cross was a symbol of distaste and even of disgust. Can we elaborate what he meant? It is a fundamental hermeneutical principle that we allow the context to determine the meaning of the text. We should never isolate a text from its biblical context if we are desirous of understanding it. So since my text, Galatians 6:14, is part of the conclusion of the Epistle to the Galatians, it is, I suggest, in that epistle that we find the clues we want for understanding why Paul gloried only in the cross.

Acceptance with God

The first clue is this. We glory in the cross for our acceptance with God, or, our justification. Some years ago I found myself in the city of Durham in the north of England. I was worshiping in the cathedral that morning and the preacher was the well-known New Testament scholar, H. E. W. Turner, whose book, *Jesus, Master and Lord*, is still read today.[3] In the middle of his sermon I was arrested when he said, "How can I, a lost and guilty sinner, stand before a just and holy God?" I say that I was arrested because New Testament professors don't usually ask themselves embarrassing questions in the pulpit. But he did and it was a good question to ask. Indeed it is the most important of all questions

2. J. C. Ryle, *Home Truths* (London: Thynne, [n.d.]), pp. 19-20.
3. Henry E. W. Turner, *Jesus, Master and Lord: A Study in the Historical Truth of the Gospels* (London: Mowbray, 1953).

because the fact is that we cannot enter into the presence of God in his holiness in the tattered rags of our own morality. All those who have seen a vision of the glory and the holiness of God have been over-whelmed by the sight. That surely is true of us still.

Other religions, by contrast, assure us with one voice that it is per-fectly possible to enter into the presence of God in our own morality. It is perfectly possible to accumulate merit and commend ourselves to God. One of the most colorful speakers at the first Parliament of Reli-gions held in Chicago in 1893 was Swami Vivekananda from India, founder of the Ramakrishna Mission. In the middle of his speech he said, "It is a sin to call a man a sinner."[4] "You are not sinners," he said. "You are children of God. You are angels." He went on to say, "No sinner needs a savior. We can easily save ourselves. It is a sin to call a man a sin-ner." We say, on the contrary, that it is not a sin to call a man a sinner; it is the sober truth. So only the Bible of all the world's religious books in-sists that we are sinners under the judgment of God, that self-salvation is utterly impossible, that our need points us to the cross instead.

Since we are allowing the epistle to determine the meaning of our text, we must look back to chapter 3 of Galatians, one of the great chap-ters on the atonement in the New Testament, and to verse 13 in particu-lar: "Christ has redeemed us from the curse of the law, having become a curse for us." Bishop Blunt in his commentary on Galatians wrote, "The language here is startling, almost shocking. We should not have dared to use it."[5] We reply to the bishop that such words may shock and startle, but that is no reason to jettison them. We have no liberty to do so. The point is that the apostle Paul did use them, and so we have to come to terms with them. "Christ has redeemed us from the curse of the law, having become a curse for us." In other words, the only way that we can be redeemed from the judgment that God's law pro-nounces on those who disobey it, is that Christ bore it in our place. He became a curse instead of us. He endured in his own innocent person the condemnation that we deserved.

Of course, we need to hedge this round with every possible safe-

---

4. Swami Vivekananda, *Speeches and Writings,* 3rd ed. (Madras: G. A. Nateson, 1893), pp. 38-39.

5. A. W. F. Blunt, *The Epistle of Paul to the Galatians in the Revised Version* (Oxford: Clar-endon, 1925), pp. 96-97.

guard, and we have to be very careful that people do not misunderstand this or misstate it. We must never suggest that God the Father showed any reluctance to come to our rescue. We must never indicate that Jesus was some third party who intervened between the Father and us in order to do for us what the Father was not willing to do. No: it was God himself who took the initiative. "God was in Christ reconciling the world to himself" (2 Cor. 5:19). He took the initiative in his holy love, but what he did in and through Christ was to bear our sin, to endure our curse, and to die our death, in order that we might be forgiven. Wonder of wonders that should bring tears to our eyes. Moreover, sisters and brothers, the Christian life continues as it began, at the foot of the cross of Jesus. Have we learned that the cross is not an elementary stage in the Christian life that we later grow out of? Have we learned that we can never graduate from the school called Calvary? We remain students in this school, and the Lord's Supper continually brings us back to it. We glory in the cross as the way of our acceptance with a holy God.

Discipleship and Holiness

Secondly, we glory in the cross for our discipleship, because the cross is the way of holiness, as well as the way of forgiveness. While Galatians 6:14 mentions only one cross, it refers to three crucifixions on the one cross: God forbid that I should glory in anything but the cross of our Lord Jesus Christ by which he was crucified, by which the world has been crucified unto me, and I have been crucified unto the world. Three crucifixions on one and the same cross. Paul has already introduced this notion earlier in the letter. For example, in 2:20, "I have been crucified with Christ, nevertheless I live." Or in 5:24, "Those who belong to Christ have crucified their fallen, self-indulgent nature with all its passions and desires."

Now, there are nuances between these verses. They do not say precisely the same thing. Nevertheless, they express the same fundamental truth: if Christ died as our substitute, instead of us, so that we might not have to die, as the New Testament obliges us to affirm, he also died as our representative, so that when he died we also died with him. It is by bringing together Christ the substitute and Christ the representative and not affirming either at the expense of the other, that we can begin to understand this second truth about glorying in the cross.

These words are Paul's elaboration of what the Lord Jesus himself taught when he called us to take up our cross and follow him (Mark 8:34-35, *par.*). If we had lived in those days in Roman-occupied Palestine, and if we had seen a man in some country lane carrying a cross, we wouldn't have needed to run up to him and tap him on the shoulder and ask what he was doing. No, we would have recognized him immediately as a condemned criminal on his way to execution, because the Romans compelled condemned prisoners to carry their own cross to the place of execution. So if we take up the cross and follow Christ, there is only one place to which we can be following him, and that is the place of execution. To quote H. B. Swete, one of the great commentators on Mark's Gospel, to take up the cross is to "put oneself into the position of a condemned criminal on his way to execution."[6] It is, in other words, a dramatic figure of speech for self-denial. Bonhoeffer in *The Cost of Discipleship* said that when Christ calls a person, he bids that person die.[7] Christ calls us to die to our own self-centeredness in order to live for him.

So cross-bearing and crucifixion are Jesus' dramatic figures of speech for self-denial. They come into direct collision with the Human Potential movement, and with the New Age movement, which has jumped on the bandwagon of the Human Potential movement and is concerned only with self. Shirley MacLaine, the high priestess of the New Age movement, is absolutely infatuated with herself. I have read, I think, three of her books and came across this: "I *know* that I exist, therefore I AM. I *know* that the God-source exists. Therefore IT IS. Since I am part of that force, then I AM that I AM."[8] Is this infatuation with self not blasphemous? It's perfectly true that Jesus taught that his followers would find themselves and fulfill themselves, but he taught that the only road to self-discovery is self-denial and the only way to

---

6. Henry Barclay Swete, *The Gospel According to St. Mark: The Greek Text with Introduction, Notes, and Indices* (London: Macmillan, 1902), p. 182.

7. Dietrich Bonhoeffer, *The Cost of Discipleship*, trans. R. H. Fuller (New York: Macmillan, [1937] 1959), p. 99: "When Christ calls a man, He bids him come and die. . . . In fact, every command of Jesus is a call to die, with all our affections and lusts. But we do not want to die."

8. Shirley MacLaine, *Dancing in the Light* (New York: Bantam, 1985), p. 420.

find ourselves is to lose ourselves in loving. It is one of the great paradoxes of the gospel.

The old Authorized King James Version puts it like this: "Whosoever will save his life shall lose it; but whosoever shall lose his life for my sake and the gospel's, the same shall save it" (Mark 8:35). I used to think this was a reference to martyrdom, the loss of your life. But let me put it in modern language. If you insist on holding on to yourself, and if you refuse to let yourself go, and if you are determined to live for yourself, you will lose yourself. But only if you are willing to lose yourself, to give yourself away, in love for God and in love for the neighbor, then in the moment of complete abandon when you think everything is lost, then the miracle takes place that you find yourself. You only find yourself by losing yourself in loving. That is the message of the cross.

So we glory in the cross for our acceptance, and we glory in the cross for our discipleship. We have a constant tendency to trivialize Christian discipleship. We sometimes think it is nothing more than becoming a bit religious and adding a thin layer of piety to an otherwise secular life. Then scratch the surface or prick the veneer and there is the same old pagan underneath. Nothing has radically changed. But in fact, becoming a Christian involves something so radical that no imagery could do it justice except death and resurrection: dying to the old life of self-centeredness and self-indulgence and rising to an altogether new life of holiness and love in which the world has been crucified unto me and I have been crucified unto the world.

Message and Mission

Thirdly, we glory in the cross for our message, because the church is called to mission and you can't have a mission without a message. What is our message for the world? It is the story of the cross; it is the fantastic truth of a God who loved us so much that he came after us even to the desolate agony of the cross. He came after us in Christ in order that he might seek and find and save us. That is our message. In Galatians 3:1, the apostle sums up his mission in the words, "We publicly portrayed Christ crucified before your eyes." That is what we did, he says, when we came to Galatia. The cross had become the focus of his message and he had, as it were, placarded Christ crucified, as if on a public billboard.

Neither the Galatians nor Paul actually saw Christ crucified; they weren't there. But through his preaching, the apostle Paul brought the past out of the past and into the present, making the historical event of the cross a contemporary reality (which is also what the Lord's Supper does). As a consequence the Galatians could now see the cross in their imaginations. They could understand that he had died for their sins, and they could kneel before the cross with great humility to receive from his hands that gift of eternal life, which is absolutely free and utterly undeserved. This preaching of the cross, which was the center of Paul's message in Galatians and elsewhere, was a stumbling block to some and foolishness to others. Why? Because it undermines our self-righteousness and challenges our self-indulgence. That is why it is so unpopular.

It is in this connection that Paul contrasts himself with the false preachers, the "Judaizers." The contrast that he paints in Galatians 5 and 6 between the Judaizing preachers and the gospel preachers is very dramatic. The Judaizers preached circumcision, which was apostolic shorthand for preaching self-salvation by obedience to the Law. On account of preaching circumcision, they escaped persecution for the cross of Christ. But Paul preached Christ crucified, that is, salvation through Christ alone, and so he was always being persecuted.

The very same choice lies before us. We are either "Judaizing" preachers or we are gospel preachers. Either we flatter people and tell them what they would like to hear about themselves; we develop what I sometimes like to call a pussycat ministry — we stroke them until they purr with delight — as we flatter them, and as a result of that we escape persecution. Or we tell them the truth, which they don't want to hear, about sin and guilt and judgment and free salvation, and then arouse their hostility. In other words, either we are unfaithful in order to be popular, or we are unpopular in order to be faithful. I doubt very much indeed if it is possible to be faithful and popular at the same time. I think we have to choose.

For our acceptance before God, for our daily discipleship, and for our message for a needy, alienated, and lost world, we like Paul should glory in nothing but the cross. It seems to me that all human beings are born boasters. There seems to be something in our inherited constitution that leads us to boast. We need to glory in something in order to boost our own ego: so we boast about our possessions or our car or our yacht or our salary or our gifts or our church or our preaching ability or whatever it is. In the last resort, there is only one alternative. Either we glory in ourselves and in our own achievement, whatever it may be, or we glory in Christ and his achievement on the cross. There is no possibility of compromise, and the hallmark of authentic Christianity is to glory only in the cross. I pray that God will give us grace to be able to recite and echo Paul's great statement, "God forbid that I should glory in anything except the cross of our Lord Jesus Christ, by which the world has been crucified unto me and I have been crucified unto the world" (Gal. 6:14).

I Will Proclaim the Name

(Exodus 34:6-9)

Michael P. Knowles

1998

How is it possible to preach in our day? We search in vain for cultural examples on which to model our understanding of the task. Thanks to the recent pranks and pratfalls of certain individuals and the steady decline of ecclesiastical influence in our day, the role of the preacher is not currently held in universal esteem. So what other models are there? Who else in our culture proclaims anything resembling good news for us to hear? Television journalists bring news of triumph and tragedy; sports announcers tell us who won or lost; politicians make promises for their spin-doctors to reinterpret; and more prominent than anyone else, advertisers assure us that one more acquisition will make for a fuller life. Not that we ever really believe them. When contemporary culture teaches us to be wary of those who bring "good news," is it any wonder that we have such difficulty coming to grips with the task of preaching in our day? That so many feel so unsure of what they preach, and why?

So it's time to swim upstream again, because our models for this task lie not within the cultures of the modern or postmodern age, but further back in time, rooted in an ancient vision of what it means to be called by God to do something you may or may not want — or feel particularly well equipped — to do. Paul provides one example of such a call, with his bad temper, his tendency to boast, and his awkward admission that he really didn't deserve to be called an apostle because he had persecuted the church of Christ. Not that a shady past kept him from preaching. Before him, there's Peter, who, in effect, tells Jesus to get lost, because he doesn't feel worthy to be in the presence of one so great. And judging by his later conduct, Peter's estimate of his own character turns out to be sadly accurate. Yet neither did that stop *him* from becoming the first and most powerful preacher of the infant church.

Prior to him we can trace a line of reluctant prophets. Jeremiah, for example, stages the equivalent of a sit-down strike so as not to have to carry out the task he has been chosen and born to do. In the end, he can't hold the words in: not even being imprisoned, beaten, and thrown down a well can silence the voice of God within him. At the very head of the line stands Moses, in Jewish tradition the greatest prophet of all. Moses, who answers God's call by saying, more or less, "Here am I, send my brother." An inspiration for every first-time preacher who has stood, trembling and dry-mouthed, before a congregation that desperately hopes the speaker has something to say.

But do you notice what worries Moses most? "Who am I," he stutters, "to confront Pharaoh?" "I'll be with you," says God. Moses' next question is even more revealing: "If I go to your people and they ask me who has sent me; if they want to know what right I have to speak to them about God, what shall I say?" He's really more worried about what the congregation will think. He's terrified that they'll say the kind of thing we all fear: "We know him, he's just the carpenter's son; we remember him from Sunday School; the family used to live just down the street. We know this preacher too well to think that he or she has anything new to say." "Besides," says Moses, "I'm not what you'd call articulate; I trip over my own tongue."

We know what happens next. Moses goes, however reluctantly; and Pharaoh lets the people go, even more reluctantly. We know that. You'd think the story might end there. But miracles alone, however miraculous, can't sustain a congregation in the long run. I speak from experience. Something deeper has to happen. There must be something more for the preacher to say. For Moses, it takes thirty more chapters of the book of Exodus, and several months to find out exactly what. His discovery comes at a point when the people are sullenly disobedient, in theological disarray, and Moses has begun to despair. Nothing like a little congregational revolt to send the pastor to prayer.

As I see them, Exodus 33 and 34 lie at the heart of the life of faith and the task of proclaiming the things of God. Moses sets out in weakness, obeys with deep self-doubt, and after a few months discovers that he really doesn't know how to lead these people. He really doesn't know the One who has called him. Not unlike one or two of my Anglican friends, colleagues in ministry who report — with some embarrassment — that they were ordained first and converted later. So Moses says, "If I have found favor in your sight, show me your ways, that I might know you. Show me your glory" (Exod. 33:13, 18).

I find deep wisdom in the assurance that the task of the preacher and leader of God's people begins not with knowledge of God, but with ignorance; with a kind of provisional and personal *via negativa,* a "not-knowing" that fuels the search to know. There's nothing like preaching week after week to make you discover how much you really don't know, above all how little you know the One of whom you speak. It's a preacher's prayer, a pastor's prayer: "I need to know your ways."

But the beauty of this encounter lies in the Lord's reply: "I will proclaim my Name":

> And the LORD passed before him and proclaimed,
> "The LORD, the LORD, a God compassionate and gracious,
> slow to anger, and abounding in steadfast love and faithfulness,
> keeping steadfast love for thousands, forgiving iniquity
>   and transgression and sin,
> But who will by no means clear the guilty. . . ."

> Then Moses quickly bent his head to the earth, and worshiped, and said, "If I have found favor in your sight, do not abandon us the way we have abandoned you; forgive us and take us for your people." (Exod. 33:19; 34:6-9)

I am convinced that preaching and the proclamation of the gospel are not matters of eloquence, although a little eloquence doesn't hurt. They are not matters of structure and logic, much as I try to convince my students that structure and logic are indispensable. They do not depend in the first instance on deep learning, cultural relevance, or even pastoral sensitivity, much as these are qualities no self-respecting sermon wants to be without. Preaching and proclamation are not even matters of exegesis and interpretation alone, much as a sermon that lacks either of them is no sermon at all. And that is because texts, even the sacred texts of Scripture, are not ends in themselves. As a colleague once told me, not many congregations want to know about translation variants from the Septuagint. Scripture is not an end in itself, to be left dissected on the exegetical examining table. It is a living record of the revelation of God's character, God's nature, in the course of human history — a record and revelation of a character that devolves with grace and power upon the lives of subsequent generations. The first evidence of that fact lies within Scripture itself, as the language of Exodus 34, and the qualities of God's name, are recited again and again throughout the Old Testament, and on into the New.

The great challenge of preaching is to name the Name; to proclaim the character, the identity, the nature of God; to know God's name and God's ways. The preacher's task, in simplest form, is to proclaim the Name. More years ago than I care to remember, I read a short story by science fiction writer Arthur C. Clarke, entitled "The Nine Billion Names of God," in which a group of Buddhist monks, believing that history will come to an end when they have named all the names of God, program a computer to accomplish the task for them. As they look up, the stars begin blinking out, one by one.[1]

In Judeo-Christian tradition, by contrast, the names of God are comparatively few and simple, though profound. And to name them is not the end, but the beginning of history. Because there is nothing more dear to the human spirit than to know the Name and the ways of the One about whom (not necessarily *for* whom), but *about* whom we claim to speak. All the details are there in the book of Exodus, in God's words to his reluctant and stuttering servant, Moses. More than anything else, once they have begun to ask ultimate questions, people want to know whether God's presence will go with them, the way we know God's presence was with Moses and Israel, was evident in Christ, was with the early church. People want to know whether this God will be with them and what this God will be for them. They want to hear in our words the words of the living God, "My presence will go with you,

---

1. Arthur C. Clarke, "The Nine Billion Names of God," *Star Science Fiction Stories #1,* ed. Frederik Pohl (New York: Ballantine, 1953), pp. 188-95; reprint, Arthur C. Clarke, *The Nine Billion Names of God: The Best Short Stories of Arthur C. Clarke* (New York: Harcourt Brace Jovanovich, 1967), pp. 3-11.

and I will give you rest." People of all kinds and convictions long to discover for themselves whether this God, the God of Abraham, Isaac, Jacob, Moses, the prophets, and ultimately Jesus, is indeed "compassionate and gracious, slow to anger, and abounding in steadfast love and faithfulness, forbearing many, forgiving thousands, faulting few." Who would not want to know a God like this? Who would not hasten to take refuge in the assurance that God is "gracious and forgiving, slow to anger"? Who could not find comfort in the knowledge that this God overflows with "steadfast love and faithfulness," in the affirmation that God keeps his promises and is unfailingly consistent and true?

This is how God acts throughout history, in the book of Exodus when God's people have broken the covenant and worshiped foreign gods; in Lamentations as the people depart into Exile; in the Son whom we crucified; in the life of every congregation. God's ways are ways of faithful love and mercy at moments when we are in no position to demand them; not overlooking or ignoring injustice, but making possible a new beginning each morning of each new day. People will come a long way to hear about a God like this, to hear a preacher who will name and proclaim the Name of God, who will answer the question of every seeking and spiritually hungry heart: "O Lord, show me your ways, that I might know you."

Yet the terrible irony is that naming God's Name is not something we are naturally able or inherently likely to do. Because God says, "I will proclaim the Name." Why is this God's prerogative alone? Because it is not for the creature to define the creator; for the clay to say, "I think I'll make me a potter." It's no accident that in Hebrew tradition, the four letters of God's name, *YHWH,* the name God spoke to Moses, are to this day considered too holy to pronounce. God's Name is the only word in Hebrew Scripture that the scribes purposely and consistently leave without any indication of its proper pronunciation, just in case anyone should try to articulate it, to reduce the magnitude of God to a mere word. Because to declare, to define, the name, the nature, the character of God is something only God can do. It is God who says, "*I* will proclaim the Name."

And that, you recall, is the whole point of God's Name in the first place. For when Moses, in great trembling and fear before the burning bush, says, "Tell me your name," God replies, "I am who I am; I will be who I will be" (Exod. 3:14). At least, that's our best guess as to what those four letters of God's Name actually mean. But something else is at work here, just below the surface. In the Ancient Near East, to know someone's name is to apprehend their very essence, and to know the name of your god gives you access to godly power. If you can call on their name, you have them in your power. But this God is different. The name of this God gives nothing away; it is its own guarantee: "I will be who I will be." It's not what Moses wanted, but it's enough, so after one or two failures to forestall the inevitable, off he goes to carry out the purposes of this unconstrainable, uncontrollable God.

One is tempted to conclude that if it is God's prerogative alone to proclaim the Name, then there is nothing more to say, and we can all go home. But just before we pack up our preaching gear, we should pause to recall once more that God's declaration of the Name is the beginning, not the end, of Israel's history. God may refuse to be named, reduced, contained in a box of human making, but to leave the matter there would be to miss the whole point of the encounter. The fact that the preacher is not free to define God does not lead to silence, or to agnosticism. It simply means that we are constrained by God's pronouncement of that Name: by the character of which it speaks, and by the ways and deeds of this God in history that demonstrate its deepest meaning. For while our naming of the Name cannot define God, God's naming of the Name can and does define us. Therefore God's Name is the beginning, not the end, of the preacher's being, and the preacher's task.

Much the same dynamic is at work in the words of the Apostle Paul, who trembles at the task of speaking God's truth before the world. We are the aroma of life to the living, he declares, and the aroma of death to those who have chosen death. "Who is sufficient for these things? Who is adequate for such a task?" (2 Cor. 2:15-16). Not Moses, not Paul, not you or me. Which is as it should be:

> For God chose the foolish things of the world to shame the world; God chose what is weak in the world to shame the strong; God chose what is low and despised in the world . . . to reduce to nothing things that are, so that no one might boast in the presence of God. (1 Cor. 1:27-29)

"We are treated," Paul says, "like scum, the dregs, the lowest of the low" (1 Cor. 4:13). I love Eugene Peterson's rendering: "We're something everyone stands around and stares at, like an accident in the street. We're the

Messiah's misfits." If that is how Paul describes his own ministry, his own call to preach, then others who have heard a similar call should take note. "We are *not* competent," he continues in Second Corinthians, "We are not competent of ourselves to claim *anything* as coming from us; our competence is from God, who has *made* us competent to be ministers of a new covenant; not a covenant that kills or brings death, but a covenant that brings life by the Spirit of God" (2 Cor. 3:5-6). Jesus tells the disciples as much in John 15: "Just as the branch cannot bear fruit by itself unless it remains attached to the vine, neither can you unless you remain in me . . . because apart from me you can do nothing, *nothing*" (John 15:4-5).

So here is the strange dynamic of being called to preach and to proclaim the Word, the deeds, the Name of God. It begins with the realization that this is not something you are competent or able or — some days — even willing to do, and that for at least two reasons. First, because only God can define the divine identity; and second, because there is nothing in us that sets us apart or makes us able anyway.

But these things never end the way we expect them to. It is as if we hear the call to the foot of the holy mountain, and just when we begin to tremble with awe and fear, we hear the voice of Jesus calling, "Come up higher, friend." It is as if we take off our shoes, knowing that we stand on holy ground, only to discover that Jesus wants to wash our feet. It is as if, once we realize that our lives are spiritually wanting and our ministries barren, *then* Jesus begins to bear fruit in us.

So for those who hope to proclaim the Name, it helps to know what you don't know, and what you haven't heard, in order to have ears to hear. It helps to know what you lack, and what you're incapable of, in order for Christ to supply the much that's missing. I am willing to propose that this is the universal pattern of Christian proclamation, of Christian ministry, of Christian pilgrimage as a whole, and the experience of all those who come to know the Name of God. It's there in Moses, in Jeremiah, in Peter, Paul, and the words of the Psalmist:

> I waited patiently for the Lord; He inclined to me and heard
>   my cry.
> He drew me out of the pit of tumult, out of the miry bog,
>   and set my feet upon a rock, making my steps secure.
> He put a new song in my mouth, a song of praise to our God.
>   (Ps. 40:1-3)

This is the song of one who has known his or her need, seen God's ways, knows God's Name, and now has something to proclaim. This is the song of one who has nothing to offer God, not even ears to hear:

> Sacrifice and offering you did *not* desire, but you have dug out
>   my ears for me.
> Burnt offering and sin offering you have *not* required;
> So I said, "Here I am . . . I delight to do your will, for you are
>   my God."
>
> (Ps. 40:6-8)

The movement of this Psalm — this Psalmist — is surely universal: from calling and waiting to hearing to speaking; from need, to encounter, to proclamation; by way of ignorance, incomprehension, and emptiness, to the grace and compassion and fullness of God, even to being given gracious words to proclaim. This is the experience of the first disciples, who abandon their Master only to have their dejection and defeat transformed by the news that God has triumphed anyway. It is the path they travel from their own first calling, through the events of Easter to Pentecost and the proclamation that ensues. It is Jesus' own experience, and the truth that he proclaims: "Whoever wants to hang on to their life will lose it, but whoever loses their life for my sake and the gospel's, will save it" (Matt. 16:25).

Because that's how you get to know the Name. It's not just an unpronounceable mystery, an almost-evasion of identity, "the One who is." Not just a list of attributes and characteristics, however appealing they may sound: mercy, steadfast love, forbearance, forgiveness, justice. No, those who have heard the Name, those whose ears God has opened, know that these are the ways of God toward each and every one of us and all creation. Those who have heard the Name are able to say with John the Evangelist, "We have beheld his glory, full of grace and truth; we have seen him and heard him and some can even say they have touched him" (cf. John 1:14; 1 John 1:1). This is what we testify to and proclaim; that the ways and the Name of God have gotten personal, have grabbed hold of us, and given us something to say.

At least in the pages of Scripture, lots of other people get to have their say, but not once do the Gospels directly report the words of Joseph, Mary's husband. In fact, we know of only one word that Joseph actually spoke. The angel says to him, "Joseph, son of David, do not be afraid to take Mary as your wife. . . . She will bear a son, *and you shall name him Jesus,* for he will save his people from their sins" (Matt. 1:20-21). It was his right to name the child. It is the only word we know he spoke: "Jesus." But what a word. It was enough. He knew the Name. So he spoke, and so must we. That is the preacher's task.

What Are We About?

(Zechariah 2:1-5; 1 Corinthians 3:10-23)

ELIZABETH R. ACHTEMEIER

1999

What is it that we as members of the church of Jesus Christ are called to be? What is it that we are about? In answering those questions, I want to stretch your imagination for just a moment. You are, in the congregation of the Christian church, a little advance colony of heaven. You see, God has a kingdom in heaven, a kingdom of joy and righteousness and peace and goodness which he wants to establish all over this globe. He wants his kingdom to come on earth even as it is in heaven. And you in your congregation are a little advance colony sent by God to live the life of that kingdom in your present time and place. Like Captain John Smith sent by the crown to claim the little town of James — Jamestown — for the rule of the British, you are Christians sent by God to claim your towns and villages and cities for the rule of God. You are God's beachhead on the shores of this present darkness; God's pioneers invading a wilderness of sin with the good news of the gospel. Or in the metaphors of our Scripture readings, you are those sent by God to be the beginnings of the city of God on earth. You are the forerunners of a new Jerusalem, of a new Zion, of a city which has foundations whose builder and maker is God.

Now, the church has always thought of itself in that way, as the beginning of the new Jerusalem on Zion's hill. And so we sing it in the familiar hymn, "O Zion, Haste, Thy Mission High Fulfilling,"[1] and we take that as a command to the church. As God's new Zion we do indeed have a mission. You and I have been redeemed from our slavery to sin and death by the cross and resurrection of Christ. We have been set free to live the life of his kingdom. We have been given God's Spirit to guide and to empower us in living out that life. But that is not an end in itself. We have a mission, a mission not only to be the beginning of God's new Jerusalem, but to build it up, to expand its city limits, to push it out into the countryside, and to claim all those around us for the rule of God.

That brings us to our Old Testament text for the day. For in that vision of the prophet Zechariah, we have a picture that could be a symbol of you or me. The year is 519 BC. The Israelites have returned from Babylonian exile, but the capital city of Jerusalem is in ruins and so it is going to be rebuilt. In this vision, the third one of Zechariah, a young man sets out to plan the new Jerusalem. He takes his tape measure to mark out the dimensions of the new city of God in order to erect its walls. Do you know what he does? He plans the new Jerusalem by measuring the dimensions of the old. He takes his little yard stick and laboriously measures the outlines of the walls of that old city in Palestine founded by the Canaanites and Kings David and Solomon.

He is a good deal like us in that lack of imagination, isn't he? Heaven knows your denomination has been a force for good in this country but there is always the temptation in such a situation to sit back and rest on our laurels. We grow tired of mission, you see, and so after a while we just want to be content the way we are. What were our church membership figures last year, we ask. Well, let's just try to keep them up to that and not show a decline in numbers. After all, many denominations are slipping in membership, so let's just keep it that way and not worry about bringing in other kinds of people. After all, they probably wouldn't feel comfortable in our fellowship anyway. Build up the new Jerusalem, yes! Build up the church of Christ! But build it only according to the measurements of the old Jerusalem we have always known.

Now such an attitude is, according to our texts, not sufficient for God. For in Zechariah's vision, an angel is sent after that young man

---

1. "O Zion, Haste, Thy Mission High Fulfilling" (1868, rev. 1871), by Mary Ann Faulkner Thomson (1834-1923).

with the tape measure and the angel tells him, "Jerusalem shall be inhabited as villages without walls because of the multitude in it" (Zech. 2:4). In other words, the church is to have no human limits on it, no membership rolls with which we are ever satisfied, no walls of class or custom or race that shut out anyone from our fellowship, no dimensions of self-satisfaction that make us content as we are. There are hundreds of people out there, people whom your congregations know, with whom they work every day, or whom they entertain, or who live not a mile from your church, who desperately need to hear the good news of Christ. And they will come if your people will speak to them of their faith, and befriend them with the love of Christ, and invite them to come into your congregation.

Indeed, friends, God has a vision according to our prophet, a vision of the whole earth turned into the city of God. A vision of multitudes from every people and tongue streaming into the new Jerusalem of the church because your congregation and others like it have gone forth with their money and missionaries and message and obeyed their Lord's command to make disciples of all nations. No human limits on the church of Christ. No walls for the new Jerusalem. That is the first guideline from our text as you seek to be God's new Zion of the Christian church.

But let's be very clear about it. The church, the new Jerusalem, does have dimensions that set it off from its surroundings. It's not like every other community in the world, indistinguishable from Toronto or New York or Paris. No, it has a measure and a cornerstone whose name is Jesus Christ. It is built upon his words and deeds as its only foundation. He is the rock upon whom the whole structure depends and if you remove him from the church's foundation, the whole community will crack and crumble and come crashing down. Too often the church in our time has sought to be like the society around it. We want to be relevant, we say. Or we want to be able to communicate with modern men and women. And so we have sometimes abandoned our sure foundation for the shifting sands of popular opinion, following the latest in marriage and morals, in lifestyle and belief, in what we trust and what we want, until the church has become indistinguishable from any other social or service club and the city set on a hill that we are supposed to be has moved down into the valley of death and can no longer be found by anyone searching through the darkness.

But our New Testament lesson puts it very clearly. "No other foundation can anyone lay other than that which is laid which is Jesus Christ" (1 Cor. 3:11). Therefore, Paul says, let each citizen of the city of God, of the church, take care how he or she builds on that foundation, for each person's work will become manifest, and the fire will test what sort of work each has done. The church, the city of God, has dimensions and a foundation upon whom alone it must depend: Christ the measure of all we do and say. Christ the rock upon whom we build and expand. Christ the cornerstone of every action and belief. For unless our leadership of the church is grounded in our personal and heartfelt trust in him, unless his commandments and compassion become our guide in every decision that we make, we will have forfeited our citizenship in the city of God, and our Lord will tell us, "I never knew you." The new Jerusalem, the church, has dimensions because God its ruler sets the limits of them. Not everyone who says to him, "Lord, Lord," can enter into its life. Christ the cornerstone and the only sure foundation. Christ the measure of all we do and say. That is the second guiding biblical word from our text for our life as the church.

Now we should further note from our Old Testament text that the church, the beginning of the city of God, has no earthly defenses. Certainly the name of the game in our time is power, as it has always been. It is the most powerful military nation that need not worry about its enemies. It is the powerful multinational corporation that can run its competitors out of business. It is the powerful political bloc that can put down the opposition to its programs. So we in the church are always tempted to want to have such power through the use of lobbyists in the halls of government, and propaganda in the media, and massive spending campaigns. We would like to make things go our way. Heaven knows, the church has lots of enemies; it always has. It struggled to life in the catacombs of Rome and it has always been in that position. Defending itself against the Nazis, the Ku Klux Klan, the Marxists, and lately even against the tax agencies, the Muslims, and the Moonies.

Indeed, the church has always had to fight off a fifth column in its own midst, those who want to dilute its doctrine, and turn its liturgy into a celebration of merely human life, and make its ethic identical with that of any decent humanitarian. Yes, from Hitler to the modern atheist philosopher the church has always had its enemies and we in the church would like to have enough power just to squelch their voices.

Indeed, even on a personal level we would like to have that power. What one of us would not like to have the authority and prestige that would put down anyone who disagrees with us? But according to our Old Testament lesson, the new Jerusalem of the church has only one source of power and only one source for her own defense. "'For I will be to her a wall of fire round about,' says the Lord" (Zech. 2:5). God is our power and defense in every circumstance and it is he who will preserve his church. In the words of the hymn:

> On the rock of ages founded,
> What can shake thy sure repose?
> With salvation's walls surrounded
> Thou may'st smile at all thy foes.[2]

We may smile at all our foes, for the church of Christ has been attacked and buffeted and battered in every generation. Diocletian and Hitler and Mao Tse-Tung tried to wipe it out and could not do so. The church has been "afflicted in every way, but not crushed; perplexed, but not driven to despair; persecuted, but not forsaken; struck down, but not destroyed" (2 Cor. 4:8-9). It never will be banished from the face of this globe until its knowledge of its risen Lord covers the earth like the waters cover the sea. For God is our ruler and Christ is our rock and the very gates of hell shall not prevail against this little colony of heaven.

So when you become discouraged in your congregation, good Christians, and when you pastors and future pastors face those low moments in your ministry that every one of us knows; when all of you think that your love and work and thought are producing no results whatsoever; when all of the voices of secularism seem to drown out the herald of Zion that you are; when the enemies of Christ appear more numerous than his disciples and friends; when you are tempted to give up the struggle that is the Christian way of life and just to capitulate to the ways of the world around you, then remember God is your wall of fire round about you and his power to preserve cannot be defeated.

Finally, our Old Testament text says one more thing about the new Jerusalem, the church. "I will be the glory within her," God promises. Glory. How tempted we are to try to seek it for ourselves. If power is the

---

2. "Glorious Things of Thee Are Spoken" (1779), by John Newton (1725-1807).

name of the game in our time then surely glory is its nickname. And we all know how the rules of the game are played, don't we? Why don't you come and join our congregation? You can't find a prettier church building in town. Our choir is first rate. Or our youth group is great. We have a lot of fun together. Or even, God forgive us, our church is the leading church in this community and that's where you can meet the right kind of people. Thus we try to make ourselves glorious and to attract persons to our membership on that basis. Like those in that ancient story of the tower of Babel in Genesis, we want to make a name for ourselves. We ministers are certainly not immune from that attempt. Our teaching, our personal manner in the sick room, our list of advanced degrees, our skill and eloquence in the pulpit — sometimes we think that these are all we need to build up the new Jerusalem of the church.

But the Christian church, the new Zion of God, has only one source of glory and that is the presence of her risen Lord in her midst. "Lo, I am with you always," he promised (Matt. 28:20). Consider who he is: the Son of God with the grace and mercy and love of the Father made incarnate in his flesh; the crucified one who bore the nails and the scorn and the crown of thorns to forgive us every evil thing that we have ever done; the risen, triumphant Lord of life whom death itself could not defeat; the King of kings whom no power of this world could conquer, whose church now circles the globe and whose cross is raised above even the most humble hamlet. *There* is the glory of God, friends, the glory of God shining in the face of Jesus Christ, and his is the only light that can never be extinguished.

People will never come into the new Jerusalem of the church if all we hold up before them is our architecture or our fellowship or our worldly power. No, the Zion of God, the church, will be built up only as men and women can say, as Zechariah later puts it, "Let us go with you, for we have heard that God is with you" (Zech. 8:23). God in Jesus Christ in our midst: our glory, our gospel, our good news. Let us tell that to our neighbors and towns and cities. Let us proclaim Christ throughout the earth. Let us make him the focus of all our activities as Christians. Christ the One for all the world. Christ our cornerstone and foundation. Christ our defense. Christ our glory. With that message build up the church. Amen.

A Divine-Human Dance

(Exodus 3:1-12)

Donna E. Allen

2000

In the book of Exodus, the third chapter, the first twelve verses, we find these words as recorded in the NRSV:

> Moses was keeping the flock of his father-in-law Jethro, the priest of Midian; he led his flock beyond the wilderness, and came to Horeb, the mountain of God. There the angel of the LORD appeared to him in a flame of fire out of a bush; he looked, and the bush was blazing, yet it was not consumed. Then Moses said, "I must turn aside and look at this great sight, and see why the bush is not burned up." When the LORD saw that he had turned aside to see, God called to him out of the bush, "Moses, Moses!" And he said, "Here I am." Then he said, "Come no closer! Remove the sandals from your feet, for the place on which you are standing is holy ground." He said further, "I am the God of your father, the God of Abraham, the God of Isaac, and the God of Jacob." And Moses hid his face, for he was afraid to look at God. Then the LORD said, "I have ob-

Previously published online in the *McMaster Journal of Theology and Ministry;* http://www.mcmaster.ca/mjtm/.

served the misery of my people who are in Egypt; I have heard their cry on account of their taskmasters. Indeed, I know their sufferings, and I have come down to deliver them from the Egyptians, and to bring them up out of that land to a good and broad land, a land flowing with milk and honey, to the country of the Canaanites, the Hittites, the Amorites, the Perizzites, the Hivites, and the Jebusites. The cry of the Israelites has now come to me; I have also seen how the Egyptians oppress them. So come, I will send you to Pharaoh to bring my people, the Israelites, out of Egypt." But Moses said to God, "Who am I that I should go to Pharaoh, and bring the Israelites out of Egypt?" He said, "I will be with you; and this shall be the sign for you that it is I who sent you: when you have brought the people out of Egypt, you shall worship God on this mountain."

A divine-human dance. When we consider this theophany, this story, this event, this appearance of God, we are gripped by the extraordinary. Oh come on, there is nothing ordinary about this story. Nothing ordinary! God is present. God is visible in a bush that does not burn. God is present. God is heard through a voice. A voice in conversation with Moses. God is present in this story event. This is an extraordinary story.

The community that gave birth to these words captures for us an experience of a rather intimate God: God coming to creation in images that make us smile. As we try to imagine a burning bush that is not consumed, our attention is tuned in to the extraordinary. And rightly so, for there is nothing ordinary about an appearance of God. In fact, in the story, when we the readers are impressed with the presence of God, everything changes. Holy ground suddenly emerges on a mountainside. Shoes that were good for walking must be shed to worship. A neck once stretched to see the flame now bows to honor the phenomenon. Transformation! A rickety staff becomes a source of strength. Moses' stagnant speech from a stuttering tongue becomes an eloquent arrow for liberation. Nothing stays the same in the presence of God. Everything changes. Transformation!

Helpfully, the authors of the story raise a question for us. In between each line, I hear resonating the question, "Who is this God?" Who is this God? Who is this God that burst onto the scenes of human story in the form of a burning bush? Who is this God? Who is this God that speaks out of nothing, a voice that commands Moses into conversation? Who is this God that declares that we shed sandals because simple sand has become holy ground? Who is this God? It is a God who sends people on road trips without compass, or map, or destination, like Abraham. This God is a God who touches a barren woman's womb and gives birth to babies for her who would have none, like Sarah. This God is a God who puts a fortress around a fugitive like Jacob. This God is a God who keeps a dreamer's dreams alive, like Joseph. This God is a faithful God. A God of intimate action. A God of human history.

I am intrigued that Moses would first of all have the audacity to move in the direction of a bush. A bush that was on fire. Right away, immediately, I admire Moses. I would not have gone that way, but I admire Moses. The notion that God speaks to Moses and Moses engages in conversation with God speaks to the intimate image of God the writers give us. An intimate God. An accessible God. Intriguing. The reality that God declares who God is through history. Through *human* history. I am the God of Abraham, of Sarah, of Joseph, and the list goes on. That is God's nametag. The story is intriguing. The intrigue increases, for this God engages Moses in conversation with the revealing declaration, "I have seen the oppression of my people, I have heard their cries, and I have known their suffering." God declares, I have seen their affliction. I have heard their cries. I know their suffering. If we are not careful, we will miss the good news of the text. The good news! Now, as my cousin would say, it gets *good-er.* That's the first good news in the text. That God has seen the affliction of God's people. God has heard the cries. God knows the suffering people. To the oppressed, this is good news!

My ancestors cry out in the Negro spiritual, "Nobody knows the trouble I've seen, Nobody knows my sorrow. Nobody but Jesus!" Oh, that is good news. If you are pressed to the margins of society, if you can imagine in the midst of despair, that you serve a God who sees affliction, who hears cries, and who knows suffering, that is good news. The good news of the story reminds us that something is about to happen. In the presence of God, change is bound to occur. Oh, that is the good news of the witness of the text. God sees affliction, hears cries, and knows suffering. Look! Listen! *Know* God's response. The God of Exodus declares that human liberation involves human responsibility, human obligation, human vocation. "So, Moses, I have heard, I have seen, I have known. Now you go." Hey, I figure that's what Moses deserves for walking up to the burning bush in the first place. Go, Moses, you go!

The divine-human dance. Truly the divine-human dance that we are repeatedly invited to join. God hears, sees, and knows suffering. God's response is to beckon a dance partner. "Moses, oh Moses, I have heard, I have seen, I know. I want you to go." Now hope is floating in the air. Perhaps only gentle glimpses of hope. Like a breeze in the summertime, just enough to bend a blade of grass, to shake a leaf on a tree. Hope is in the air. Moses cries out, "Who am I? Who am I that I should go to your people? Who am I that I should tell Pharaoh to let them go?" This too is our response to the divine invitation: "Who am I?" "Who am I that I should respond to God?" Get ready for some more good news, because God will respond to our cry! God declares nothing about Moses and everything about God. God says to Moses, "I will go with you." Let us dance! Can you not hear, echoing through history, God calling us, to be God's partners in a divine-human dance? And we, like Moses, have the audacity to say, "Who am I? Who am I? I am a single mother. I have scarcely raised my own children, just got my high school diploma, trying to get to college, thinking about seminary. Who am I? I am a dad. I have always worked with my hands. If you look at my nails, they are short and forever tinted from the hard labor I have done. Feel the calluses. I am no theologian. Who am I? I barely earn enough to keep food on my table, and coming to school is a stretch of my imagination. So every time I show up I must be dreaming. Who am I? That I should plunge in the snow and think I can overcome ice. Who am I?"

Who are you? God's response to us is, "I will go with you." It is as if God says to us, "I know who you are. I am glad about it. But the point is not who you are but who is with you. I will go with you." The divine-human dance. God makes it clear that God leads and we follow. God directs and we move with God. The dance is worth dancing because the partner is worth dancing with. Ministry calls us into a divine-human dance that began long before we dared to become Reverend, Deacon, Elder. Ministry, ministry and the work, work, work of the people of God is a divine-human interaction. We have been invited to dance with God. We are privileged. The divine-human dance has been moving before we were born and it rolls on through us. We feel the weight of the witness of history nudging us along. We are not the first ones to struggle with a sermon on Saturday night, to go to bed hoping and praying that something will happen while we sleep. We are not the first ones to make it to the church, knowing the manuscript is lacking every principle of preaching we have ever been taught. We are not the first ones to dare to preach, knowing the words we have make little sense to us, let alone when they fall out of our mouths to our people. We are not the first ones to break open the word of God, to read the words and try to make sense of the notion that we should turn the other cheek, go the second mile of the way, give away our coat. Oh, we are not first to be seduced to this miracle called ministry. In the divine-human dance we serve a God of liberation who involves human hands, human hearts, in a divine-human dance.

God says to us, do you want to dance? Do you want to dance? Do you want to dance? Dancing with God is a compelling image because it suggests a certain order to the movement. If you have ever danced, you know, depending on your partner, you really don't know exactly what you will do until you are doing it. You really don't know when you're going to end, and you don't know where you're going to be on the floor when this particular dance is over. All you know is that you have agreed to do this thing together. You give yourself away to the moment. In the space of uncertainty there is a spontaneity. There is creativity. And when you are clear that you are willing to dance with God, it is miraculously true that the first step to dance with God is one where you repeatedly lose your balance. You repeatedly give yourself over to God's beckoning. You repeatedly surrender to God's nudge, God's push. You repeatedly fall into God's hands, willing for God to guide you in dance. The divine-human dance. The dance wherein we surrender to God's will. Amazed, inspired by a God who hears, sees, and knows.

So why would anybody want to dance with God? If the dance means you'll be engaging in work, why would anyone want to dance with God? If the dance means you'll be laboring for God. Well, you'll want to dance with God, because in that dance your relationship with God reflects a knowing that you cannot have without God. You don't know yourself until you've given yourself to God, and allowed God to guide your life. You don't know the extent of your ministry until you've released your grip on it, and allowed God to shape you. You don't know the celebration in your sermon until you've let it fly on the wings of the moment of worship. You don't know. It's true; it does not yet appear what we shall be, but if we would start to dance with God, glimpses of God's presence, God's reign will break out all around us. It's true. Eyes have not seen and ears have not heard. It has not entered into the hearts of men and women what great things God would do if we would surrender to dancing with God, let ourselves go to God's lead, God's direction. Moses' question, "Who am I, that I should go?" brings God's affirming response, "I will go with you." We do not go into our ministry alone. We do not venture into service by ourselves. But we go with a God who goes with us, with us. With us to the pulpit, with us to the nursing home, with us to the hospital, with us to the home of the bereaved. God goes with us. With us when we dare to dance with the homeless, dance with the hungry, dance with the hurting. God goes with us when we find ourselves among the least of them. God is there with us. You shall miss a step or two, and you shall fall out of rhythm and sync with God and you shall lose your rhythm and timing. You shall not be able to keep up, but rest assured. In this divine-human dance God is with you, dancing with you, and you are not alone. So God says to us today, "Do you want to dance?"

Divine-human dance as an image of our ministry also compels us to consider that we are not puppets. We have not lost our will. We have not lost our ability to create and do in ministry. No, we are engaged in ministry with God. In fact, more often than not when we become puppets, it is because we have surrendered our will to the institution we honor. We have surrendered our will to rules and regulations that we choose to worship. We surrender our will to laws and things that bind us. We create bondage where God moves with creative liberation. We throw up barriers and restrictions where God casts them aside and makes a path for dancing. We put down who shall and who shall not. Who's good enough and who's not good enough. Who can come and who cannot. Where God just beckons all who will dance, "Let's dance." We bring limitations where God gives an invitation for inclusion. But maybe you don't know the limitations that some of us encounter. Some of them are captured in those "-isms." We bring the limitation of sexism, we bring the limitation of racism, we bring the limitation of classism, we bring the limitation of heterosexism. We set up boundaries where God pushes them away and invites all who will come to come and dance with God. Divine-human dance is a place for possibility, endless opportunity, an in-breaking of God's interaction in human history.

So the God of Exodus is a God who understands human liberation, involves human responsibility, human obligation, human vocation. God is our leading partner. We rest not on the notion that the church is a source of salvation in the world. We rest not on the suggestion that preaching is the means of salvation. We rest not on any human effort as the definitive source of liberation. No. But we understand, at least from Exodus, that God calls humanity to serve humanity, to set humanity free. It's really very peculiar. The people are oppressed by other people, and God calls one of the people to set the people free. It's nothing we would elect to do on our own and nothing we could achieve. But that's how God works. Let us just face it. It really is the good news, but you might not be excited about it — what God does, God often does through us. That's right. Doesn't look good. Never has. History was confounded by a young Jewish boy, the least of them, a carpenter's son, born to a young woman, growing up on the margins of society, born in a manger, running around talking crazy about the reign of God. We never like God's partners. I'm glad it doesn't matter, because God keeps dancing anyhow. It's strange, it's awkward, but that's what God does. God uses us to set us free. God uses us to liberate us.

God calls us to set us free. So it is a divine-human dance. It is God who calls us to dance. It is God who calls you to dance. We are clear that we are following God, but we'd best also be clear that God calls us to get involved. So we want things to be different in our churches. We want things to be different in our institutions. We want things to be different in our community, in our neighborhood, in our world. Well, I want to know, do you hear the music of liberation? For if you do, you'd best believe God your partner is beckoning you to dance. You want things to be different in the community; do you hear the music of liberation? God your partner is calling you to dance. You want the world to be a better place to live, better for your children and your grandchildren. Well, don't you hear liberation music? God is calling you to dance. You want the church to be changed, transformed — don't you hear liberation music? God is calling you to dance. The good news is that we serve a God who sees, hears, and knows. A God who calls us to set us free. Peculiar, but just like God. Not very popular, but just like God. Strange, but just like God. Miraculous, miraculous, and just like

God. If we can imagine a better world, it's because we hear the music of liberation. If there shall be a better world, it's because we choose to dance with God. God is calling us into partnership, calling us into ministry, calling us. The God of Exodus declares, "I have seen, I have heard, and I have known, and I send you." Who are you? It doesn't matter. I am going with you. A divine-human dance. A divine-human dance. So God calls us today. Do you want to dance?

Why Bother?

(Acts 17:16-31)

CLEOPHUS J. LARUE

2001

Splattered across the front doors of a trendy restaurant in Palo Alto, California, were these words: "This is a bad place for a diet!" That most visible, in-your-face sign said to me that there are certain places where some requests are out of order. That there are certain times when some pleas are in poor taste. No matter how noble, how life-giving, how worthy they are in and of themselves, there are simply certain times and certain places where some pleas are unseemly. And in like manner, we could splatter across the pages of our text today, a similar warning: "This is a bad place for the gospel!"

For whether one considers Acts to be a bona fide historiography or simply a piece of well-crafted Hellenistic literature, the gospel in Athens comes off sounding like a bunch of misplaced hooey. Athens, after all, has seen and heard it all! This great, proud city was still considered the cultural and intellectual capital of the Roman Empire. It was a city steeped in art, literature, and history. Athens had its names and its heroes and it was not easily impressed with the "here," with the "new," or with the "now." It was, after all, the place where Socrates, Aristotle,

Previously published online in the *McMaster Journal of Theology and Ministry;* http://www.mcmaster.ca/mjtm/.

and Plato had lived and talked, and still counted among its sacred places was the Academy of Plato, the Lyceum of Aristotle, the Porch of Zeno the Stoic, and the Garden of Epicurus. Athens. The voices of her poets had been heard throughout the civilized world, and the hands of her artists had filled her streets and temples with images of the gods. It was then that while strolling the streets of Athens you were more likely to meet a god than you were a man or a woman. Her myriad buildings and works of art stood in silent testimony to her former grandeur and greatness.

Even though Luke goes to great lengths to create this scene where Paul is standing face to face with the philosophers on their own turf and in their own town, the gospel still seems out of place in Athens. The gospel still seems to be out of its league in Athens. Athens still seems to be a bad place for the gospel of Jesus Christ! Athens. Athens seems all the more a bad place when you consider how Paul got there in the first place. Athens was a temporary stopover. Paul did not arrive in Athens by way of some grand missionary plan. He arrived there through happenstance and rerouting born of necessity, because the work God had called him to do had not gone well in other places. Because the work that God called Paul to do had not gone as Paul had prayed or planned. He did not arrive in Athens on a set schedule. He arrived in Athens on a wing and a prayer, trying to redo what unforeseeable circumstance had brought. So he did not arrive in Athens fresh and friendly. He arrived there disheveled, unkempt, bedraggled, woebegone, battle-scarred, and road-weary. Because he's already in a bad mood, immediately upon his arrival in the city, he does not see a city filled with beautiful works of art. He's already in a bad mood. He sees a city full of idols! Yes, he probably could have been in a better mood and yes, he probably would have been better received had he expressed some initial aesthetic appreciation for the works of art he found in the home of Hellenism's literati and intelligentsia. But when you've been stoned in Lystra, jailed in Philippi, threatened in Thessalonika, and run out of Berea, it's understandable that you might not be in a sightseeing mood when your friends finally drop you on the outskirts of Athens.

Let me say here parenthetically, to the preachers, that sometimes we do our best work under life's most austere and trying circumstances. Sometimes we do our best preaching when life is hard and the load is heavy. Sometimes we do our best work when life finds us in a place we would prefer not to be and a place where we hope not to stay long. So when life finds you there, do like the apostle Paul: do not bemoan your plight, but go forward with the work God has called you to do. Lift up your head and lift up your heart and go forward with the work God has called you to do!

Well, back to Athens. He does not arrive in Athens by way of some grand plan, but through happenstance. And even though he arrives there under this tension and uncertainty and adversity, he continues to press the case of Jesus Christ. But Paul's arguing and preaching — and Conzelmann says these are one and the same — his arguing and preaching are not well received in Athens. When the people of Athens first heard Paul speak, they said with some derision and not a little contempt: "What does this babbler have to say? What does this seed picker, what does this one who gets just enough of an idea to talk about it in a superficial manner, what does he have to say?" Before the Athenian elitist, Paul (some would say our first theologian, I don't know); before the Athenian elitist, Paul, God's international gospel globetrotter; Paul, the greatest preacher this side of Jesus Christ; before the Athenian elitist, he comes off sounding like an outgunned pipsqueak. Taking on a fight, he must surely know that he cannot win. Look at him, he is in hoity-toity Athens. He did not intend to be there, he is not well received there, he is not in a good mood there, and his preaching is just so-so . . . I know that feeling!

Paul is invited to appear before the Areopagus Court, and I do believe it was an invitation and not an arrest. It would be easier to preach as an arrest: I could get more "Amens" out of an arrest, but I believe it was an invitation. You know that Christians like to be in jail! They put one of my students in jail many years ago for misusing credit cards and when I went to see him, he said, "Rev. LaRue, I know how Paul felt." I said, "I don't think so." So even when he is invited to appear before the Areopagus Court, his sermon/speech does not go over very well. For when he is done preaching, there are no mass conversions, there are no triumphalist claims to undisputed victory. Luke, who records this sermon, said of Paul's preaching when he was through — a very strange word. He did not use an all-inclusive term like "great," or "many," or "all." When Paul was done preaching before the Areopagus Court, Luke said of his preaching, the word he used was "some." "Some." When he was done preaching, Luke said "*some* scoffed, others said, 'We will hear you again,' and *some* believed." Wow! May I say it again: in Athens where he did not intend to be, where he is not well received, where he is not in a good mood, the preaching is so-so even by account of some of his friends. The question almost jumps out at you, "Why bother, why bother?" Paul, why put yourself through this? Why try to preach the gospel of Jesus Christ to these people? This is a bad place for the gospel. These people are not interested in the gospel. Why? Why don't you leave these highfalutin Athenians alone and go on to Corinth, where you just might be appreciated? Go on to Corinth where you just might win some friends and influence some people. Why bother? And then when you consider that the critical scholars say this whole scene is a literary construction created by Luke simply for the purpose of telling a story and making a point, okay, what's the point? It's not the obvious point, because the obvious point is that there are some people and some places where you are wasting your time trying to tell them the good news of what God has done for us and for our salvation. There are some people and some places where you are simply spinning your wheels trying to get them to see life as it is to be lived from God's perspective. So what is the point?

Well, maybe there is a not-so-obvious point and maybe in this not-so-obvious point there is good news. For running like a thread throughout the whole Luke/Acts schema is this notion of the universality of the gospel. There is this universal theme running throughout Luke/Acts. This universal offer of salvation was first begun by the Messiah, who preached good news to the poor and to the downcast and the downtrodden, and this universal offer was picked up by his prophetic successors. The conversion of the Gentiles throughout Luke/Acts is the clearest expression of Luke's conviction that all people will be saved through the grace of God. So in Acts you have good news being preached to poor widows and proconsuls, to jailors and to sailors, to merchants and to military officers. Yes, to kings and to philosophers. This gospel is to be proclaimed to all, even when it is only received by "some." There is a universal appeal to this gospel. It is for all! I sometimes worry that those who consider themselves most faithful in our day seem to me to be the least sure about the universal appeal of the gospel. I sometimes worry that those who proclaim themselves to be the true inheritors of the Christian faith seem the most determined to turn this faith to a truncated, privatized religious hope, palatable only to a feeble few. This gospel is for the whole. This is a universal gospel. Now, that's easy to say when you are ministering in the midst of a Jerusalem Pentecost experience. That's where most of the young seminarians think they are going when they graduate.

But the challenge is to be able to say it when ministry finds you in a disinterested Athens. For if you cannot say it in a disinterested Athens, then what you are really saying is that you don't trust God to be at work in tough situations. What you're really saying is that the power is in you and not in God. What you're really saying when you cannot preach this message to a disinterested Athens is that you don't trust God to be at work to effect God's redemptive purposes in the lives of men and women, boys and girls, no matter who they are or where they may be. It is our responsibility to preach this good news in all places to all people. To preach the good news of the coming reign of God. To preach the good news that God can change and transform lives even in this twenty-first century. To preach the good news that this is God's world, and even when all evidence is to the contrary that one day this world shall conform to God's will and God's way. It is our responsibility to tell that story, for in that story is the bread of life. Speak the good news of what God has done for us and for our salvation in the person and work of Jesus Christ. Tell that story. I say to the seminarians, don't try to be so deep and profound, just get the story straight! There's power in the story. Just tell it! That he was born in Bethlehem, brought up in Nazareth, baptized in the Jordan, tempted in the wilderness, preached in Galilee, arrested in Gethsemane, tried in Caesar's court, died on Calvary's cross, and rose from Joseph of Arimathea's brand-new tomb. Just tell the story! Tell it when you're up and tell it when you're down. Tell it when all is well and tell it when all is hell! Tell it when it is widely received and tell it when it is nowhere believed! Tell the story! There's power in the telling of the story! Tell it until sinners are justified, tell it until hell is terrified, tell it until Jesus is magnified, tell it till God is satisfied! Amen.

And He Has . . .

(1 Corinthians 1:1-17)

STEPHEN C. FARRIS

2002

First Christian Church in Corinth was a church in trouble. It was a church divided against itself. The Christians there fought; they fought about everything you could possibly imagine.

They fought, for example, about favorite ministers. Some lined up behind Paul, who had founded their church. Others preferred Cephas — that's Peter in Aramaic, by the way. Peter, after all, had been the Lord Jesus' closest companion.

Others stood for Apollos; he was famous for his pulpit eloquence — you would definitely invite him to preach on anniversary Sunday.

Others, a truly spiritual group, claimed proudly, "I belong to Christ!"

Now there is nothing seriously wrong with admiring ministers and there is something positively right about declaring allegiance to Christ, but in a situation of church conflict, being right is never good enough if there is no love — but that would be another sermon and Paul won't get around to that point until chapter 13.

But as I say, the Corinthians fought about everything. They fought

Previously published online in the *McMaster Journal of Theology and Ministry*; http://www.mcmaster.ca/mjtm/.

about basic Christian doctrine, whether the resurrection had already happened. They fought about the gifts of the Holy Spirit: Was speaking in tongues allowed in church and were people who spoke in tongues spiritually superior to other Christians?

And when they weren't fighting about the resurrection or about speaking in tongues, they were sleeping around. Paul says a little later that some of their sexual behavior was so appalling that it even shocked the notoriously lax pagans of Corinth. Christians getting involved in sexual scandals? Have we heard headlines about that kind of thing in recent years?

And when they weren't sleeping with one another, they were suing one another.

They even managed to get drunk at the Lord's Table.

I ask you, when was the last time you saw somebody get drunk at the Lord's Table in one of our churches? Even if we use wine instead of grape juice, your elbow would give out with all those little cups . . .

Here's the worst thing I've heard about a Lord's Supper in our day. A young man went to be the associate minister of a fair-sized church. It turned out that one of his first duties was to prepare the elements for communion. On Saturday evening in the church kitchen, he cut up the bread into little pieces, put them on a tray, and stuck the tray in the fridge. Then he looked about for the grape juice but couldn't find any. Eventually he did find a bag with purple crystals that tasted like grape. He mixed the crystals with water until the mixture tasted about right, poured the juice into the little cups and put it all into the refrigerator. The next day was communion; the minister lifted the bread and said "This is my body." Then he lifted up the cup, saying, "This cup is the new covenant in my blood. . . ."

And the congregation raised their little cups to find . . . Jello!

That's the worst I've heard in a contemporary church, but in Corinth they got drunk.

Indeed, I know of no contemporary church with as many troubles as the church in Corinth. In any remotely similar situation, our church authorities would move in like a flash, removing the minister, firing the deacons, perhaps closing the place down and starting over. They were a bad lot, the Corinthians: drunks and sex fiends and argumentative troublemakers.

Paul ought to let them have it.

But instead, Paul thanks God for the church in Corinth. "I give thanks to my God always for you." For you Corinthians, for the drunks and sex fiends and argumentative troublemakers, Paul gives thanks to God!

Paul does not see them just as drunks and sex fiends and argumentative troublemakers. He calls them "saints." Our English translations are a bit misleading at this point. We read "To the church of God at Corinth . . . called to be saints" (NRSV), as if they ought to be saints but, of course, they really aren't, at least not yet. But there is no form of the verb "to be" in the original Greek. They are simply the "called saints" . . . *already*. The call has already taken place; they "are sanctified," he says, made holy, made saints, *already*. Perhaps only a person of the spiritual insight of Paul could perceive it, but that is what they were: saints.

Now, Paul does not use the word "saint" the way we commonly use it. To us a "saint" is a spiritual superstar, the religious version of Michael Jordan or Mark McGwire. You get to be a saint by hitting seventy spiritual homers in a season. Mother Teresa might be an example. A person becomes a saint, we think, because of his or her own spiritual achievements. It is human effort that counts.

There is an old story about a young boy taken for the first time to a Gothic cathedral. He looked up at the stained-glass windows, the morning sun blazing through their magnificence, and asked, "Who are those people?" Told they were "saints," he replied, "Ahh, I see. Saints are people the light shines through!"

Yes! *"Through,"* not *"from."* Not their light but God's. And I suppose that if the light is the light of a gospel about a God who loves and forgives even sinners, maybe the light can shine even through the Corinthians, because they sure are sinners.

The Corinthians aren't saints because of their own efforts and achievements. Spiritually speaking, they aren't superstars; they're scrubs. Humanly speaking, they're still drunks and sex fiends and argumentative troublemakers.

But they have been called — by God.

They have been sanctified — by God.

Paul says, "in every way, you have been enriched . . . by God." He says, "I give thanks to my God always for you because of the grace of God that has been given you in Christ Jesus."

They are saints, not because of their own efforts but because God has chosen them, has reached out and called them and made them his own. And who was Paul to disagree with God?

Dear friends, troubled churches are not just a first-century phenomenon. I say, "There are a lot of troubled churches out there," and you reply, "Tell me about it!"

I'm going to make an assumption about you as a congregation. I imagine that a few of you are seekers, but I also imagine that the vast majority are regular, faithful, committed churchgoers.

You know about the Mount Cashels and the Jimmy Swaggarts and the Bakkers.

You know about the fights over inclusive language and feminine imagery for God and homosexuality.

Above all you know about the small-time pettiness that infects so many of our congregations. You know that we Christians don't just fight over the big issues of life; we fight about the color of the new carpet.

You know about the troubles because you know about the church. A critic of the Christian church (and there are many) would, without looking very hard, still be able to find drunks and sex fiends and argumentative troublemakers.

That's not the whole truth, even humanly speaking, but this is not the main thing I want to say here. The main thing is this: it does not matter in the end what the critic sees in the church, because God looks at the church and sees saints.

We like to think sometimes that we are our own creators, self-made men and women. But even in purely human terms that's not true. It is often, very often, the case with us humans that we are what the most important people in our lives think we are. I understand that with most children — but particularly with little boys — they become what their kindergarten and first-grade teachers think of them. If those teachers think the child is wonderful and able and full of promise, it is very likely that the child will turn out well. If they think of the child as a little troublemaker with no promise whatsoever, well, you know what will likely happen.

I remember taking my mother out to lunch one day. As we left the restaurant we saw a fine little boy, perhaps four years old, standing handsome and neatly dressed, by the restroom doors. My mother, who has been partial to little boys for forty-seven years now, bent over and said to him, "You're a fine young man, aren't you!"

He looked up at her and confidently replied, "Yes. That's what my mother says too!"

That's a child who will turn out well.

Of course we should strive with every sinew and every muscle to make the church a more fit instrument for God's freeing, saving purposes, but that's not the main thing. The main thing is this: the most important Being there is looks at us and sees saints. And, as a result, God's light still shines through the church. It still may be the case that if God's light is a gospel about love and forgiveness for sinners, then we don't serve all that badly as windows.

The light in the church does not arise from what we have chosen, or the fact that we have called on God; it arises from this: that God has called us and chosen us.

This language of call echoes the old Presbyterian language and the old Baptist language of election and even of predestination: the doctrine that God calls us and chooses us before we ever choose God. Old John Calvin called this the *"comfortable* doctrine of predestination."* If we ever do think about the doctrine these days, most of us don't find it very comfortable at all. But there it is for our comfort: that God's choice of us is more reliable and more dependable than our choice of God.

On the day when our faith burns like little more than a candle guttering in the socket, when our Christian life has diminished to almost nothing, God's love for us is stronger than ever. God's call, God's choice, is firmer than ever. And in that choice we may rest secure.

There are very few times in parenting when there is a completely right answer, but I do know of one. I have been told that in a family where there is an adopted child as well as biological children, the adopted child will eventually ask the mother whether she loves the adopted child as much as the ones born from her body. There is a right answer to that question.

It is this: "Of course I love you. I chose you."

Yes, God sees the troubles in the church.

But God looks at us and says, "Of course I love you. I chose you."

Not drunks or sex fiends or argumentative troublemakers, but saints. Not failures but the called of God, the chosen of God, the loved of God, the church. Saints! And maybe, just maybe, eventually we'll live up to what we are.

In the meantime, may I tell you just one story about a saint? During the Second World War it was not just Jews who were sent to the Nazi concentration camps. In those dreadful camps were gypsies, homosexuals, Poles, communists, socialists, Protestants, Catholics, and people who had simply been in the wrong place at the wrong time. One such person was a Polish Roman Catholic priest named Maximilian Kolbe. For some reason the Nazi guards became displeased with the prisoners in Maximilian Kolbe's hut, and announced that they would immediately execute one out of ten prisoners, their names to be drawn by lot. One unlucky prisoner to whom the lot fell was a young Polish man, a husband, the father of young children.

Maximilian Kolbe volunteered to take the young man's place and was executed.

Some years ago the pope went back to Poland to declare Maximilian Kolbe a saint of the Roman Catholic Church. There was a special guest at the magnificent ceremony in his honor — an old Polish man, now a grandfather.

Of course he was there. Of course he was there!

After all, wouldn't you be there? Wouldn't you be there at a ceremony in honor of somebody who died for you?

You are.

And what is more, you're here as a saint. Because to be a saint, you don't actually have to die for somebody.

Somebody has to die for you . . .

And he has.

Not Peace but a Sword

(1 Kings 3:16-28; Matthew 10:32-39)

JOHN L. BELL

2002

The Crying Game

If you have never seen the film *The Crying Game*,[1] then permit me to spoil for you one of its most memorable moments.

The film is — among other things — about the relationship between an IRA terrorist-with-a-conscience and a hairdresser he meets while on a mission to undermine the government in London. He sees her through the hairdresser's shop window, and later develops a relationship by becoming one of her customers. She is of Asian extraction and is the perfect foil to his brusque, unsophisticated Celtic manner. You feel — as a viewer — that she is the means of his redemption as an individual if not as a terrorist.

In the course of their relationship, intimacy develops, though she is

---

1. Channel Four Films/Miramax (1992), directed by Neil Jordan; with Stephen Rea, Jaye Davidson, Forest Whitaker, Adrian Dunbar, and Miranda Richardson.

A previous version of this sermon was published online in the *McMaster Journal of Theology and Ministry*; http://www.mcmaster.ca/mjtm/. "Not Peace But a Sword," from *Hard Words for Interesting Times* (Glasgow: Wild Goose Publications, 2003); text by John L. Bell, copyright © 2003 Wild Goose Resource Group, Iona Community, Glasgow G23DH Scotland.

hesitant to be bedded on the first occasion that might be possible. But in a subsequent encounter, the camera offers the view of the terrorist as he gently and lovingly undresses his girlfriend. By page three standards she is not very stunning, for she is a slightly built creature. However, as he moves down to her nether regions the audience — who have become the terrorist undressing his beloved — gasp to discover that she is kitted out with a penis. She is not female at all but a transvestite, and he and we have been oblivious to this possibility.

Were it to happen in real life, one can imagine the agonizing incredulity as what appeared to be one reality was suddenly revealed to be quite the opposite. It's the kind of moment in which personal history and future prospects are all up for reinterpretation. The mind does somersaults trying to make sense of what has been and what now is to come.

Is it a moment reserved only for fiction? Certainly not.

A Malign Surprise

It is the kind of moment that was visited on the personnel manager of an engineering firm in an Ayrshire town, in the mid-1970s. It was the era when indigenous industry was being bought up by multinational corporations. Often large local businesses, employing a substantial proportion of the town's labor force, were being snapped up by national or international predators.

Economic rationalism being one of the in-vogue practices, it was not long before the patents that had been purchased were transferred elsewhere, and more lucrative production plants in England, France, North America, or Taiwan produced what had once been the town's originals.

The personnel manager was asked to make a list of over a hundred men who could be deemed surplus to requirements. It was a grueling task because he had to identify men he knew and trusted, who had gone through the firm with him, who were his friends — as well as newcomers with no long-term loyalty. When he presented the list to his superior, he was told to add his name at the bottom.

How would he feel?

How would he feel as thirty years of devoted service to a local industry were pulverized? What did this say about the value of his work, about the integrity of the new owners? And what did it mean for his future — and for that of his family in a town where the dole-queues were lengthening each day with middle-aged men doomed, it seemed, to perpetual redundancy?

It's the kind of moment when all that has been and all that is to come suddenly needs to be reinterpreted.

A Holy Shock

If we can, in any way, empathize with the fictional IRA soldier or with the real personnel manager in Ayrshire, we may be able to share the shock of Jesus' first disciples when they heard him say the words: "I did not come to bring peace — but a sword."

Suddenly and without warning all that they have presumed to be true about him, all that they have identified as winsome and contradictory in his teaching is turned on its head — and he begins to sound like a terrorist.

What has happened to the one who embodied reconciliation, who preached not just love of the neighbor, but love of the enemy? What has happened to the one who was presumed to value families, as in further utterances he indicates that his purpose is to come between father and son, mother and daughter — and this despite his encouragement of others to honor their parents? What has happened to the one who, in his consorting with foreign women, in his embracing of diseased people, in his invitation of outsiders into closed-session banquets, indicated that he had come to end division, not to instigate it?

Why does Jesus say this?

There are a number of possibilities . . .

The Divine Prerogative

One is that he was using the divine prerogative. What divine prerogative?

I refer to the habit God reveals in dealing with the children of Israel whereby when they think they have God "sussed," when they think that they know exactly the mind of God or can envisage the personality of God, God forces them into a double-take.

They think that God is a male warrior, then God reveals that he or she is in fact a midwife.

They imagine God as being steely and dispassionate, and discover tears on God's cheek.

They depict God as eternally passive, then Jacob, limping, witnesses to God's penchant for wrestling.

And, as such diverse figures as Abraham and Jonah discover, the inscrutable mind of God sometimes changes when compassion or divine whim determine that the presumed judgment, the advertised punishment, will not in fact be fulfilled.

Maybe Jesus was exercising the divine prerogative.

The Hard Man

Or maybe Jesus was refusing to allow himself to be seen as a soft touch.

For I imagine that then, as now, there would be devotees and admirers keen to domesticate Christ and make him the lapdog of religion rather than God's agent provocateur.

In some parts of the country and the world where I work, I am constantly aware of how the radical, transforming, cutting-edge gospel of Jesus is transubstantiated into hedonistic pap, as new consumer-friendly churches and some older traditions try to make Christianity as soothing and succulent as possible. The gospel, castrated of its seminal power, becomes a mere balm. One goes to church not to be confronted with the awesome mystery and amazing grace of God, but to get what makes you feel good — as if the Maker of all things could be reduced to a saccharine spoonful of spineless piety.

Then, as now, there would be people desperately keen to ensure that Jesus was a meek and gentle guru. And maybe he just blew a fuse — which would not be irregular. Jesus does get angry, even if few sermons and fewer hymns mention his righteous indignation.

"I did not come to bring peace but a sword."

Maybe he said it because he was exercising the divine prerogative . . . maybe he said it to indicate that he was not a soft touch.

The Gospel Truth

Or maybe he said it because it is true.

For the purpose of God in history, as I see it, is not to ensure that the prejudices as well as the wisdom of one generation transfer without question to the next. The purpose of God in history is to challenge and convert what have been malpractices, defective ideologies, and fond though misguided assumptions about the world and its people and its Creator. And if this means that there is a breach required between father and son, mother and daughter, then God reserves the sole right to let that happen.

God does not countenance a marriage being dissolved because of the predatory behavior of a third party. God does not remain indifferent when the state or the advertising industry drives a wedge between parent and child. While it is difficult from Scripture to validate the kind of Victorian family values many of us are presumed to espouse, it is clear that God meant covenanted relationships and familial relationships to be respected.

But God also reserves the right where one generation has got it wrong to prevent the deficiencies or the prejudices or the misinformation of that generation from being transferred to the next.

Two months ago, when I was in Nepal, I met a man who knows this intimately. His name is Chitra. He is a university graduate in economics who was in a respected position in the Communist party and had a civil service post. He became a Christian through attending the funeral of a distant relative, and from that day on, all things changed. The sword was swung: his grandmother forbade him to enter her house, his predominantly Hindu village ignored him, his father disinherited him and told the police he was an enemy of the state, the Communist party threatened to kill him. And all this happened because he had done nothing other than to declare his love for God and his love for them even in the face of their rejection.

Sometimes I wish that the same sword would swing again, though not perhaps in as menacing a fashion as it did within the household of Chitra. For I am convinced that in this new century there are practices and presumptions espoused by my generation that are contrary to the revealed will of God, but yet are never on the agenda of many Christian people.

For almost two months on either side of New Year, I was working in four continents, and everywhere I went people were lamenting the vagaries of the weather. Now, as a Scot, I should have found this perfectly acceptable. But it was indeed exceptional.

In the Upper Clarence region of New South Wales, farmers were selling off their cattle or their land because of a nine-year drought, which was exacerbated by the battering of the land just after New Year by hailstones the size of a fist, doing twenty million dollars' worth of damage in two hours.

In Auckland, New Zealand, where it was cloudy and rained on New Year's Day, I met an inhabitant who said that the season used to be the best of the year, but in the past decade sun and fine weather have no longer been guaranteed during the holiday season.

In Waterloo, Ontario, two weeks later, people were reporting a snowfall more severe than anything known in the last forty years.

Meanwhile much of England was drying out from irregular dousing, while in the Netherlands people feared what would happen should the polar icecap continue to melt and the sea level around the "low countries" continue to rise.

Of course we know what it is and we know the cause. But is the next generation — or indeed this one — going to continue with the wisdom of its progenitors who believed that you can do what you like to the earth and still survive?

I hope that in the Christian Unions of university colleges that produce the future captains of British industry, there will be some discerning people who will read again John's Gospel and stumble over the realization that the incarnation did not happen because God loved humanity. I do not read anywhere in John's Gospel that God so loved privatized religion that he became incarnate; I read that God so loved the *world*. I do not read in the letter to the Colossians that all souls or all religious people are connected through Christ; I read that *all things* — the world, its creatures, the cosmos, the powers and principalities — *all things* cohere in Christ.

We need in this day and age a radical appraisal of that creeping dualism that separates the concerns of Christian faith into legitimate and illegitimate categories. No, we don't need an appraisal, we need Christ to come with a sword and hack to bits this false but comfortable divide!

I hope that students of Scripture, lay and professional, will discern in the Psalms, in Jeremiah, in Isaiah, in the teaching of Jesus, in the Revelation of St. John, the gospel injunction to care for the earth rather than to abuse it. I hope that these same people will create havoc in their households and their classrooms and the boardrooms they may one day enter, so that in the avaricious privileged world there may be heard voices of conviction and commitment challenging our presumptions that we should go for endless growth despite the empirical fact that that road destines others to endless poverty.

Christ did not come here to bring peace but a sword — when the future of the world is at stake.

And I hope that in this nation, as elsewhere, there will be people of the generations after mine who will not be afraid to indicate to the church that in its quest for self-preservation and the iconization of the past, it has sold short the gospel.

I hope there will be young people in our churches who, not out of cant or faddishness, but out of love for God and the people of God, will not be afraid to say to their parents' generation as regards Christian witness or church practice: "You got it wrong."

For the word and person of Jesus are a sword intended to cut through the lies with which we comfort ourselves and to reveal the truth we avoid at our peril.

The Sword and Solomon

And this essential separation of pretense from honesty and iniquity from justice is something that is at the root of that rather irregular story in the book of Kings in which Solomon shows the wisdom for which he is famed.

He is confronted with two female prostitutes, each of whom has recently given birth to a male child. The one mother smothered her child while she slept; the other mother had no such mishap. But both women lay claim to the living child and maintain that the dead child belongs to the other.

So Solomon calls for a sword and suggests that the living child be cut in two in order that both women get a half. One woman agrees with the verdict; the other pleads for the child's life and says that it should be given to her adversary. Then Solomon awards the baby to the one who was willing to surrender her claim in order to save the child's life. For clearly she was acting selflessly, out of love, while the other was acting selfishly, out of wickedness.

The sword in Solomon's hands was there to determine how much each woman loved.

The sword in Jesus' hands has exactly the same intention. For on the day when we answer to God for how we have conducted our lives, the definitive question will not be about our theological orthodoxy or our squeaky-clean character reference. It will be "How much did you love? How much? How much did you really love?"

The Power to Submit

(Ephesians 5:21-33)

DIANE McLELLAN WALKER

2003

A couple of years ago I had a wedding in a little country church, a tiny place that might seat eighty as long as nobody exhaled. At the rehearsal, the groom introduced me to the two men who would be acting as his attendants. These two men were brothers, friends of the groom whom he had met through their mutual hobby of motorcycle racing. They were from Georgia and they looked and sounded like a Canadian-generated stereotype of the "good old boy." They were big, beefy men with big, beefy gold jewelry. The one named Buddy — I kid you not — had a brush cut straight out of 1963. The other brother had the improbable pompadour of a television evangelist. They wore jeans and serious kicking cowboy boots and they had belt buckles the size of subcompact cars. They both addressed me as "Ma'am" without a soupçon of irony.

As they sat, squashed in the pew, chatting with me after the rehearsal, the one brother explained that he was a Southern Baptist. He asked to be told about the church he was in, a congregation of the United Church of Canada. So I gave him a thumbnail sketch about how the Methodists and Presbyterians and Congregationalists had come together earlier in the century. Then he asked, with a twinkle in his eye, "So, I wonder, would you preach here on First Corinthians 14:34-35?" We smiled at each other knowingly, and some of you are laughing because of course that is Paul's injunction for women to keep silent in churches.

The next day, after the wedding was over, he paid me what I'm sure he thought was a high compliment. He told me that my homily about marriage was "Real good! Real good!" — something that wouldn't sound at all out of place in his own church. As time goes by I'm starting to think of it as a compliment as well. But he did give me a great gift that day. He got me thinking about why it was that I had never preached on 1 Corinthians 14:34-35. It's not because it isn't in the lectionary, because it's been fifteen years since I've preached from the lectionary. So what was it? Cowardice? An assumption that the issue was solved, therefore irrelevant, and therefore unworthy of my attention? I'd been preaching for twenty-five years and I had never got to this text. And why was that? Was it because it was too hard? Too challenging? But hard texts are good for us. They stretch us. They poke us squarely in the assumptions. Ephesians 5:21-33 is a hard text.

It is a hard text for me to hear because "Submit to one another out of reverence for Christ" immediately gets me riled. I think that by nature I must be one of the most inherently unsubmissive people ever to walk in shoe leather. I am opinionated, and combative, and bossy, and I am all too often addicted to getting my own way. People who know me know that I'm telling the truth. I actually had insubordination listed as my offense for being thrown out of a history class in grade thirteen. Although I think that saying to the teacher, "Insubordinate to you? That'll be the day," may have had something to do with the length of the suspension. I may be only five foot four but I'm tough.

So I stink at submission. I absolutely stink at submission and I'll bet I'm not the only one. There is something to be said for the mellowing of middle age, and — more importantly — for the sanctifying work of the Holy Spirit over time, so I am a little better at submitting now than I was at seventeen. But I still don't like it very much.

"Submit to one another out of reverence for Christ." It's too hard to hear and it's too hard to live. All the more reason for taking a careful look at it. Sometimes preachers are accused of preaching to the choir, of convincing the already convinced. But I've found the sermons most nourishing for the flock are the ones that the shepherds are starving for. So here it is, "Submit to one another out of reverence for Christ."

There is no denying that this passage has been wielded as a club to oppress and subjugate women. It has been widely used to support a doctrine of hierarchy, of wife subordinate and husband superordinate in Christian marriage. It has indeed been another text of terror, interpreted as a command for women's subservience under the domination of men. And maybe it is likewise terrifying for men, who are forced to think up some way of enforcing their authority without destroying their own integrity. While being a doormat is awful, being married to one is probably no barrel of laughs either.

The passage begins with a call to mutual submission, which flows into an outlining of what this mutual submission will mean for wives and what it will mean for husbands. So while submission might look different for husbands and for wives, both stand under the same injunction to submit. The act of submission within the Christian community and within the littlest church — marriage — this submission is a manifestation. It's an outward sign of being filled with the Spirit, just like all the other actions in the Spirit that are listed in this passage: speaking psalms, singing, making melody, giving thanks. All of these — including submission — are to be visible evidences of being filled with the Spirit of God.

Mutual submission is a visible evidence of being filled with the Spirit of God. Submission to one another is a duty and a joy that is offered to all Christian believers. And verse 22 says that wives are to submit to their husbands as to the Lord. Grumble. Grizzle. Sigh. And moan. This submission is not to be enforced but rather embraced voluntarily, which in my opinion makes it even worse. Should I *voluntarily* submit out of love for Christ? Should Christian wives submit to their husbands "as to the Lord"? Should I — gasp — give in?

Within marriage, each partner willing to go halfway to meet the other is a sure recipe for disaster. If you are only willing to go fifty-fifty in marriage, I suggest that a business partnership is a better choice. Because giving in to the other and compromising our own needs or wishes is absolutely necessary to making relationships work. That's why we see women knitting at hockey games. It's why you see men standing outside of gift shops in tourist hotspots. They should be tethered like horses. They just stand there and wait. The really smart shopowners put out benches: the husband bench. Giving in to the other, compromising our own needs and wishes, is absolutely essential to making relationships work. Giving in is not a mark of weakness: it's a mark of strength.

What Ephesians advocates is not the relationship of a doormat to an exploiter, but that of equals who freely choose, when it's appropriate and when it makes sense, to give in to each other in love. They give in freely, freely choosing to give in. I think that, like many other people, I did not really learn what it meant to embody self-giving love until I had my first baby. Being at the beck and call (or more accurately, the beck and howl) of a totally dependent and constantly ravenous newborn gave me my first real dose of truly giving in for the other. Raising four children has been for me the truest school of sanctification, as I have learned to give up my sleep, give up my tidy and orderly existence, give up my right to privacy, even in the bathroom. Finally, I found that I had to give up my heart. But here I am in august company. Martin Luther said that walking the floor with his children at night taught him more about patience and love than all his years in the monastery.

To submit willingly is not a terror. It is a treasure. It is a profound source of joy and satisfaction. But many of us never get to experience it because we remain incapable of the sacrifice of the will that it takes. The old Adam, the old sinner, may have been drowned in the waters of baptism, but again, as Luther said, the old Adam is a mighty good swimmer.

As wives are told to submit, husbands are told to love their wives just as Christ loved the church and gave himself up for her. Now there's a high standard of love: the self-sacrificing love that goes to the cross and gives absolutely all. The husband's authority is regulated by Christ's example, and by the principle of self-giving love. There is no place at all for a husband's authoritarianism, self-assertion, or self-centeredness.

The husband is not *commanded* to be the head in this passage; he is described in metaphorical terms as the "head" of the wife. This word "head" is tricky: there are whole books on it in the library next door. If you tune in to the perspective of the Biblical Council on Christian Manhood and Womanhood, or that of Christians for Biblical Equality, you will see that the meaning of this word is very hotly contested. The "headship" passages in the New Testament are about relations between men and women, and that word is variously explained as meaning "ruler," "supreme," "governor," or "boss," but also as meaning "derivation" and "source." It can mean all of those things: even in our language, the "head" of the firm is different from the "headwaters" of a river.

The context here in Ephesians provides an important clue. The reference to Christ as "head" is in the context of his self-giving sacrifice, not in his role as Pantocrator, as the glorious ruler over all the universe. So if the husband in this context is the "head" of the wife, he is for her a source of caring and giving and self-sacrificial love that is modeled on Christ's self-sacrifice.

I've said that this passage from Ephesians can and has been a text of terror for women, and that's because the word "head" can also mean "boss." That makes it pretty clear why it's terrifying. It can be terrifying for women to think that the Christian gospel is being used to advocate a secondary place for women under the dominance of men. But here in Ephesians we see something else entirely. We see a husband being instructed to love his wife as Christ loved the church, and we all know where that got Jesus.

To be clear, the parallel between the husband and Christ lies in the sacrificial nature of love. It is true that Christ's sacrifice brings salvation, but the husband is not to be seen as the savior of the wife because Christ alone, of course, is the Savior of each one of us. Nowhere is the husband called upon to be a savior to the wife. Instead, we are to look upon the loving intimacy of marriage as a suitable parallel to the love of Christ for the church.

When we read this passage on the surface, we have a tendency to balk at it. But what a recipe it provides for us for love within marriage. Because it cuts across selfishness and ambition; it lifts up and extols the relationship-building virtues of self-sacrifice, mutual submission, and loving-kindness. But the sort of self-sacrificing love seen in Christ is simply not possible under our own steam. We can't do it. Let's remember that these instructions about submission within marriage are a follow-up instruction on how to live filled with the Holy Spirit.

I started off with a story from a wedding. That's what clergy like to do when we get together. You know, we talk shop and spin a few tales about weddings, maybe funerals. But that wedding with the fellows from Georgia was a little strange. For one thing, the bride had her mother as her attendant, which is a little unusual. Even stranger was the fact that the bride and her mother wore identical dresses, except that the bride's was white and her mother's was black. And the two women also had identical hairdos and makeup. It was a little weird.

But for all the weird things that happen at weddings — and if you go to a lot of weddings, they get weirder — I must confess that what strikes me as the weirdest of the weird is that we still see brides swathed with veils covering their faces. After all, that custom goes back to the time of arranged marriages when everyone wanted to make sure that the official paperwork was done and dusted before the groom got a look at the bride. Lest he be less than satisfied with her and want to back out of the deal. It strikes me as more than passing strange that we still see brides all swathed in veils. Women who are entering into "the estate of matrimony" by their own free choice, with their own credit history, and a marriage contract in hand, still choose to walk up to the groom all bundled up in yards of tulle as if he's never seen her face before. It really stretches credulity when they've already been living together and have two or three kids. So why the veil? After all, what could you possibly be hiding at this point?

But for us, we who are the bride of Christ, we know there's plenty to hide. We've got every reason in the world for a half dozen yards of heavy-duty veiling. What else could hide our unsubmissive natures, our addiction to getting our own way, our inability to give in for the sake of our marriages, for the sake of our friendships, for the sake of our families, for the sake of our workplace relationships, for the sake of our Christian community? Only Christ can tear away the veil because he has already made us holy. He has cleansed us "by the washing with water through the word" (Eph. 5:26). What Christ has accomplished on the cross makes us radiant without stain or wrinkle or any other blemish, but holy and blameless instead (Eph. 5:27). He feeds us. He nourishes us from his own body, his own blood, for we are members of his body (Eph. 5:29-30).

In ancient times, when the people of Israel came to the temple to make their atoning sacrifices on the altar of the Lord, the animals they brought had to be prime, without stain, blemish, or wrinkle. Now Christ has, once and for all, made that sacrifice of his own stainless, blemish-less, wrinkle-less self, paying the price for all sin. He submitted himself to the cross and he offers us that same power to submit. The power to submit! This is a profound mystery, that we will be given the power to submit within marriage, within friendship, within Christian community. May that grace and that power, that wondrous mercy be with you this day and always.

In the name of the Father and of the Son and of the Holy Spirit, Amen.

Good Guys, Bad Guys, and Us Guys

(Luke 18:9-14)

HADDON W. ROBINSON

2004

When I was a boy growing up in New York City, one of the nicest ways for me to spend a Saturday afternoon was at the matinee of the neighborhood theater. A group of us would arrive early and warm up on a series of cartoons. But we really went to see the cowboy movies.

We liked those movies because they were so predictable. The bad guys always wore gray and rode dark horses. Whenever they spoke, they spoke with a snarl. The good guys always wore white hats and rode white horses. And from time to time, they would stop and sing to us with their guitars.

On Sunday, if we managed to make it to Sunday School, it sometimes seemed that the same people who had written the screenplay for the movie had also written some of our Sunday School lessons, for the characters we studied there were also very gray and very white. We knew, for example, that had we been there for the showdown in Egypt between Pharaoh and Moses, Pharaoh would have been dressed in gray and Moses in white. And it was no surprise to us that David sang with a harp, because in our minds that was a kind of old-fashioned guitar.

Previously published as *Preaching Today,* Tape No. 80 (1990); this transcription was kindly supplied by the author. [*ed.*]

As I grew older, though, I grew tired of those cowboy movies, just because they were so predictable. They didn't deal with real people living in a real world. Instead, they usually dealt with cardboard characters in a tissue paper play.

In turning from some of those stories of our childhood, many of us have unthinkingly turned from some of the ripping good stories Jesus told. We have heard them too many times. As a result, we've concluded that Jesus, like the cowboy movies, dealt with caricatures rather than real characters.

Take the story in Luke chapter 18. As soon as we get a line on the cast of characters, we have made up our minds. We know that one of the men was a Pharisee, and like Pavlov's dogs, we have been conditioned to think of all Pharisees as evil. So, mentally we proceed to color him gray. On the other hand, the other fellow in the story is a tax collector. We recognize that tax collectors were not the best of men, but we suspect that in this story, at least, we're dealing with a good guy in disguise.

But had you stood there on that ancient afternoon when Jesus first told this parable, you would not have come to any such naïve conclusions. In the eyes of good and decent men of that day, the Pharisee was a religious and a moral success. He could stand in the temple and pray, "I thank you that I am not like other men, extortioners, evildoers, adulterers. I tithe all that I take in. I fast twice each week." I'm sure he was praying sober truth. In business, he had not made his living by driving his neighbor to the wall. His word was his bond. When he made a promise, you could count on it. And in a day as sexually loose as our own, he had not sacrificed upon some wayside altar.

Measured by any conventional standard, ancient or modern, the Pharisee was a religious success. He says that he fasted twice each week. That was far more than the Old Testament had asked. In the ancient law, the people of God were asked to fast once each year — on the Day of Atonement. But in his devotion to his religion, this Pharisee would not be held to that. So, twice each week, on Monday and Thursday, he denied himself food.

He also says he gave a tithe of all that he took in. I suspect he is saying more than that he was a tither. That would have been characteristic of a great many people of his day. I think he is saying he tithed those things the law did not ask him to tithe. Perhaps each year he figured up his net worth and gave a tenth of that to God.

This Pharisee was in deep earnestness about his religion; you had to be serious about it to make yourself as uncomfortable as he made himself. God was as real to him as the shekels in his pocket, and he was willing to lower his standard of living a bit for him. And his religion had done him good: the people in the community respected and admired him as an outstanding citizen, a contributor to the community.

In fact, even the tax collector who came to services on that ancient Sabbath admired and respected the Pharisee. Jesus said when the tax collector entered the temple, he stood far from this noble leader of the religious community. He did not feel worthy to stand by his side.

If you think this tax collector was merely a good-natured chap willing to admit his limitations, you do not understand the place of tax collectors in the first century. Whenever Rome wanted to tax a province, it sold the right to tax to the highest bidder. And once a man purchased the right to tax, he was free to take anything the traffic would bear. He usually discovered it could bear a great deal. You couldn't do business without doing business with a tax collector. You couldn't move your goods from town to town without stopping by his desk.

As a result, extortion was built into the job; injustice was part of the trade. Tacitus, the Roman historian, says that once he visited a village that had had such an honest tax collector the village erected a monument to his memory. Some men are traitors by one craven deed of cowardice, but a tax collector was a traitor all day and every day. He was despised by most people. Instead, he spent much of his time with extortionists, evildoers, and the sexually loose.

If both of these men, the Pharisee and the tax collector, were running for public office, we would do our best to elect the Pharisee. If the tax collector got in, we would feel that corruption had invaded our society. If both of these fellows were courting your sister, you'd be pleased to have the Pharisee as a brother-in-law, but hardly the tax collector.

It's not so simple, then, to discover why Jesus decides the verdict as he does. It's not easy to see why he turns our values upside down, why he commends the person we would condemn and condemns the person we would commend. But he's not dealing with caricatures; he's dealing with characters. To understand this story, then, we've got to look at it more closely.

When we do, we discover that the Pharisee and the tax collector are both in the temple. Certainly Jesus is not criticizing them for that. In the temple the daily sacrifices were offered. In the temple men and women, through these sacrifices, came into a relationship with God. We also see that both of them are praying, and Jesus is not giving them low marks for that. In fact, in the previous parable, Jesus told a story whose purpose was that men and women ought always to pray and not to faint.

But as we listen to the prayer of the Pharisee, we begin to get a little uneasy. He says, "I thank you that I am not like other men, extortioners, evildoers, adulterers. I fast twice each week. I give a tithe of all that I take in. I thank you especially that I'm not like that tax collector." What upsets us is that we feel this man is conceited. If you and I were going to give him a bit of spiritual counsel, we would urge him to be more modest. We'd say to him, "Look, what you pray is true, but you ought not pray it in public. It sounds bad, conceited. You ought to be careful how you pray."

In the assortment of sins that men and women commit, one of the sins we don't like (at least in other people) is the sin of conceit. We like our heroes modest, and conceit has a way of putting us off. When the back runs seventy yards, scores a touchdown, and then is interviewed on television, we like him to say he made the long run because of the good line in front of him. We don't like him to say, "I'm the best runner in the National Football League."

Or, let's say you and I play tennis, and you beat me in three straight sets and then come bounding over the net, saying, "Look, Robinson, I don't know what you play, but it isn't tennis. Next time you want exercise, get somebody else to give it to you." I'm willing to admit you're a better tennis player than me. (I guess everybody else would admit it, too.) What I don't like is to have you admit it. I like you to tell me that you got in some good shots, that you were particularly up on your game that day. Conceit has a way of rubbing me wrong.

Or, let's say you discover that on a test you've gotten a fat C-minus. As the person next to you looks at his blue book, you ask, "What did you get?"

He says, "Oh, I got an A. That was an easy exam. I didn't even study for it. Got an A! You didn't have any trouble with it, did you?" You're willing to admit the other person's a better student than you; it's obvious to the professor. What you don't like is to have him say it. You don't like his conceit. It puts you down. It rubs you wrong.

But, as far as God is concerned, conceit never makes it into the big leagues of sin. Conceit is a minor matter. It's often a way of talking. It's often just bad judgment.

A young woman went to her pastor and said, "Pastor, I have a besetting sin, and I want your help. I come to church on Sunday and can't help thinking I'm the prettiest girl in the congregation. I know I ought not think that, but I can't help it. I want you to help me with it."

The pastor replied, "Mary, don't worry about it. In your case it's not a sin. It's just a horrible mistake."

That is often true of conceit. There are people who talk big because inside they feel small. It's a way of covering up feelings of inadequacy. As far as God is concerned, conceit is a lot like acne: disturbing but not fatal.

The trouble with this Pharisee was not conceit, not pimples on the skin. The trouble was in the bloodstream. He is standing in the temple — in the presence of God — and thinking that the differences that matter among men matter with the Almighty. The problem with the Pharisee was pride.

Luke tells us that Jesus told this parable to those who were confident of their own righteousness and looked down on everybody else. One of the symptoms of self-righteousness is a critical spirit, because one of the ways we feed our self-righteousness is by comparing ourselves with others. We usually look at their vices and think of our virtues, and that, we assume, gives us special standing with God. We have a way of cutting other people off at the knees and putting ourselves up on stilts. In comparison, "we seem to stand tall."

Whenever you hear somebody always criticizing other people, see it as a manifestation of a self-righteous spirit. It's a kind of insanity that says, "If I pull your house down, my house stands taller." That is self-righteousness and the way proud people feed their pride.

Pope Gregory the Great said of this Pharisee that he was like a man who had killed an elephant, but who was killed by the elephant's fall. The stench, the smell that comes out of this passage — this horrible aroma that has about it the brimstone of hell — is the smell of grace gone sour.

Here was a man with benefits: he had a knowledge of the Scriptures; he had been brought up in a good environment; his religious life had contributed positively to his character. But he took those things for granted; he thought that the good things given to him made him a creature of special merit and put him in special standing before God. Even though he thanks God, he is really practicing self-congratulation. He is saying, "Lord, you have made a good soup. But you couldn't have done it without good material like me to work with." That's the smell of grace gone putrid.

You can smell it in the life of young men and women. Many young people are brought up in a good environment, perhaps a Christian home. They're enabled to go to a Christian university. They have advantages that many others don't have. But soon they take those advantages and turn them into virtues. They begin to look at these "virtues" and compare themselves with others. They feel that as the mass of people go, they're pretty special, special to others and special to God. That's the stink of grace gone putrid.

You can see it in schools, seminaries, and Christian colleges. Across the years, some institutions have been true to truth. By God's grace they have the truth. By God's grace they've been true to truth. But in order to show how true they are, they begin to look at other schools, pointing out other schools' flaws and defections. When they do it, there are no tears streaming from their eyes; their hearts are not broken. No, they feel they're pretty special, the objects of God's blessing because they deserved it. That is the smell of grace gone putrid.

This Pharisee was in the presence of God, and in the presence of God he thought that the distinctions that mattered among men mattered with the Almighty. In the presence of God, he had a good eye on himself, a bad eye on his neighbor, and no eye on God.

"But the tax collector," Jesus said, "stood far off and kept beating his breast." That was something that women did, not men. "And he would not even look up into heaven." He looked down at earth. When the standard way to pray was to look up into the heavens, he kept beating his breast saying, "O God, be merciful to me, a sinner."

You say, "All right, he was humble. But after all, he had a lot to be humble about: he was a tax collector." But you can have left-wing Pharisees and right-wing Pharisees, like the Sunday School teacher who, after teaching this story, said, "Now, boys and girls, let's bow our heads and thank God we're not like that nasty Pharisee."

This tax collector could have stood in the presence of God and said, "O God, I thank you that I'm not as other men are. I especially thank you I'm not like that Pharisee. I don't pray long prayers in public. I don't pray like a religious type. I know I have sinned, and I'm willing to admit it. And even if I had done all these things, at least you know and I know that I'm not a hypocrite."

I think a man is as stupid as he is rotten who thinks that by taking the bandages off the putrid sores of his life, he becomes a creature of merit. I don't know why we think hypocrisy is the worst sin in the world, and why we believe that by living shabby lives, but not being hypocrites, we become creatures who enjoy special favor from God. I could wish that some people would take a short course in guile and cover up those sores.

A few years ago, two men held up a bank in Dallas. For reasons I do not know, only one of them wore a mask. In ten or fifteen minutes they were captured. Can you imagine one of those men standing before the judge and saying, "Your Honor, I admit I robbed the bank. I admit that I did it. But at least I went in there without a mask. I was not a hypocrite. Everybody saw who I was." That doesn't make it with a judge in Dallas. So, if you want to play the game of Pharisee, you can play it from any position on the board. This tax collector stood in the presence of God, and in the presence of God he kept beating his breast, saying, "O God, be merciful to me, a sinner."

One of the benefits of living in God's presence is this: when you really see God, you see yourself; when you see yourself, you see your sin; when you see your sin, you cry out to God for grace and forgiveness, and you receive it. The saint is always more aware of his need of God than his successes in God, always more aware of how far he has to go than how far he has come.

Job is described by the biblical writer as the most righteous man of his day. When he suffered, his friends told him he was suffering severely because he had sinned badly. Job denied that, refused to accept that. Then, at the end of the book, Job receives a vision of God. When he sees the vision, Job responds, "I have heard of you with the hearing of my ear, but now my eye sees you, and I repent in sackcloth and ashes" (Job 42:5-6). Seeing God, he saw himself; seeing himself, he saw his sins; seeing his sin, he saw his need of grace and forgiveness. And he cried out to God for cleansing.

Isaiah was the cream of young manhood of his day. But in an hour of national and personal crisis, when a mighty king had died, Isaiah stood in the temple and caught a vision of God, high and lifted up, his train filling the temple. And when Isaiah caught that vision of God, he said, "Woe is me. I am undone. I am a man of unclean lips. I live in the midst of a people of unclean lips" (Isa. 6:5). When Isaiah saw God, he also saw himself; when he saw himself, he saw his sin; when he saw his sin, he saw his need of forgiveness and grace. And he cried out to God for cleansing.

In Paul's first letter to his young friend, Timothy, he says, "Here is a trustworthy saying that deserves full acceptance: Christ Jesus came into the world to save sinners — of whom I am the worst" (1 Tim. 1:15, NIV). Did you notice the verb? It is not "I *was* the worst, back there on the Damascus Road, when I was persecuting the church," but "I *am* the worst of sinners. Now that I have preached the gospel across the empire, now that I have established churches in the major cities, now that I have suffered persecution for God — I am the worst of sinners." Why does he say this? Because a verse later he says, "Now, to the King eternal, immortal, invisible, the only God, be honor and glory for ever and ever" (1 Tim. 1:17).

If you live in the presence of God and live in the light of his holiness, you will see your sin. And when you see your sin, you see your need of forgiveness, and you cry out to God for grace to cleanse you.

You never outgrow your need of grace or forgiveness. The most respected professor on your faculty, who has lived with God for scores of years, needs God's grace just as much as the pimp or prostitute on a skid row who is coming to Jesus Christ for the first time. The more you know of God's light, the more you see your own shadow. And the more you become aware of your need of God's grace, and the more often you cry out for God's cleansing and grace, the more you realize how much God gives you.

H. G. Wells was no friend of the church, but sometimes he served us well. Years ago in the *New Yorker*, he told a story about an Episcopalian clergyman. (He could have told it about a preacher from any denomination.) This Episcopalian bishop was the kind of man who always said pious things to people. When troubled folks came to him, he found that a particularly helpful thing to say, if said in a right tone of voice, was, "Have you prayed about it?" If said in just the right way, it seemed to settle things.

The bishop himself didn't pray much; he had life wrapped up in a neat package. But one day, life tumbled in on him and he found himself overwhelmed. It occurred to the bishop that maybe he should take some of his own advice. So, one Saturday afternoon he entered the cathedral, went to the front, and knelt on the crimson rug. Then he folded his hands before the altar (he could not help but think how childlike he was).

Then he began to pray. He said, "O God — " and suddenly there was a voice. It was crisp, businesslike. The voice said, "Well, what is it?"

Next day when the worshipers came to Sunday services, they found the bishop sprawled face down on the crimson carpet. When they turned him over, they discovered he was dead. Lines of horror were etched upon his face. What H. G. Wells was saying in that story is simply this: there are folks who talk a lot about God who would be scared to death if they saw him face to face.

Yet that is where we are called to live. That is the secret of humility — not looking inward at your deficiencies or weaknesses, not looking outward at other people, comparing yourself with them, their vices against your virtues, their virtues against your vices. Humility comes from looking up into the face of God — who is holy love and loving holiness — to see ourselves and our need of forgiveness, to cry out for grace for daily life. Seeing God is to see ourselves. And to see ourselves is to understand what humility is.

Isaac Watts captured it when he wrote,

When I survey the wondrous cross
On which the Prince of Glory died,
My richest gain I count but loss,
And pour contempt on all my pride.

Forbid it, Lord, that I should boast,
Save in the death of Christ my God;
All the vain things that charm me most,
I sacrifice them to His blood.[1]

---

1. Written in 1707 and published (under the heading, "Crucifixion to the World by the Cross of Christ; Gal. 6:14") in *Hymns and Spiritual Songs* (London, 1707). [*ed.*]

Permissions

Excerpt from *Les Misérables* by Alain Boublil and Claude-Michel Schönberg; lyrics by Alain Boublil, Herbert Kretzmer, and Jean-Marc Natel. Copyright © Alain Boublil Music, 1985 ASCAP. Used by permission of Alain Boublil Music.

Excerpt from "The Impossible Dream (The Quest)"; lyrics by Joe Darion, music by Mitch Leigh. © 1965. Used by permission.

Excerpt from *Unexpected News: Reading the Bible with Third World Eyes*. Copyright © 1984 Robert McAfee Brown. Used by permission of John Knox Press.

"Not Peace But a Sword," from *Hard Words for Interesting Times* (Glasgow: Wild Goose Publications, 2003); text by John L. Bell. Copyright © 2003 Wild Goose Resource Group, Iona Community, Glasgow G23DH Scotland.

New Revised Standard Version Bible, copyright © 1989, Division of Christian Education of the National Council of the Churches of Christ in the United States of America. Used by permission. All rights reserved.

Scripture quotations marked (NIV) are taken from the *Holy Bible, New International Version®*. NIV®. Copyright © 1973, 1978, 1984 by International Bible Society. Used by permission of Zondervan. All rights reserved.

Scripture quotations marked (GNT) are taken from the *Good News Translation — Second Edition* © 1992 by American Bible Society Used by permission.

Index of Names

Index of Names

Calvin, John, 62, 118, 121, 148-49, 158, 184, 230
Campolo, Anthony, ix, xiv, xix, 29
Camus, Albert, 124, 177
Carey, Joyce, 14
Carter, Jimmy, 188
Casserley, Langmead, 125
Celsus, 135
Cephas. *See* Peter, Simon
Channing, William Ellery, 4
Chloe, 151
Cicero, 44, 131
Clarke, Arthur C., 201
Cone, James H., 15-16
Constantine, 14
Conzelmann, Hans, 223
Cornelius, 125
Cosgrove, Charles H., 141
Cotton, John, 4
Craddock, Fred B., 10, 46-47, 146
Cronkite, Walter, 174
Cullmann, Oscar, 40

David (King), 183, 206, 208, 246
Davis, H. Grady, 46
Diocletian, 211
Dixon, William Macneile, 177
Dodd, C. H., 75
Douglass, Frederick, 187
Doulos, William Lane, 88
DuBois, W. E. B., 182-83

Edwards, Betty, 90-91
Edwards, Jonathan, 4
Einstein, Albert, 183, 187
Eisenhower, Dwight D., 188
Eliot, Thomas Stearns, 30, 34
Emerson, Ralph Waldo, 174-75, 180
Epicurus, 222
Esau (Patriarch), 59, 63

Fant, Clyde, 10
Farris, Stephen C., x, xv, xvi, xxi, 140, 154, 226

Fee, Gordon D., 136
Feld, Eddie, 52
Fielder, Cecil, 187
Finney, Charles, 4
Fishbane, Michael, 84
Ford, Michael, xvii
Forsyth, Peter T., 133, 190
Fosdick, Harry Emerson, xiv, 5-6, 82, 171, 188
Frazier, E. Franklin, 19
Frost, Robert, 175
Fuller, Reginald, 67
Funk, Robert W., 76

Gadamer, Hans-Georg, 104
Gandhi, Mahatma, 25, 182
Gardner, Erle Stanley, 60
Garrison, William Lloyd, 187
Gladstone, William, 128
Gladstone, John N., x, xv, xvi-xvii, xviii, xix, 174
Gomes, Peter, 51
Graham, Billy, 44
Greene, Graham, 170
Gregory the Great, Pope, 250
Gurganus, Allan, 50

Hall, Douglas John, 13
Halverstadt, Hugh, 141
Handel, George Frideric, 28, 185
Hatfield, Dennis D., 141
Hauerwas, Stanley, 54
Hayakawa, S. I., 99
Haydn, Joseph, 185
Hays, Richard B., 76
Henry, Carl F. H., 109
Hiltner, Seward, 43
Hirsch, E. D., 123
Hitler, Adolf, 92-93, 210-11
Hoge, Dean, 48
Holmes, Oliver Wendell, 54
Hopkins, Gerard Manley, 91
Huggins, Charles, 103
Humboldt, Wilhelm von, 62

258

Index of Names

Index of Names

Index of Scripture References